MANDATORY SEPARATION

MANDATORY SEPARATION

Religion, Education, and Mass Politics in Palestine

SUZANNE SCHNEIDER

STANFORD UNIVERSITY PRESS
STANFORD, CALIFORNIA

Stanford University Press
Stanford, California

Printed in the United States of America on acid-free, archival-quality paper

Library of Congress Cataloging-in-Publication Data
Names: Schneider, Suzanne, 1983– author.
Title: Mandatory separation : religion, education, and mass politics in Palestine / Suzanne Schneider.
Description: Stanford, California : Stanford University Press, 2018. | Includes bibliographical references and index.
Identifiers: LCCN 2017022011 (print) | LCCN 2017047749 (ebook) | ISBN 9781503604520 (electronic) | ISBN 9781503604148 (cloth : alk. paper) | ISBN 9781503604155 (pbk. : alk. paper)
Subjects: LCSH: Religious education—Palestine—History—20th century. | Jewish religious education—Palestine—History—20th century. | Islamic religious education—Palestine—History—20th century. | Education and state—Palestine—History—20th century. | Education—Political aspects—Palestine—History—20th century. | Palestine—Politics and government—1917–1948.
Classification: LCC BL42.5.P19 (ebook) | LCC BL42.5.P19 S35 2018 (print) | DDC 296.6/8095694—dc23
LC record available athttps://lccn.loc.gov/2017022011

Typeset by Bruce Lundquist in 10/14 Minion Pro

For my parents, Mary Sue and Joel Schneider, with love and gratitude

CONTENTS

Acknowledgments ix
Note on Transliteration xiii

Introduction: The Politics of Denial 1
1 Religious Education in the Modern Age 19
2 Educational Modernity in Palestine 41
3 Education and Community under Sectarian Rule 71
4 New Schooling for an "Old" Order 97
5 The Boundaries of Religious Knowledge 129
6 Border Clashes 161
Conclusion: The Invisible Cross 197

Notes 205
Bibliography 237
Index 251

ACKNOWLEDGMENTS

Nearly seven years ago, this project began innocently enough in a decision to participate on a panel about education in Mandate Palestine at the Middle East Studies Association's annual conference. Organized by Liora Halperin and Hilary Falb, the panel offered the initial impetus to try to grapple with the overlapping impulses evident within modern attempts to reform Jewish and Islamic education. Since that time, my approach to the subject has undergone numerous revisions and acquired new points of nuance thanks to the insights of many other friends and scholars. Yet I would be remiss if I did not begin by acknowledging the pivotal role that our humble panel played in shaping this work and by stating my gratitude to Liora and Hilary for their collegiality and friendship.

Many other colleagues, friends, and mentors have served as sounding boards in the years that followed, providing both helpful suggestions and much-needed critiques. In particular, Rashid Khalidi offered innumerable ideas that helped facilitate my research and frame the project as a whole. Uri S. Cohen has been both a sharp reader of my work and a constant source of encouragement for well over a decade. And Richard Bulliet, whom I have had the distinct pleasure of knowing for nearly all of my adult life, has and continues to be a teacher, mentor, and friend all rolled up into one. Columbia University served as my academic home during the early stages of this project, and I owe a special thanks to Taoufik ben-Amor, Timothy Mitchell, Dan Miron, Gil Anidjar, Elik Elhanan, Maheen Zaman, Valentine Edgar, Yitzhak Lewis, Seth Anziska, Yuval Kremnitzer, Roni Henig, and Jessica Rechtschaffer for their insights, companionship, and myriad forms of assistance.

My research for this project was also supported by a number of other key institutions, including the Institute for Israel and Jewish Studies and the Middle East Institute at Columbia University, as well as the Palestinian American Research Center. Their support enabled everything from language training to research trips, and I owe their respective staffs my heartfelt thanks. Finally, the

Center for Religion and Media at New York University served as an incredibly hospitable home in which to work on this manuscript. In particular, I want to thank Angela Zito, Kali Handelman, and Adam Becker for all they did to welcome me and facilitate my work.

There are still others who have provided needed direction, logistical support, and constructive criticism. Kate Wahl of Stanford University Press has offered sound advice and patiently ushered this work through its many iterations. The two anonymous readers of the manuscript challenged me at every turn to refine the book's argument and structure. Yotam Hotam has been a patient reader of many chapter drafts and a source of good cheer. Laura Schor has served as both an intellectual companion and personal mentor as I worked my way through this project. Yuval Dror was kind enough to share many rare archival sources with me and to offer other important suggestions. And Chananel Bejell made many trips to the Central Zionist Archives on my behalf. Still other individuals aided in my research in one way or another, and I thank Ela Greenberg, Khader Salameh, Ellen Fleischmann, Ayala Gordon, Elon Goitein, Qais Malhas, Gila Feinblum Brill, and Amiel Shefer for all their kindness and assistance.

This project has had its fair share of intellectual challenges, but in many ways they pale in comparison to those presented by having twins in the midst of my research. I acknowledge the many friends and family members without whose emotional and logistical support this project would have never reached fruition. My parents have long exhibited selfless concern for their children and now extend the same sense of unconditional devotion to their grandchildren. My siblings and their spouses have offered years of love, advice, and patient support. Gloria Rivera loved our babies as if they were her own and was a constant source of calm and reassurance. My in-laws, Lisa and Yaron Reich, have offered endless support in various forms, while my brothers and sisters-in-law have supported my intellectual pursuits with gracious cheer and needed jest. I owe special thanks to Yehuda and Arielle Reich and Leora and Aharon Bejell, who have looked after me during my many trips to Jerusalem. And to the living legends Drs. Leon and Rosalie Reich, who spent many hours with their great-grandchildren while I snuck away to write, I owe my deepest gratitude and affection.

Beyond merely offering words of support, my friends have been sources of strength, inspiration, and needed distraction. To Elizabeth Marcus, Daniel Lee, Rebecca Miller, Josh Levine, Jordan Salvit, Ori Rokach, Eliana and Lev

Meirowitz-Nelson, Joanna Kabat, Steven Meltzer, Tracy Massel, Adam Zachary Newton, Miriam Udel, Erica Borghard, and Jason and Janna Canavan, my love and most genuine thanks. And I would be remiss not to acknowledge a number of new friends who have enriched our lives on the other side of the East River: Noah and Nava Greenfield, Lonnie and David Firestone, Tamar Huberman, Mike Clarfeld, Tehilah Eisenstadt, Simon Feil, Manoah Finston, Nathalie Gorman, Howard and Shosh Goller, and many others who make our community the wonderful and sustaining place that it is.

Over the past few years, Brooklyn has become not just a personal home but a professional one as well thanks to the tireless efforts of my fellow colleagues at the Brooklyn Institute for Social Research. To Ajay Singh Chaudhary, my intellectual collaborator, co-conspirator, and dear friend, thank you for all that you do to make our work possible and our world better. I also have the good fortune to spend my time working (and laughing) with, learning from, and thinking alongside Abby Kluchin, Danya Glabau, and Rebecca Ariel Porte. Thanks to all of you for the long hours spent as we continue to engineer not only a new type of scholarly work but also a new model of collegiality. Finally to Audrey Nicolaides, who supports us all with her unique combination of intelligence, technical skill, and humor, I extend my heartfelt gratitude.

Last but far from least, I thank Jonathan Reich for all his love, patience, and encouragement. It was the happiest of accidents that you stumbled into my Arabic class all those years ago, and it is my great fortune to still have you by my side. May we have the privilege to grow old and cranky together. Finally, to our smart and spirited daughters, Charlotte and Sophia, thank you for the absolute splendor you bring to our world. I look forward to the day when you can read this book and challenge me about its details.

NOTE ON TRANSLITERATION

In transliterating Arabic and Hebrew words into English, I have relied on a simplified version of the style guidelines issued by the *International Journal of Middle Eastern Studies* and *Encyclopedia Judaica*, respectively. In the interest of greater legibility, most names that are clear to English readers (e.g., Ibrahim) have been written without diacritical marks.

MANDATORY SEPARATION

INTRODUCTION

The Politics of Denial

SEVERAL YEARS AGO IN JERUSALEM I had the opportunity to attend a *ḥumash mesibah*, a celebration during which five-year-old boys in an ultra-Orthodox Jewish school, or *ḥeder*, received their individual copies of the Torah (*ḥumash*). The program was conducted in Yiddish with a tall barrier separating excited mothers, grandmothers, sisters, and aunts from the men up front. Plates with the presiding rabbi's kugel circulated through the audience. For all these traces of *yiddishkeit*, it would be hard to characterize this as a traditional affair. To begin with, the rabbi was escorted into the event by a security detail wearing Bluetooth headsets. A stage had been erected whose level of set design would outshine many private school productions in the United States. The young boys performed—in costume—a fully choreographed song-and-dance routine before receiving their *ḥumashim*. Flat-screen televisions broadcast the performance throughout the audience, ensuring that even the women seated in the back could get a close-up view of their budding Torah scholars in matching silver hats.

While Yiddish is not a language I speak, I was nonetheless able to deduce that this "traditional" ceremony within the most "traditional" of Jewish communities was a wholly modern affair, notwithstanding popular depictions of Israel's ultra-Orthodox communities as the living embodiment of medieval Jewry. Instead of somehow residing outside the experience of modernity, this small anecdote illustrates the ways in which the new can animate—rather than replace—the old. It is an observation to which I have continually returned in my attempt to make sense of my multifaceted object of inquiry: the nature of Jewish and Islamic religious education in Palestine during the years of British rule, which began in the final months of the First World War and lasted until May 1948. It was precisely during this period, perhaps more so than during any other in the history of modern Palestine, that the nature of education underwent a seismic shift from a decentralized practice managed largely by religious communities to a formalized system of schooling centrally administered by state or quasi-state institutions.[1] Far from ensuring the continuity of tradition, as proponents sometimes claimed, this shift could not occur without radically transforming the form and function of religious education—and arguably religion itself.

This book aims to better understand the nature of this transformation by posing a series of historical and conceptual questions to archival records, school syllabi, textbooks, newspapers, and personal narratives. How did religious education function within the ideological and administrative frameworks used to govern Palestine? What were the features of "modern" religious education as outlined by Jewish, Arab-Muslim, and colonial educators, and in what ways did this education differ from customary forms? How did each party conceive of the proper relationship between religious traditions and nation-building projects? In short, what were the content, form, and purpose of religious education as it developed into a discrete type of schooling in modern Palestine?

Surveying this dynamic period, this book argues that the British Mandatory government supported religious education as a supposed antidote to nationalist passions at the precise moment when the administrative, pedagogic, and curricular transformation of religious schooling rendered it a vital political tool for Zionist and Palestinian leaders. I show that the Government of Palestine viewed religious schooling within both Jewish and Muslim communities as a means of preserving (or reconstructing) the "traditional" order in which respect for the sacred was regarded as both an integral facet of individual character and a collective counterweight to mass politics. In part, this perception grew out of past experiences in India and Egypt, where the strategic support for religious elites, institutions, and legal codes had, by the late nineteenth century, morphed into a sort of "imperial best practices" for managing the unruly masses. Yet we can also detect traces of a distinctly liberal notion of religion as a code of ethics that could be separated from politics, commerce, and material life. Colonial officials who associated religious education with the status quo did not, by and large, detect the interpretive flexibility that gave this form of education its revolutionary potential. Indeed, it was as if by meddling in the messy business of mass politics, "religion" left its proper ontological field and became something else entirely.

In contrast to these colonial designs, Jewish and Muslim communities in Palestine offered competing educational models within which religious knowledge was explicitly tied to their respective political goals. Far from representing the natural heirs to long traditions of religious learning within Jewish and Islamic contexts, the interconnected rise of mass politics and mass education, I argue, produced opportunities to link religious identity to political action in novel ways. Based on a case study of al-Najāḥ National School and the writings of its former headmaster, Muhammad 'Izzat Darwaza, I argue that one way to articulate this relationship was to stress the mutually constitutive nature of Islam and Arab identity and, moreover, to do so in a way that did not alienate Palestinian Christians. For their part, I argue that Zionist schools tried to inculcate a new form of Jewishness that challenged the liberal construction of religious affiliation as distinct from political identity. Thus, far from accepting a colonial view of religion, politics, and education as discrete practices that were best kept separate, educators from both Palestinian and Zionist communities sought to use new and dynamic forms of religious education as a means of advancing their nationalist projects.

In formulating this argument, I have drawn theoretical and methodological insights from three primary bodies of scholarship in the fields of religious studies, Middle East history, and science studies, respectively. The first consists of those works that have, over the past two decades, revolutionized the study of religion and secularism as abstract categories. It was not so long ago that scholars spoke of the world as divided into different but functionally comparable religions and posited that a society could arrive at modernity only by adopting a secular orientation that purged the public sphere of religious values. However, in the years since José Casanova's important intervention, *Public Religions in the Modern World*,[2] scholars from a wide range of disciplines have challenged social scientific models that linked secularization with modernization, questioned the universality of secular reason, and highlighted the particularism inherent in the modern concept of religion itself. Of particular note here are works by Talal Asad, Jürgen Habermas, Charles Taylor, Timothy Fitzgerald, Tomoko Masuzawa, Gil Anidjar, Brent Nongbri, and Saba Mahmood, as well as the compilations edited by Craig Calhoun, Mark Juergensmeyer, and Jonathan VanAntwerpen.[3]

Despite this growing body of scholarship, historians of the Middle East have not, on the whole, taken the consequences of these interventions into serious consideration. How, for example, does our understanding of Arab political movements in the twentieth century shift if we take a critical stance toward the avowed secularism of many of their leaders? In what way were they secular? Which intellectual positions are assumed within (and concealed by) this claim? One of the overarching claims of this book is that if we are to describe these projects as "secular"—and I remain unconvinced that given its popular connotations, the term reveals more than it obscures—we must also be ready to excavate the rather different configurations of the self and the citizen that they envisioned. That is, if secularism in its normative sense is not a neutral political model but rather the outcome of a particular set of conflicts between the early modern state and different Christian churches, we must also grasp that the division of human life into "religious" (spiritual, private, voluntary, and nonjudicial) and "secular" realms bears traces of the Christian political and social order out of which it evolved. Historians have only just begun to examine the ways in which non-Christian communities, in Palestine and elsewhere, navigated this conceptual terrain. This is in part, as Jonathan Gribetz argues, the result of a general historiographical tendency to assume that nationalism is the most critical category for studying the early Zionist-Arab encounter and that religion (like race) is of only tangential concern. Moreover, "the blinding effects of secularization theory" and the "secularist nature of much nationalist historiography" have obscured the extent to which religion, race, and nation were fluid categories instead of clearly demarcated zones of identification or political mobilization.[4]

These considerations should be of particular interest to historians of education and nationalism in the Middle East in light of the association of national education with secularism. Certainly for an earlier generation of thinkers like Ernest Gellner, nationalism was a force that seemed to march hand in hand with the secular public school, just as the division of individuals into their private and public selves offered a mode of overcoming religious difference for the sake of common citizenship.[5] It is understandable then to find that scholars often assume the secularity of Zionist and Arab national projects, including their cultural and educational aims. Yet as I argue in the final chapters of this book, just because Jewish and Muslim leaders and educators in Palestine viewed their task through a radically different lens than did their religious forebears, the national systems of education they endeavored to construct could hardly be said to play by the normative rules of (Christian) secularism. In lieu of attempts to remove religion from the public space to facilitate a nonconfessional politics, we instead encounter concerted efforts to mobilize religious texts and traditions in furtherance of the national project. Taking stock of this history also gestures toward certain continuities that joined the nationalist tumult of a century ago to the religiously inflected discourses of the present. Rather than view religion as something that faded and then mysteriously returned late in the twentieth century, the educational history of Jewish and Muslim communities during the Mandate period highlights the interpretive flexibility inherent in religious traditions and the ways in which they can be selectively mobilized in different ways by each generation.

I found these theoretical insights particularly useful in trying to analyze the critical role of religion in structuring Palestine's educational system as a whole.[6] As it turns out, governing Palestine on sectarian lines generated a number of particular challenges and contradictions in regard to defining the content and purpose of religious education, difficulties that stemmed largely from contested, and sometimes contradictory, understandings of religion itself. Was religion a set of beliefs or a communal designation? What types of knowledge and facets of life were religious in nature? And who decided? Out of the difficulties inherent in answering such questions, I arrived at an important consideration, the instability of religious education as an analytic category, one whose development as a distinct conceptual object hinged on a redefinition of formalized learning, on the one hand, and the emergence of the secular as a separate sphere of human experience, on the other. It followed that because the boundaries that distinguish the religious from the secular are porous, historically contingent, and contested, a study of religious education in Palestine should not limit its analysis to the educational endeavors of the usual suspects. Thus, rather than look primarily at schools managed by Orthodox Zionists,[7] the Supreme Muslim Council,[8] or communities in the Old Yishuv,[9] I have tried to move away from an institutional analysis toward a genealogical one that interrogates the criteria by which knowledge is labeled as "religious" in nature and the consequences, both material and hermeneutic, of this designation.

Second, I have been inspired by recent works of Middle East history that challenge the long-standing tendency among historians to assume the separateness of Jewish and Arab societies in Mandate Palestine. Scholars of Jewish education in Palestine have generally worked within the "dual society" model pioneered decades ago by Moshe Lissak and Dan Horowitz, which regards the *yishuv* (prestate community) as an autonomous body that existed in isolation from its surroundings. Though not without merit, this methodological approach nonetheless reifies one of Zionist historiography's most sacred myths: that of self-sufficiency.[10] Studies of Jewish education in the *yishuv* have therefore devoted little attention to the points of dependence and influence that linked this history to practices pursued by the Government of Palestine, missionary bodies, or Palestinian Arabs.[11] At the other end of the historiographical spectrum, scholars of Palestine have endeavored to showcase the history of Palestinian Arab society as a multidimensional entity that existed prior to and independently of its conflict with Zionism.[12] There is much to say in favor of this method given that comparisons of Palestinian Arab society to the *yishuv* are fraught with methodological difficulties due to radical differences between the two populations in terms of literacy, educational level, and occupation.[13] However, despite their merits, such studies tend to reinforce the dual society narrative that, particularly when dealing with the Mandate period, obfuscates our understanding of the forces that bound Palestinian and Jewish communities together, however unhappily. Is there a compelling alternative to isolationist and comparative approaches?

I have found the sociological model pioneered by Gershon Shafir, which examines the formative (though often unstated) impact of Jewish-Arab relations on Israeli state and society, more promising. As Shafir points out, "Those aspects of their society which Israelis pride themselves on being the most typically Israeli," including the former hegemony of the labor movement and kibbutz farming, are in fact consequences of Zionism's early struggles with the Arab economy in Palestine.[14] In a similar vein, Zachary Lockman has argued the merits of a relational approach to the history of Mandate Palestine that posits that "the histories of Arabs and Jews in modern Palestine can only be grasped by studying the ways in which both these communities were to a significant extent constituted and shaped within a complex matrix of economic, political, social and cultural interactions."[15] Though the difficulties embarking on this course of historical study cannot be understated, some of the most compelling studies of modern Palestine have employed a relational framework.[16]

This project adopts a similar approach in attempting to account for the transformation of Jewish and Arab-Islamic education during the Mandate period. Thus, my research stresses the discursive, administrative, and financial structures that caused these educational systems to develop relationally.

While accounting for the distinctiveness of each, I attempt to show that treating these systems in isolation presumes certain social structures that were still in the process of formation. In this respect, my project differs from the work of historians who have assumed that Jewish and Arab systems of education under the Mandate were mere continuations from the Ottoman past, in which Palestine's population frequented schools in a largely sectarian fashion. In contrast, I argue that the segregation of Jewish and Arab schooling assumed a new and dramatically influential form during the Mandate period due in large part to the political and pedagogic concerns pursued by both the Palestine government and the communities themselves. Moreover, rather than project communal separatism onto the past as the preexisting reality, I have tried to examine the administrative, legal, and financial means through which Arab-Jewish divisions were concretized and the role of religious difference within this scheme. Indeed, this study invites us to view national and religious difference as factors acting in concert with one another rather than assume that either served as the dominant category of differentiation between Palestine's communities. By examining the tensions inherent in the sectarian management of education in Palestine, I hope to demonstrate the lasting significance of these policies—which established a new matrix of relations between mass education, religious knowledge, and political action—for thinking about political identity in the broader Middle East.

The third body of scholarship on which I have drawn comes from the world of science and technology studies and, in particular, the theoretical interventions of the French philosopher Bruno Latour. In his 1991 text, *We Have Never Been Modern*, Latour describes the apparent separation of the natural world from the social one as the defining marker of the period we call modernity. Outlining what he terms the "Modern Constitution," Latour details a series of assertions and denunciations about nature and society, a compendium of claims that alternate between stressing the transcendence and immanence of each. A key component of this conceptual order has been the growing sense of separation between us "moderns"—who have dispelled myths and potions in favor of scientific reason—and primitive peoples among whom nature and culture remain hopelessly intertwined:

> You think thunder is a divinity? The modern critique will show that it is generated by mere physical mechanisms that have no influence over the progress of human affairs. You are stuck in a traditional economy? The modern critique will

> show you that physical mechanisms can upset the progress of human affairs by mobilizing huge productive forces. You think that the spirits of the ancestors hold you forever hostage to their laws? The modern critique will show you that you are hostage to yourselves and that the spiritual world is your own human—too human—construction.[17]

Latour is not a thinker that scholars of secularism have frequently drawn on, but I have found in the notion of the Modern Constitution a productive model for thinking about divisions between the religious and the secular, and the political and the scientific. The idea that we moderns have managed to purge our social and political systems of irrational forces—religion chief among them—in ways that *others* have not remains the central animating claim of Western exceptionalism. This is not to say our God is dead; rather, as Latour argues, a key feature of the Modern Constitution is the "crossed-out God," removed from the dual social and natural construction but "presentable and usable nevertheless." As he continues, "No one is truly modern who does not agree to keep God from interfering with Natural Law as well as with the laws of the Republic. God becomes the crossed-out God of metaphysics, as different from the premodern God of the Christians as the Nature constructed in the laboratory is from the ancient *phusis* or the Society invented by sociologists from the old anthropological collective and its crowds of nonhumans."[18]

What is of crucial importance is that this neat system of division between nature and society, the rational and the transcendental, us and them, is both illusory *and* useful. It is precisely this sense of separation (purification, in Latour's terms) that serves to mask, and indeed facilitate, the proliferation of ideas and practices that transgress the boundaries between these supposedly distinct worlds. These "hybrid" forms must be vociferously defined for the conceptual order to function, and thus Latour argues that modernity is not distinguished by its *success* in separating the natural world of neutral facts from the socially constructed one composed by human agents but by the *claim* that it does so. Thus, "the modern world," Latour argues, "has never happened, in the sense that it has never functioned according to the rules of its official Constitution alone."[19]

In addition to offering a different framework for approaching the claims of secularism, the concepts of separation, transgression, and denial are also helpful in thinking about modern forms of education. If education in the premodern world was by and large a communal responsibility that was clearly intertwined with the social environment, the "science" of modern pedagogy and the emergence of a professionally trained class of teachers meant that education at the beginning of the twentieth century was increasingly conceptualized as distinct from both politics and society. In many instances, it was through the right form of education that reformers hoped to correct the backward social practices of the home. With these insights in mind, we should not find it strange that the Mandatory government refused to acknowledge the obvious link between pedagogy and politics. Rather, a Latourian approach enables us to avoid the anachronistic projection of our own sensibility on the past. Instead of finding it contradictory (or idiotic!) that colonial administrators could possibly *overlook* the political dimension of educational practices—or likewise, the political power of religious traditions—we should try to excavate the epistemic order in which such thoughts were not just possible but obvious. It then becomes clear that we are dealing with a larger matrix of colonial power that held as self-evident distinctions between pedagogic need and social engineering, civic action and mass politics, national pride and national chauvinism, and "true" religion and religious fanaticism. This framework mobilized the languages of scientific fact, educational best practices, and universal values in service of what I will call a "politics of denial," the expression of power through policies that insist they have nothing to do with politics. In each instance, the "purification" of these categories marched hand in hand with acts that violated the boundary meant to preserve their separation. Following Latour, transgressions of this kind must be diligently denied, a fact that becomes most evident when we consider British views of Christian schools in Palestine as the value-neutral meeting ground for temperamental Semites.

Here we come to see that the apparent differences between the approach to religious education that the Mandatory government pursued, on the one hand, and those of Jewish and Muslim educators, on the other, were more discursive than material. Education served as a political tool within the schools maintained by each group. So too did religious texts, values, and worldviews freely mingle with questions of political power and animate political struggles. "The less moderns think they are blended, the more they blend."[20] I endeavor to show that, while British colonial officials in Palestine refused to acknowledge the "hybrid" nature of their own educational policies, Zionist and Palestinian leaders embraced these transgressions—across the boundaries between the individual and the communal, the pedagogic and the national, and the political and the religious—as foundational to the construction of a new future.

PALESTINE UNDER BRITISH RULE: THE NATIONAL HOME PROJECT AND ITS DISCONTENTS

"The British entered Palestine to defeat the Turks; they stayed there to keep it from the French; then they gave it to the Zionists because they loved 'the Jews' even as they loathed them, at once admired and despised them, and above all feared them." The academic historian can add much to these words by Tom Segev, but few would be able to summarize the contradictory impulses that characterized British rule in Palestine so efficiently. The fruits not of "diplomatic interests but of prejudice, faith, and sleight of hand," the 1917 Balfour Declaration still ranks among the most influential and controversial documents in the history of the modern Middle East.[21] Assuming the form of a letter to Lord Rothschild from the foreign secretary, Arthur James Balfour, it read:

> His Majesty's government view with favour the establishment in Palestine of a national home for the Jewish people, and will use their best endeavours to facilitate the achievement of this object, it being clearly understood that nothing shall be done which may prejudice the civil and religious rights of existing non-Jewish communities in Palestine, or the rights and political status enjoyed by Jews in any other country.

Purposefully vague—using the language of "national home" rather than "state"—the declaration nevertheless offered the Zionist movement an imperial lifeline by committing the world's foremost empire to the principle of reconstructed Jewish life in the historic Land of Israel.

Modern Zionism emerged as a political and cultural movement among European Jews during the final decades of the nineteenth century. Composed of numerous and often competing strands, Zionism nevertheless committed itself to the idea of a Jewish national renaissance. Emerging out of the romantic nationalism that swept Europe during the nineteenth century, and a growing sense of disillusion regarding the possibilities for full Jewish emancipation within European states, many in the movement looked to Palestine as the site for reconstituting the Jewish people along national lines. Though the first Zionist Congress convened in 1897 after the publication of Theodor Herzl's *Der Judenstaat* (The Jews' state), the movement's early leaders and thinkers were divided over the nature of their goal. For highly assimilated Jews like Herzl and Max Nordau, Zionism was chiefly a political fix to the problem of anti-Semitism, with the envisioned state assuming the form of Vienna on the Mediterranean. Conversely, the "cultural" arm of the movement asserted that such a state would not really be Jewish at all; rather, Zionism should stress above all the cultural renaissance of the Jewish people and the Hebrew language, the ethics of the biblical prophets, and the organic—even cosmic—links between the Jewish people and the Land of Israel. While political leaders in Europe debated, the pioneers of the Second Aliyah (wave of immigration, extending from approximately 1904 to 1914) focused on building a new physical presence in Palestine along with the educational and cultural institutions necessary for a Hebrew revival. The material conditions were crushing, and the onset of the First World War brought plagues of locusts and famine alongside political deportations for many Jews whose countries of citizenship were now at war with the Ottoman Empire. The Balfour Declaration arrived at a critical point to offer new life to the fledgling movement. The occupation of much of Palestine by British troops in December 1917 seemed to offer assurance that His Majesty's Government possessed the practical means to honor this "contract with Jewry."[22]

Much has been written about the declaration, the motivations behind it, and the British relationship to Zionism; for our purposes, it is important to note that this was merely one of Britain's many wartime promises. With forces trapped in an extended stalemate in the trenches of western Europe—where each new confrontation seemed to bring an unprecedented loss of life but only minor territorial advantage—both sides looked to gain an upper hand in other theaters of war. With the Ottoman Empire fighting on behalf of the Central Powers, its vast territories appealed to the Allies in terms of both a potential military breakthrough and, perhaps more important, postwar spoils. Britain had occupied Egypt and parts of the Sudan since 1882 and also maintained bases in southern Arabia; both served as strategic positions to ensure the passage of ships from India through the Suez Canal. Meanwhile, France maintained its own sphere of influence in the Middle East, stemming largely from its support for Maronite populations around Mount Lebanon and its self-appointed role of "protector of Catholics" in Ottoman lands. Long seeking to enlarge their imperial holdings throughout the Middle East, both powers took it for granted that, in the event of an Allied victory, they would parcel up Ottoman lands as compensation for the crushing costs of the war.

In 1916, Britain and France concluded the infamous Sykes-Picot Agreement, which divided the Ottoman territories into two zones of control: Zone A, encompassing modern-day Syria, Lebanon, southeastern Turkey, and parts of northern Iraq, would be awarded to France; Britain would assume control of

Zone B, consisting roughly of the territory south of Acre in present-day Israel and extending eastward through Transjordan and Iraq. With British-Zionist talks already in full swing, the agreement carved Palestine out of the two zones with the understanding that some sort of international accord would decide its fate. Even as these negotiations were ongoing, Sir Henry McMahon was busy concluding a separate agreement with Hussein bin Ali, the sherif of Mecca, to raise an Arab revolt against the Ottomans. In exchange, McMahon agreed that Britain would recognize an independent Arab state in the Arabic-speaking provinces of the Ottoman Empire, excepting "the districts of Mersina and Alexandretta, and portions of Syria lying to the west of the districts of Damascus, Homs, Hama and Aleppo," which "cannot be said to be purely Arab."[23] Perhaps needless to say, this assemblage of wartime agreements could not all be reconciled, and the reality that emerged from the peace conferences was a largely colonial one despite being cloaked in new terms.[24]

Those terms included the League of Nations Mandate system, a three-tiered categorization scheme that divided the Central Powers' former colonial holdings as well as the Ottoman Empire's Arab provinces according to their level of civilizational progress.[25] Article 22 of the League Covenant stipulated that "advanced countries" would provide tutelage to "peoples not yet able to stand by themselves under the strenuous conditions of the modern world."[26] Ever committed to the "sacred trust of civilization," France and Britain eagerly assumed Mandates for Syria and Lebanon, in the former's case, and Palestine, Transjordan, and Iraq in the latter's. The former Ottoman territories were classified as Class A Mandates, meaning that they were supposedly the closest to attaining the capacity for self-government. The administrative systems that were erected in Iraq, Syria, Lebanon, and Jordan reflected this status through the appointment of local leaders and bureaucrats who were receptive to such "tutelage." Indeed, though British systems of imperial governance displayed more variety than is commonly assumed, by the 1920s officials increasingly embraced the idea of indirect rule wherein British advisers would guide local officials in the creation and implementation of "correct" policies. Here the anomalous case of Palestine was most jarring, as local Arab officials could obviously not be entrusted with implementing the Zionist project. Thus, unlike the situation in other Class A Mandates, the upper-ranking administrative class in Palestine was almost entirely British; with important exceptions, Arab and Jewish officials were usually employed only as lower-level bureaucrats or inspectors.[27]

Despite the vigorous protests of Palestinian leaders—and material realities on the ground, in which the Arab population represented approximately 88 percent of the total population—the League of Nations Mandate for Palestine included the Balfour Declaration as part of its official text and therefore served to concretize the British commitment to Zionism. Any wavering based on the practical impossibility of implementing the Jewish national home project without prejudice to the rights of the "non-Jewish communities" could henceforth be interpreted as a breach of contract that jeopardized Britain's claim to Palestine. What ensued was an acute case of muddling through with little strategic sense as to how discrete policy choices were linked to long-term political outcomes. This was particularly evident in the realm of education planning, where the policies pursued were at direct odds with anything other than the country's partition, even as officials often spoke about schools as sites for inculcating common civic virtues.

The Colonial Office appointed as director of education Humphrey Bowman, a seasoned colonial officer who attended Eton and Oxford before supervising education departments in Sudan, Egypt, and Iraq.[28] Bowman was highly sympathetic to the Arab cause in Palestine and wary of political Zionism, though he did not share in the outright anti-Semitism expressed by some of his colleagues. He served from 1920 to 1936, when he retired and Jerome Farrell, his longtime assistant director, assumed his post. Farrell was more caustic than his predecessor and had little sympathy with the national aspirations of either the Jews or Palestinian Arabs. He became famous for his long, frank dispatches to the Colonial Office, which contain both considerable insight into the problems that plagued educational planning and frequent displays of antipathy toward Palestine's various "Semites." Indeed, Bowman initially expressed a great deal of reservation about Farrell's suitability for the post, describing him as a man who "rather despises Arabs, but works well with his colleagues (except G.A.) [George Antonius]," whom he famously forced out of his high-level post at the Department of Education.[29] In Bowman's words,

> He [Farrell] likes to rule the roost and does not really take much notice of any opinion offered him by anyone. He is too good for the job, he thinks, and is too well qualified academically that he deserves a better post, but in a country where the lack of sympathy for the ruled does not count for too much. Here, sympathy and understanding is everything and that happens to be one of my few qualifications for the job.[30]

Though Bowman softened toward Farrell over time and admired his administrative efficiency, there was no doubt he felt that his junior colleague lacked the proper sensitivity and disposition for the job, a verdict with which it is hard to disagree. Following the riots of 1929—which ostensibly erupted because of a dispute over the nature of Jewish access to the Western Wall in Jerusalem—the Arab Executive called for a general strike and encouraged students to stay home from school. It was in this context that Bowman recounted with horror how Farrell dealt with the political tension in Nablus: "Having heard that all boys in secondary classes of Salahiyah [school] were absent on Wednesday, went there on Thursday with a British policeman and ordered 50% of the boys caned by him. Result: boys left school, joined general rabble, made a riot and were arrested. Beaten again by police in barracks. Result: general strike in Nablus by parents against sending children to school on Saturday."[31] Jerome Farrell served as education director until the end of 1946, when Bernard de Bunsen, a former inspector, succeeded him. I mainly discuss the views and policies associated with the first two directors, as de Bunsen filled the post for only eighteen months before the Mandate terminated. Two groups of school inspectors, for the Arab and Hebrew public systems, respectively, rounded out the Department of Education's staff. The inspectorate included a number of noteworthy figures, such as Sheikh Hussam al-Din Jarallah—who was chosen by the ulema of Palestine to assume the title of grand mufti before the British appointed Haj Amin al-Husseini[32]—and the budding scholars Abdul Latif Tibawi, Joseph Bentwich, and Shlomo Dov Goitein.

In addition to the Department of Education of the Government of Palestine, there were other administrative bodies about which a word of explanation is required. Article 4 of the Mandate for Palestine stipulated that "an appropriate Jewish agency shall be recognized as a public body for the purpose of advising and co-operating with the Administration of Palestine in such economic, social and other matters as may affect the establishment of the Jewish national home."[33] An actual Jewish Agency was not established until 1929, but the executive arm of the World Zionist Organization's Jerusalem office (referred to throughout as "the Zionist Executive") assumed its functions in the interim. In addition, in 1926 the Jewish community of Palestine secured recognition of its representative body, Knesset Israel, through the Religious Communities Organization Ordinance. Unless they opted out, all Palestinian Jews were included in the electorate of Knesset Israel and collectively chose representatives to serve in a parliamentary body called the Va'ad Leumi (National Council).

The executive council of the Va'ad Leumi played an active role in Zionist politics and—though officially recognized as the head of a religious community—"was composed of politicians, not religious leaders" who "functioned in strictly secular fields."[34] I have much to say about this strict secularism in later chapters, but here it is worth noting that the Va'ad Leumi remained rather weak in comparison to the Zionist Organization until the 1930s, when the center of Zionist political power began to shift decisively to the *yishuv*.[35] The Jewish Agency served as the chief administrative body for Zionist schools until 1932, when control over the *yishuv*'s education was transferred to Knesset Israel.

Conversely, the League of Nations Mandate for Palestine recognized no Arab political body that would parallel the Jewish Agency because the Mandate did not recognize the Arabs of Palestine in *national* terms at all, preferring to regard them as a motley crew of Christians, Muslims, Bedouins, and Druze with no unifying features or political identity outside their religious communities. The Balfour Declaration reflected this reality by pledging to protect only the "civil and religious rights" of the Arab population. Faced with the recent departure of Ottoman religious functionaries—and ever wary of appearing to meddle in the religious affairs of subject populations—the British opted to create a new position, the grand mufti of Palestine, to oversee Muslim courts, charitable endowments, and other communal functions. Rather than offer a counterpart to the Jewish Agency, the muftiship was envisioned as a parallel office to that held by the Greek patriarch.[36] The grand mufti was recognized as president of a larger communal governing body, the Supreme Muslim Council, which would eventually emerge as the leading force in the Palestinian struggle against British and Zionist forces. The Supreme Muslim Council did maintain a network of schools, though most of Palestine's Muslim children who had access to formal schooling attended government schools. We encounter each of these groups as we examine their respective visions for Jewish and Islamic religious education in a time of mass politics.

CHAPTER OVERVIEW

Mandatory Separation showcases the ways in which colonial administrators sparred with Jewish and Muslim leaders regarding the political function of religious education. Because this is not an institutional analysis, I have chosen to organize chapters thematically rather than strictly chronologically. Chapter 1 serves to contextualize the activities of Jewish and Muslim educators in Palestine by taking stock of the "enlightenment" projects in which education reform emerged as a key tenet. By distinguishing between the transmission of sacred knowledge and modern systemic schooling, this chapter highlights the novelty of "religious education" as a site for the production and disciplining of moral and political subjects. I further argue that grappling with this history requires us to bear in mind three overlapping developments and considerations: the modern conceptualization of "religion" as a set of beliefs and practices segregated from other realms of human experience (e.g., politics, commerce, and culture); the political nature of modern education as a tool for character formation and civic training; and the rise of new type of mass politics in Palestine that linked religious education to national identity.

Chapter 2 further contextualizes this inquiry by outlining key aspects of the Mandatory government's administrative apparatus and its policies related to the provision of education. Although British officials strove to immunize Palestine's schools against the destructive influence of "politics," I argue that such rhetoric serves to mask the inherently political nature of modern schooling and elides over the very real consequences of policies that were supposedly guided by pedagogic need. Rather than insulate Palestine's schools from the surrounding tumult, I detail how the provision of education during the Mandate period contributed to the division of Palestine into competing Arab and Jewish spheres, each with its own national language, public school system, and administrative machinery. Chapter 3 moves this general discussion into the legislative realm by examining both the sectarian management of education in Palestine and the tensions present within this form of governance. Based on an analysis of debates surrounding the Palestine Education Ordinance of 1933, this chapter argues that the Mandatory government created a category of exception for religious schools and those managed by "religious" communities. This administrative structure functioned to the advantage of schools managed by the Zionist Organization and, later, the Va'ad Leumi, which were given a large degree of autonomy based on their dual status as both public and religious entities. Conversely, linking educational autonomy to religious community weakened Palestinian attempts to create a *national* school system that united children from different confessional backgrounds.

Chapter 4 looks more concretely at how this legislation impacted religious schools by comparing the Department of Education's attempts to reform "old-fashioned" Islamic and Jewish schools into clean, efficient, and pedagogically sound sites for producing model citizens: moral, productive, and decidedly nonpolitical. Discarding the more typical approach of considering Jewish and

Arab schools separately, this chapter highlights certain common assumptions about the purpose of education and the role of religious instruction in combating nationalist passions. I argue here that the government's education administrators ultimately related to Palestine's Jewish and Islamic communal schools (*ḥederim* and *katātīb*) in similar ways by promoting a view that linked the preservation of authenticity to the introduction of novel curricula and pedagogic practices. Thus, this chapter demonstrates the creative interplay between the "new" and "old" as ideas that animate, rather than replace, one another.

The final two chapters detail what might be called points of transgression: those uses of religion and education that violated the boundaries—between civic engagement and mass politics, pedagogic need and social engineering, individual ethics and public religion—that framed key components of colonial thought. Chapter 5 consists of an extended study of the Palestinian educator Muhammad 'Izzat Darwaza and the educational program he pioneered at al-Najāḥ National School in Nablus. In this context, I argue that even leaders associated with certain features of secular modernity did not acquiesce to the severance of religious values from political activism. Chapter 6 rounds out the analysis with a case study of curricula used in Zionist schools, which the Government of Palestine consistently derided for being both excessively political and insufficiently religious. I argue that this designation serves to obscure our understanding of what was truly noteworthy about Zionist education: the attempt to construct a synthetic national identity that imagined a new type of Jewishness freed from the restrictions of Europe's secular political order. In Palestine, many argued, one need not be a Jew only at home.

The Conclusion returns to the concept of a politics of denial by considering one final case for discussion: the frequent praise of Christian missionary schools among British officials as a safe meeting ground for the unruly natives. This example serves to highlight that claims of this sort, which characteristically denied that such schools meddled in the nasty business of politics, typify a form of colonial power whose strength lies in assertions of its own neutrality. Finally, in closing, I offer some thoughts about the contemporary association between religious education and political radicalism and suggest an alternative framework for approaching the study of religious traditions.

1 RELIGIOUS EDUCATION IN THE MODERN AGE

The secular is itself a sphere of transcendental values, but the invention of religion as the locus of the transcendent serves to disguise this and strengthen the illusion that the secular is simply the real world seen aright in its self-evident factuality.

—Timothy Fitzgerald, *The Ideology of Religious Studies*

LONG A SITE OF CROSSROADS AND PILGRIMAGE, Palestine in the early twentieth century nurtured educational ideas and practices that often, though not always, originated elsewhere. Whether it was the latest developments in German educational theory, Sayyid Ahmad Khan's efforts to develop the empirical sciences in India,[1] or the "lessons" derived from Egyptian schooling, educators of all stripes tried to assimilate global insights into their local contexts. Looking more narrowly at Islamic and Jewish education, we must begin by appreciating the extent to which developments in Palestine were linked to debates and processes that began several decades earlier in places like Berlin, Cairo, and Istanbul. After all, education reform was a key tenet not only of colonial regimes but of modernist platforms propagated by Jewish "enlighteners" (*maskilim*) in the late eighteenth century and, beginning in the early nineteenth century, by Muslim reformers spread from South Asia to North Africa.[2] In general terms, both movements sprang from a sense of the inadequacy of the existing religious and social order to meet the challenges of the modern world—the latter being represented by the cultural, economic, and political might of western Europe.[3]

While bearing their individual nuances, which are too expansive to detail here, it is nonetheless true that these reform projects were characterized by an overarching concern with the narrowness of traditional curricula centered on the study of religious texts. It was, reformers claimed, the neglect of subjects like philosophy and the natural sciences that had caused communities to sink into a state of subordination—either literally colonized in the case of millions of Muslims or unfit to join the communion of European civilization in the case of those Jews petitioning for membership. In both contexts, reformers were confronted with long traditions of communal education, and their efforts were often directed at the transformation of existing schools—which were increasingly viewed as the source of moral corruption and cultural decay—rather than the ab initio creation of secular public ones. In many instances, the core of this reforming impulse involved diversifying the customary curricula to incorporate the empirical sciences, foreign languages and literatures, and the emerging body of European political and social thought. This chapter surveys these overlapping geographies and modernizing impulses, the legacies of which would inform the work of Jewish and Arab-Muslim educators in Palestine as they looked to construct—though not without key changes in orientation—their respective visions for the role of religious traditions in the age of mass politics.

Even as we are attentive to certain points of continuity, we must begin by appreciating the novelty inherent in modern religious education under state or quasi-state supervision and, correspondingly, question the sense of timelessness that is often ascribed to religious learning. For instance, in his 1965 book *Education in Israel*, Joseph Bentwich, a former assistant director of education for the Government of Palestine, offered a conventional view of Jewish education through the ages: the medieval school (*ḥeder*) gave way to modern ones founded by European *maskilim*, which in turn yielded to the Zionist school system and that of the State of Israel.[4] Extending the historical arc back in time, Bentwich explained that Jewish education for boys already existed on a widespread, if not universal, level by the fourth century CE. A parallel account of the history of Islamic education written by Abdul Latif Tibawi—who was, incidentally, Bentwich's colleague in the Department of Education during the Mandate period—appeared in 1972.[5] Though in many ways a thoughtful and nuanced account, the text nonetheless presents a similar evolutionary trajectory that links the medieval madrasa of al-Ghazali's time to the educational reforms of Muhammad ʿAli and the eventual founding of national school systems in postcolonial Arab states.

As evidenced in these works, it can be tempting to narrate the history of Jewish and Islamic education from a communal to state concern as an unbroken chain. Yet we would be well served by pausing to question this presumed continuity between classical, medieval, and modern forms of schooling. Certain features, such as the texts studied, seem to support the argument that contemporary Jewish and Islamic schools are the natural progeny of those that preceded them. Yet these narratives seem to take for granted what are, to my mind, radical differences in terms of the purpose, structure, and content of education that render the modern school something very different from the medieval *ḥeder* or *kuttāb*. As Jonathan Berkey has argued in his study of the madrasa, education in the premodern world was conceived of as "a pillar of *stability* rather than as a force for *change*."[6] Thus, while institutionalized learning had a long history in both Jewish and Islamic contexts, it is doubtful whether what occurred in these places was "education" in our contemporary sense of the term. In approaching religious education in twentieth-century Palestine, we must therefore first appreciate the extent to which it represented a modern innovation despite obvious points of continuity with premodern practices.

With this in mind, I argue that the growing consensus throughout the nineteenth century of education as a state, rather than merely communal, concern had significant implications in regard to creating institutions for Jewish and Islamic learning in the years that followed. Appreciating the novelty inherent in mass, publicly funded religious instruction requires us to take stock of three important conceptual pivots: first, the shifting relationship between state and subject; second, the hardening boundaries between "religious" and "secular" concerns and the corresponding interests associated with each; and third, the rise of mass politics, which I argue provided opportunities to link religious knowledge to political activism in new ways. I deal with each of them in turn, as they collectively provide the theoretical foundation for my discussion of discrete educational practices in Mandate Palestine.

RELIGIOUS EDUCATION AND THE MODERN SUBJECT

The idea that the primary purpose of education is moral fashioning, or in a more contemporary idiom, character development, has found widespread acceptance in contexts ranging from classical Athens to medieval Baghdad and contemporary America. That the responsibility for such education was historically conceived of as belonging to the child's immediate community is also clear enough. In the Jewish context, the catalyst for education can be traced to the biblical commandment for a father to instruct his children in the laws of Israel. The modern Hebrew term for education, *ḥinuch*, does not appear in the Hebrew Bible; there, words derived from the same root mean "to dedicate," "to initiate," or (less frequently, as in Proverbs 22:6) "to train." By contrast, one "learns" Torah (from *lilmod*), and even in contemporary usage the act of studying Jewish texts is referred to as "learning." Given this etymology, I prefer conceptualizing *ḥinuch* as a form of initiation, suggesting that it was through *ḥinuch* that the child assumed his full role in the community. If one remembers that learning to publicly read the Torah was a necessary stage of preparation for the bar mitzvah (literally, one who has reached the age of obligation for religious commandments, i.e., adulthood), the notion of *ḥinuch* as a form of initiation is even more compelling.

The system of learning that Jewish modernists would later denounce—with the *ḥeder* and *talmud torah* at its base and yeshiva at its apex—was already well established by the medieval period.[7] The *ḥeder* (literally "room") was a private school run by an individual teacher to whom parents paid a fee. Children traditionally began at age three by studying the Hebrew alphabet and quickly moved on to the Torah, the Mishnah (the basis of the oral law), and the practical *halachot* (laws) that they would need to function in the community in which they lived. The *talmud torah* was identical to the *ḥeder* in terms of subject matter but was maintained by the community at large to serve children whose parents could not afford the fees associated with the latter.[8] Only the most gifted students continued their studies beyond the elementary stage in the yeshiva, where learning and debating the legal disputations contained in the Talmud consumed the bulk of their energy.

Within the Islamic textual tradition, one can point to numerous hadiths that implore the believer to educate himself or herself. Famously included among the sayings of Muhammad are, "The quest for learning is a duty incumbent upon every Muslim, male and female," "Wisdom is the goal of the believer and he must seek it irrespective of its source," and "Seek knowledge even if it be in China" (a weak hadith, though this has rarely stopped reformers from quoting it). The *maktab* or *kuttāb* (plural, *katātīb*) were communal schools in which the child learned to read, recite, and write using the Qur'an as textbook—the terms *maktab* and *kuttāb* being related to the Arabic verb "to write" or "to inscribe." Pointing to the distinction between these institutions and the modern school in his study of colonial Egypt, Timothy Mitchell has argued, "Education, as an isolated process in which children acquire a set of instructions and self-discipline, was born in Egypt in the nineteenth century. Before that, there was no distinct location or institution where such a process was carried on, no body of adults for whom it was a profession, and no word for it in the language." Mitchell highlights that education in this modern sense (*tarbiyya*) must be differentiated from learning that "occurred within the practice of the particular profession," which was more akin to a system of apprenticeship.[9]

Until the early modern period, institutionalized learning in most Jewish and Islamic communities focused on acquiring literacy through the study of canonical texts, coupled with a practical understanding of the behavioral codes that ordered communal life. In its idealized form, education of this type was an

FIGURE 1. A lesson in a typical village school (*kuttāb*) in Ramah (northern Palestine), 1898. Courtesy of the Central Zionist Archives, PHG\1015590.

inquiry into the sublime, and practically, it served as a process of socialization into the community in which the child lived. For example, no business partnership or marriage would be arranged without the parties reciting *al-fātiḥah*, the opening sura of the Qur'an. Similarly, it is hard to classify familiarity with the laws of *kashrut*, or Sabbath observance, as merely intellectual exercises—or worse yet, "religious" duties—within the corporate structure of the medieval Jewish community. The fact that the *ḥeder* and *kuttāb* were useful to the communities they served was often overlooked in the modern period as Jewish and Muslim reformers came to echo the colonial distain for "literary" knowledge and to advocate an expansion of traditional curricula to include "practical" subjects. Yet it is likely that the narrow curriculum in these schools had less to do with an innate opposition to utility than with a unique understanding of what education as a practice actually entailed.

Medieval Muslim philosophers such as al-Namari, al-Zarnuji, and most important, al-Ghazali, articulated the classical expression of education as a form of ethical training that was "essential for the formation of virtuous subjects and the maintenance of a common good."[10] This did not necessarily entail opposition to other forms of knowledge per se but rather an attempt to preserve formal education as a system for developing the moral conduct that governed the individual's relationship with his fellow man and the piety that assured his devotion to God. As often occurred, the gifted student was able to study history, geography, or the empirical sciences in noninstitutional settings, or even in select madrasas; the average child would surely acquire much practical knowledge through apprenticeships or work with family members in agriculture, trade, or commerce. Formal education, however, was to be reserved for something more dignified than learning a vocation.[11] Jewish thinkers held that education was not only a form of socialization required to ensure the continuity of tradition (*mesorah*, literally meaning "that which is passed down or handed over") but represented an act of worship itself. The act of "learning Torah" constitutes a central commandment and, significantly, one that is regarded as encompassing all others. As the Talmud famously states, "These are the things for which man eats the fruit [of them] in this world but their bounty is fulfilled in the world to come: honoring one's father and mother, acts of kindness and bringing peace between men. Learning Torah is the equivalent to all of them."[12] Again, the reverence for education as a practice of transmitting sacred knowledge was not necessarily accompanied by the eschewing of practical training within premodern Jewish communities. The emergence of a large ultra-Orthodox bloc in Israel that fiercely opposed the inclusion of secular subjects within school curricula partially obscures this fact, yet one need only scratch the surface to uncover the modern providence of this "traditional" revolt.

The formal education that existed in premodern Europe was also, by and large, a practice that belonged to and functioned within the intellectual context provided by the Catholic Church. Cathedral and monastic schools constituted the most important centers of formal education throughout medieval Europe, out of which the first universities evolved during the High Middle Ages. The curriculum leaned heavily toward theology and law, though it also included medicine and the arts.[13] One important factor that distinguished the education developed under Jewish and Islamic auspices from formal schooling in Christian Europe is that the latter was largely reserved for the clergy. The most important revolution in this regard was the Protestant Reformation and, with it, a newfound emphasis on individual literacy as a means to access the Bible in an unmediated fashion.

Historians of education have long recognized the ideological centrality of the Reformation to the establishment of mass education, yet it was not until the rise of the nation-state in the nineteenth century that European governments began to support public education on a large scale. This was, according to Michel Foucault, reflective of a larger set of shifts that accompanied the growth of "governmentality," a term that signifies both a historical process and a set of administrative, institutional, and analytic practices. With regard to the former definition, Foucault argued that Europe, in the period from the middle of the sixteenth century to the end of the eighteenth, underwent a transition from sovereignty to government. Whereas the sovereign's primary interest is the perpetuation of rule over a specific territory through the use of law, the displacement of governance from the prerogative of the father to that of the state ushers in a new concern for the management of population though tactics.[14] It is therefore the population, rather than the territory, that becomes both "a field of intervention and . . . an objective of governmental techniques," that is, the object toward which the arts of government are directed.

As the rise of the market economy "invested individuals with both the authority to conduct their own productive activities and the responsibility to support the state financially," the need to unite the masses under the rubric of the nation assumed a newfound importance.[15] State-sponsored education was one of the premier vehicles for effecting this transformation, as Ernest Gellner and Eugen Weber have argued in their seminal studies of European nationalism.[16]

The rationale of the modern state, which came to view schools as a means for molding loyal, industrious, and self-disciplined citizens, both built on and fundamentally overturned premodern views of education as a path toward ethical formation or intellectual maturation. Plainly put, the nation-state's interest in mass education corresponded with the need to construct a unitary idea of the national community amid the expansion of capitalist forms of economic life.[17] The educational models it developed differed in important ways both from classical ideas that linked education to the pursuit of philosophical truth and from contemporary religious views that tied it to moral fashioning or individual salvation. Though clearly modeled on Christian virtues, the character education developed under state auspices was above all concerned with being useful, not merely to the individual receiving it but to the national community and market economy in which he or she would live and work. Arguably then, the modern state's concern for and financing of mass education are inexplicable outside the perception that public schooling constitutes an effective instrument with which to produce, in John Rawls's more contemporary idiom, both self-supporting and fully cooperating members of society.[18] It is within such a context that the population becomes both subject and object, "the subject of needs, of aspirations" but also "the object in the hands of the government, aware, vis-à-vis the government, of what it wants, but ignorant of what is being done to it."[19]

While many scholars of postcolonial studies have built on this Foucauldian perspective,[20] it has not been welcomed without some reservations that are particularly relevant for our inquiry. Among the critiques is that this theoretical frame is too focused on discourses and plans and less attentive to the gaps that separate intentions from their actual implementation. After all, Jeremy Bentham's infamous panopticon, which occupies a place of privilege in Foucault's understanding of the disciplinary society, was never built. In this regard, historical studies have been particularly important in exposing the lack of direct correspondence between top-down state planning and the lived experience of power.[21]

Reflecting this distinction, Francisco Ramirez and John Boli have argued that "state interest in mass education was shaped by the political construction of mass education, that is, by its *perceived institutional character* rather than by the actual effects of compulsory mass education on nation-state structures."[22] Thus, even if the modern state's support for education has historically stemmed from the perception that schooling constitutes an effective means of channeling the energies of the masses toward "productive" pursuits and away from political agitation, this is not to say that such attempts are always successful. Particularly in colonial settings, British administrators of Humphrey Bowman's vintage were receptive to the fact that the natives might use their Westernized education to rationalize an anticolonial revolt: they might move from being the objects of political manipulation to political subjects in and of themselves. In a similar vein, we find that the introduction of modern forms of discipline and associated technologies of rule, meant to neutralize the threat of lower classes, could also facilitate rebellion. "If schools, universities, the press, and the military barracks act as centers of revolt, it is because the spread of their unique disciplinary practices across the whole of society is accompanied by the spread of the distinctly new techniques and potentials for revolt associated with them."[23]

This distinction between what might be called subject and object education is important to bear in mind as we consider the relationship between religious education, individual agency, and state planning in Palestine. These terms serve to highlight the distinction between premodern forms of learning that idealized the individual path toward higher truths (even if only reserved for a privileged few in practice) and the types of public education the modern state developed for managing the masses. The latter has always been deeply political and indeed was coterminous with the rise of a new form of political rationality that directed itself toward the management of behavior, or in Bentham's terms, conditioning people to do what they ought.[24] Yet if we look at the modern period alone, the distinction between subject and object education can also help us understand the *limits* of state power. Those "modes of objectification that transform human beings into subjects" are far from totalizing in many instances. With regard to colonial education in Palestine, the ease with which schools—explicitly designed to keep the masses in check—could morph into centers of anticolonial agitation offers an important reminder of the gaps that separate disciplinary planning from lived experience. But even beyond this, what I am interested in here is the act of transgression itself: the barrier between subject and object education becoming the site of an improper crossing—a violation of the colonial order that was, in turn, called "politics."

FINDING RELIGION

Humphrey Bowman, Palestine's first education director, tellingly included the following quote from Plato's *Laws* as a preface to his memoir: "We are not speaking of education in this narrower sense, but of that other education in virtue from youth upwards, which makes a man eagerly pursue the ideal perfection of citizenship, and teaches him how rightly to rule and how to obey."[25] It was an uncanny statement for a man who clung faithfully to the need for character education under British auspices yet failed to register (unlike Plato) that education was fully intertwined in the political management of society. As we have seen, sentiments of this sort were commonplace in discussions regarding education in nineteenth-century England as liberal reformers pushed for an expansion of state schooling as a means of civic training. This was all the more crucial as the specter of revolutionary change—and violence—seemed to threaten to overturn the social and economic status quo. No longer was education thought to be the privilege of the elite alone, but rather, it was the masses that most required instruction to lead them away from radicalism and toward an orderly and industrious life.[26]

Religious instruction played a complementary role in this process of mass socialization, and there was no reason to suspect that its mode of moral fashioning was anything other than compatible with the virtues of good citizenship.[27] Thus, far from representing a threat to the established order, religious education constituted a cornerstone of mass education as it evolved in Great Britain. From the Sunday schools that provided the working classes with their first access to formal education in the late eighteenth century, to the dominant position achieved by Anglican schools one hundred years later, mass education was largely regarded as a symbiotic partnership between the church and state. England, along with France, lagged behind less industrialized European countries in adopting state-sponsored schooling and chose to leave education in the hands of ecclesiastical authorities throughout most of the nineteenth century. In the English context, "the principles of voluntarism that had shaped the private, religious, elitist schools . . . would not be easily overturned, especially in light of the global success to which it was believed these schools had contributed."[28] This is important to recall when contextualizing the highly privatized delivery of social services favored by the British in colonial settings like Palestine, where the administration envisioned a public school system composed of both government and private schools yet granted the latter a greater share of autonomy because of their "religious" nature.

In her work on colonial Bengal, Parna Sengupta has shown that these domestic views toward mass education and the centrality of religious instruction therein were highly influential on the English administrators and missionaries who worked in imperial settings. In Bengal, for instance, primary religious schools were deemed the most appropriate means to ensure the loyalty of the Muslim masses.[29] Yet as was the case later in Palestine, linking the public provision of mass schooling to the religious community did not merely reflect existing social divisions but functioned to bind together religious and political identity in an altogether novel fashion. In Sengupta's terms, "This particularly volatile mix of identity and schooling ensured that modern education remained a critical political arena in twentieth-century mass politics—a space in which issues of national identity and culture were constantly negotiated."[30] This is particularly important to note given the paradigmatic role of India in British colonial thinking as the premier example for apprehending both the advantages and pitfalls of native education. Indeed, references to the experience of India cast a shadow over Palestine's education administrators as they devised an educational program heavily biased toward religious instruction and agricultural training.

Despite this association of religious education with social and political stability, "religion" is not an abstract force that exists outside particular historical circumstances or exerts the same influence across space and time. The term has its own complex history that any study of religious education, particularly in colonial settings, must confront. As numerous contemporary scholars have shown, the abstract concept of religion, generally associated with belief in a deity (or deities) and ritual behaviors thought to represent certain elements of this fundamental belief, did not exist prior to modernity, to say nothing of the widespread assumption of continuity between ancient and modern "religions."[31] Likewise, the notion of "religion" as a universal category, some form of which supposedly exists in every culture, is a modern invention that often functions to hide the particularism inherent in the term itself.[32] And although "religion" appears frequently in official documents issued by the Mandatory government—ranging from statistical tables that categorize school pupils by religion or legal ordinances that grant certain privileges to religious communities—it in no way represented a stable or uncontested term, even within the relatively narrow confines of early twentieth-century Palestine.

Derivatives from the Latin *religio* were used in Roman and early Christian periods to denote a number of meanings, only one of which was related to matters of ritual.[33] As the scholar Jonathan Z. Smith has noted in an influential essay, a new phase in the word's history emerged in the sixteenth century when European colonialists began to use derivatives of "religion" with reference to non-Christian ritual practices. However, only in the eighteenth century did the normative usage of the term come to signify matters of personal faith or belief, a shift that corresponded both with the beginnings of the nation-state and the growth of European empires.[34] The construction of the nation-state hinged on the possibility of rationally overcoming all forms of public divisiveness that stemmed from differences in individual conscience, the realm to which matters of religion were now relegated. Perhaps of even greater importance was the need for emerging modern states to monopolize the use of violence within their territories, a process that required stripping ecclesiastic or corporate communities of their judicial or coercive functions. Thus, the religion that we now take for granted as a timeless feature of human society in fact emerged from the conceptual and political rearrangements that accompanied the rise of the modern European state.

As Leora Batnitzky has shown, it was only in this context that Judaism emerged as a religion, as "one particular dimension of life among other particular and separate dimensions, such as politics, morality, science, or economics."[35] In Batnitzky's estimation, the argument that Judaism represented a religion in the modern sense was made first by Moses Mendelssohn in his *Jerusalem: Or on Religious Power and Judaism* (1783), in which he made the case for individual (as opposed to collective) Jewish emancipation on the basis that, as a religion, Judaism had no true coercive power and thus could not claim political authority over its adherents. However, much in tension with his later assertion that Judaism is a religion of action rather than belief—and thus less easily sequestered to the private realm—*Jerusalem* is useful in demonstrating both the political stakes involved in rendering Judaism a religion and the great difficulty involved in doing so. The fundamental tension in Mendelssohn's text stems from precisely this lack of correspondence between a Jewish tradition built largely on public and communal actions and the Protestant contours of religion as defined in his time.[36]

In the wake of Mendelssohn's philosophical interventions, European *maskilim* took up the project of Jewish Enlightenment, taking aim in particular at the narrowness of traditional Jewish education. While it was certainly not unknown for Jews to study European languages or other secular subjects prior to this point, doing so was usually economically driven, required for a career in trade, for example, and not tied to the advancement of any ideological program. The novelty introduced by the *maskilim*, particularly in Germany, was the suggestion that such studies were valuable for their own sake.[37] This intellectual tumult emerged not only from the general Enlightenment context but also from the Edict of Toleration issued by Emperor Joseph II in 1782, which extended certain freedoms to Jews in the Habsburg Empire in an effort "to make the Jews more useful and serviceable to the State." Importantly, the edict called for the dissolution of the semiautonomous corporate structures of Jewish life (*klal*) and insisted that "the Jews in Vienna shall not constitute their own community, under their own direction; each individual family enjoys the protection of the law of the land."[38] As an artifact of secularization in Europe, and in particular the process of rendering Judaism a religion stripped of its political function, we cannot overstate the importance of the edict. Moreover, assimilation through schooling was a conspicuous goal of the declaration, which ignited a sustained debate among Jewish intellectuals with regard to terms on which Jews should seek inclusion into broader civil society.

Important in this regard was Naphtali Herz Wessely's infamous open letter in 1782 to the Jewish community, "Divrei shalom ve-emet" (Words of peace and truth), which attacked the prevailing models of Jewish education and disputed the adequacy of Torah study to meet the challenges and opportunities posed by emancipation.[39] Wessely called for the radical transformation of Jewish learning into a true system of education that would prepare Jews to assume an active role in civil society and capitalize on their newly expanded professional opportunities—in short, "to make the Jews more useful." The main thrust of the argument regarded the ethical necessity to teach *torat ha-adam* (the Torah of man, loosely translated as "human knowledge") alongside "the Torah of God, that is, God's laws and teachings." Wessely defined *torat ha-adam* as "etiquette, the ways of morality and good character, civility and clear, graceful expression," history, geography, astronomy, and the natural sciences, all of which "are inscribed in the mind of man as innate 'primary ideas' whose foundation is reason" and for which man "does not need anything divine to comprehend them."[40]

This structural distinction between the Torahs of God and man in fact reflected two tenets of the emerging secular order: that of religion as the home of nonrational faith and that of a distinct secular realm governed by reason alone. Moreover, as we can detect from this list, Wessely's critique was directed not merely at the narrowness of Jewish learning but at modes of Jewish behavior that were regarded as crude in contrast to (Christian) European civility. By severing certain types of knowledge from the Torah of God and locating them within the newly formed secular realm of *torat ha-adam*, the letter offers a real-time demonstration of how an abstract Judaism was invented as a religion in the modern sense. It also demonstrates the limitations baked into the emerging secular order, since many allegedly universal and rationally derived aspects of *torat ha-adam* were the particular social norms of well-to-do Christians in the surrounding environment. As an example of the eagerness displayed by some *maskilim* to lop off certain kinds of knowledge and conduct from the space inhabited by religion in exchange for broader social acceptance, Wessely's letter offers a useful counterpoint to the vision of Jewish education developed under Zionist auspices that would try, however self-consciously, to reconnect those facets of life torn apart by the secular.

If the rise of the nation-state provided the immediate context for the emergence of religion as a modern concept and the subsequent accommodation of Judaism within this paradigm, the global spread of colonial empires also contributed to this epistemic reordering. Much like "Judaism," a term with a long usage in Christian contexts that was only recently adopted by Jews themselves, "Hinduism," "Buddhism," and "Confucianism" are terms generated by European scholars, theologians, missionaries, and colonial administrators seeking to locate religion among the peoples they encountered.[41] Moreover, the quest to identify and classify the world's religions complemented the ongoing attempt to construct fields of secular knowledge and practices that were supposedly governed by universal reason alone. Here it is worth quoting Timothy Fitzgerald at length:

> The search for (or the invention of) religions in all societies by colonizing Europeans and Americans was proceeding hand in hand with the search for principles of natural rights, laws and markets. The discovery of religion as either the special repository of traditional values or alternatively a private realm of individual, non-political, otherworldly commitment made possible the construction of this-worldly individual freedoms, laws, and markets that were assumed to correspond to natural reason. One can see this process especially in relation to the changed meaning of the "secular" from a division within a totality of Christendom combining all created beings in a cosmic hierarchy to a fundamentally distinct and neutral (factual) sphere of nature: natural individuals, freedoms, civil society, markets, and rationality defined in terms of natural science and contrasted with the supernatural, otherworldly sphere of private soteriological commitment. In reality the neutral, factual space, "the secular"—the arena of scientific knowledge, modern politics, civil society, and Individuals maximizing natural self-interest—is itself an ideological construction, and it is the location of fundamental western values. But it is presented as a universal given to which all cultures (if they are fully rational) should conform.[42]

The construction of secularism as the proper field of politics is of the utmost relevance in understanding the dependent project of rendering religion not just practically, but definitionally, apolitical. As I argue throughout, it was on this conceptual battlefield that British administrators sparred with Jewish and Muslim educators over the proper content and purpose of religious education.

This conceptualization of religion was also fundamental to the developing discourse of European liberalism and its unique brand of religious tolerance. Liberal arguments for toleration by John Locke, John Stuart Mill, and even contemporary theorists hinge on the conjoined notions of freedom of conscience and the location of religion in the realm of that conscience. The acceptance of religious difference is thus conditional on religion not constituting a set of competing legal obligations that might challenge the sovereign for political authority. It is on this basis that Locke famously excluded Catholics, whose allegiance to the state was supposedly muddled by their simultaneous loyalty to the pope, from those to whom tolerance may be extended.[43] What is most noteworthy for our purpose is that, despite the significant distinctions among liberal theorists, they share the same fundamental concept of religion as private, faith driven, and decidedly nonpolitical; indeed, these are the conditions for its toleration. It is in this regard not surprising that contemporary nation-states whose foundations for religious tolerance were erected on such terms have been unable to develop a theory of accommodation for *public* manifestations of religious observance, as witnessed, for instance, in ongoing battles over Islam in Europe.

That an analysis of "religion" as a historical concept, and the liberal accommodation of "Judaism" within this framework, seems to propel us into a discussion of religious tolerance in regard to Muslims in contemporary times should not be that surprising.[44] Rather, as Aamir Mufti has argued in his insightful study of postcolonial India, "in the 'question' of the Jews' status in modern culture and society, as it first came to be formulated in the late eighteenth century, what emerges is a set of paradigmatic narratives, conceptual frameworks, motifs, and formal relationships concerned with the very question of minority existence, which are then disseminated globally in the emergence, under colonial and semicolonial conditions, of the forms of modern social, political and cultural life."[45] While the focus of Mufti's work is the minoritization of Muslims in India, his observations regarding the crisis of liberalism carry weighty implications for anyone working on colonial dimensions of religion, particularly religious reform. It seems evident to me that insofar as Jews, as the paradigmatic minority, were central to the construction of a liberal discourse of secularism and religious toleration, built on a very specific notion of what religion entailed, this particular historical experience is linked in crucial ways to colonial attempts to reform Islam as well.

Here, too, education served as the premier vehicle for carrying out the reformist agenda, and religious instruction often occupied a place of privilege within newly formed educational schemes. In Robert Hefner's terms,

> In the nineteenth and twentieth centuries . . . Muslim societies experienced powerful new pressures to recenter and standardize their still-plural traditions of religious knowledge. The effort was the greatest seen since the birth of the madrasa in the high Middle Ages, and was linked to the expansion of mass education and movements of religious reform. These two events converged to create conditions in which more people than ever were educated in Islam, not just through the informal interactions of everyday life, but through schools run by either state officials or reform-minded Muslims.[46]

As Gregory Starrett and Parna Sengupta have argued in the contexts of Egypt and India, respectively, we should not regard the modernization of Islamic education as a process that flowed naturally from the internal logic of the tradition itself. Despite the different contexts, these works nevertheless converge in highlighting how particularly Christian concepts of religion and religious authenticity were transplanted via modern pedagogy to colonial settings. For instance, the centrality of individual reading in school curricula cannot be understood apart from the Protestant emphasis on literacy as a tool for establishing an unmediated connection between the pupil and the sacred text. Similarly, object lessons, an influential pedagogic method that employed observation and classification, functioned within missionary pedagogy in colonial India as a means of weaning idolatrous and fetishistic Hindus away from the materiality of corrupt religion toward the abstract word of God.[47]

With regard to Islamic education, we can point to certain common themes that linked religious instruction in various zones of British influence. Among them was the long-standing European anxiety that memorization, associated with the practice of learning to recite the Qur'an by heart in *katātīb*, left the child bereft of true comprehension. This concern was not a mere pedagogic one but emanated from the idea that the Qur'an must contain some ethical core that was distinct from the ritual practices and behaviors that surround it.[48] This understanding emerged in part from approaches to religious education in nineteenth-century Britain, where reformers insisted that "true moral instruction lay in the study and understanding of 'lessons' drawn from Scripture. The text itself, aside from refining literary taste, was secondary to the conveyance of such lessons."[49] In Palestinian public schools during the Mandate period, for instance, teachers were instructed to give "the meaning of difficult words and a résumé of the general sense" of each Qur'anic passage as well as ensure that "the verses selected for the various years of study should be explained so that they may become firmly rooted in the minds of the pupils who should be led to act in keeping with the principles and precepts embodied therein."[50] Building off Brinkley Messick's observations in the context of Yemen, this emphasis on isolating the ethical content of the Qur'an overturned older modes of relating to the text's divinity as something to be embodied through recitation.[51] Thus, memorization was not merely deemed pedagogically unsound, but it compromised the modern project of relating to the Qur'an as a coherent set of dogmas and ethical precepts to be absorbed by the individual conscience, of making Islam a "religion."[52]

These pedagogic changes were not, however, simply the fruits of colonial labor. One of the recurring themes in this book is the convergence of colonial reform efforts with those propagated by Jewish and Muslim modernist thinkers who, while undoubtedly influenced by Western social and political movements, remained rooted in their respective textual traditions.[53] For instance, the Ottoman Empire, assisted by French advisers, was highly invested in creating modern schools that propagated a standardized form of Islamic education. As Benjamin Fortna has argued, it was the Ottoman state that first put "Islam to work," borrowing a useful formulation from Gregory Starrett. Fortna argues that the political crises and territorial losses of the late Ottoman period led to a renewed emphasis on Islam within schools, including the development of institutional supervision meant to ensure students' proper moral conduct.[54] Significantly for our purposes, the introduction of standardized curricula devoted to the transmission of morals (*akhlāq*) represented not merely an attempt to create a form of character education infused with Islamic values but one of the first efforts by a modern state to define Islam as a set of normative behaviors and ethical outlooks. The privileged vehicle for the dissemination of correct religion was of course the textbook, and indeed the endeavor to define Islam in normative terms received a boon from the widespread adoption of commercial printing in the nineteenth century.

From this discussion we can see that Sengupta's observation—that "by connecting religious identity so closely to modern schooling, the definitions of what constituted Christianity, Hinduism, or Islam became more narrowly defined through the standardizing of particular texts and rituals"—might also be applied to religious education in late Ottoman and Mandatory Palestine.[55] This represented only the beginning of a longer process of defining and formalizing religion that would extend well into the twentieth century, one that has had mass, state-sponsored education at its core. However, harnessing religious education to the will of the state did not represent an uncontested move; nor, to recall an earlier point, should we assume a direct correspondence between administrative attempts to shape the masses through schooling and the lived experiences of the students themselves. What is clear, however, is that the spread of public schooling helped propel another radical change in the modern Middle East, the rise of mass politics. It was this link between modern religious education and mass politics that rendered the former something very different from the pillar of political and social stability it seemed to represent in centuries past. To complete the theoretical framework suggested at the outset, we must now turn to the relationship between these two phenomena and consider how they in turn changed, irreversibly, the very nature of religious education in the twentieth century.

RELIGIOUS EDUCATION IN A TIME OF MASS POLITICS

For half a century, scholars of Ottoman political life in the Arab provinces have been guided by the late Albert Hourani's idea of the "politics of notables."[56] In brief, Hourani argued that the urban nobility formed a patriciate that functioned as an intermediary between the imperial state and the local population. While this emphasis on the elite as the locus of politics has been scrutinized in later years, particularly by scholars working on the early twentieth century, the fact that the notable classes played a disproportionate role in the political projects of both the late Ottoman and Arab successor states remains relatively uncontested.[57] Yet by the second decade of the twentieth century, this arrangement began to appear increasingly fragile. Not only had a new class of journalists, teachers, and intellectuals—products of the Ottoman Empire's nascent public school system—begun to play a more active role in discussions regarding the political future, but they were emblematic of an expansion of the public sphere that would, in time, encompass the lower classes as well. Adding to the instability, the influx of immigrants around the turn of the twentieth century—mostly European Jews, but also Christian missionaries and merchants—resulted in population segments that were not politically or socially linked with traditional networks of power and often preferred to turn to European consulates to resolve issues rather than petition the Ottoman state.

As Ami Ayalon and Michelle Campos have documented, newly formed newspapers and periodicals played a crucial role in constructing this public sphere and extending the realm of political discourse well beyond the confines of the notable classes.[58] Approximately 35 new publications appeared in Palestine between the years of 1908 and the outbreak of World War I alone, with another 180 to follow during the period of British rule.[59] The expansion of public schooling functioned as a facilitating factor in this expansion of journalistic activity, though as Ami Ayalon has argued, even the low level of general literacy—presumably a limiting factor in the emergence of a public space mediated by the press—could be circumvented through lively public readings of newspapers in coffee shops and markets.[60] Though the notable classes still controlled the levers of politics at the end of the Ottoman era, their hold on power became increasingly contested as a new generation of leaders emerged during the Mandate period. And importantly, as Weldon Matthews has shown, these were leaders who built their following not through the old patronage networks but through their highly visible roles in Palestine's expanding public sphere.[61]

Among British imperial officers, there was nothing reassuring about the rise of political activism among the masses. Consider, for instance, the following editorial from the *Times* that was preserved in Humphrey Bowman's personal papers. Written with the memory of Egypt's 1919 revolution in mind, during which Said Zaghlul led a popular uprising against the British occupation, the editorial implored the Government of Palestine to take all possible measures to prevent the unnatural intrusion of mass politics into the classroom. "In fairness alike to national safety and to the education of the young Arab it is absolutely essential that the first sign of political propaganda in the schools of Palestine should be checked without a moment's delay." As the editorial warned,

> It was through his trained choruses of excited schoolboys (paid so many piastres for each demonstration) that Zaghlul taught his parrot-cries to the Egyptian people; it was from the student class that the agents were recruited to carry out the crimes inspired by the Wafd. In fact, the authorized introduction of politics into Cairo schools—to the utter neglect of proper study and the systemic insulting of the British teacher—has had the disastrous effect on the peace of the country as it has had on the education of its children.
>
> So far the schools in Palestine have been fortunate in their freedom from such interference by the Arab leaders. . . . But there is a distinct tendency on

> the part of the Arab leaders to-day to follow the example of Egyptian agitators. It must be remembered that the Arab is not naturally a politician either by nature or by inclination, and the original leaders of the protest against the Zionist policy, weary of continued strife, are gradually drifting back to their daily tasks in the field.[62]

The evident anxiety regarding the use of schools as launch pads for mass political agitation is here countered by the reassuringly racist axiom that the Arab "is not naturally a politician," thus suggesting that the current troubles are something of an exception (fueled by a few coins) rather than an actual expression of Egyptian public feeling. This assessment of the Arab's "natural" state found its corollary in attempts to design the school curriculum around a rural bias, which was viewed as a necessary corrective to the "literary education" that had proven so disastrous in India. Furthermore, just as the editorial formulates the presence of politics in the classroom as an unnatural intrusion, censorship of the press and other means developed to combat politics are not presented as political actions in and of themselves but as necessities dictated by pedagogic responsibility and an overarching concern for children's well-being. This offers a glimpse of what would prove the greatest difficulty for British officials in Palestine: how to devise a system of mass education without allowing schools to morph into centers of political agitation.

This was not the first time such a problem had arisen within the empire. Of central concern though is the importance that officials granted to a certain type of religious education in solving it. Just as the specter of revolutionary agitation helped pave the way for public education in England, so too in the colonies did officials link quelling the populace to the proper form of schooling. For example, it was in the context of mass uprisings in British India, beginning with the frontier wars against Indian Wahhabi rebels and culminating in the mutiny of 1857, that W. W. Hunter, a British civil servant in Bengal, authored his study *The Indian Musalmans*.[63] First published in 1871 in response to a question raised by Lord Mayo—"Are the Indian Musalmans bound by their Religion to rebel against the Queen?"—the book set out to survey the grievances claimed by Indian Muslims and to recommend ways of rectifying them. Hunter identified the system of public education as one of chief policy failures, because by creating a system of schools "opposed to the traditions, unsuited to the requirements, and hateful to the religion, of the Musalmans," English governors had unwittingly created a system that chiefly catered to the Hindu population. The latter group subsequently exploited new routes of economic advancement either via commerce or government service, generating resentment among Muslim classes who still recalled their former glory as rulers of the land. "If we analyse this charge, we shall find that our unsympathetic system of Public Instruction lies at the root of the matter. The Bengal Musalmans can never hope to succeed in life, or to obtain a fair share of State patronage, until they fit themselves for it, and they will never thus fit themselves until provision is made for their education in our schools."[64]

Not only that, but the "fanatical seething masses of the Muslim peasantry," generally ignorant and with little prospect of advancement, were perfectly primed to embrace the seditious messages carried by puritanical preachers. "But it is not to any single class, however rich or powerful, that the Wahabis owe their strength. They appeal boldly to the masses; and their system, whether of religion or of politics, is eminently adapted to the hopes and fears of a restless population."[65] Indeed, it was the innate fanaticism inherent in Islam, always threatening to spill over, which heightened the need to provide Muslim children with a proper education to sublimate their energies into less hostile and more productive pursuits. Rather than attempt to integrate the existing public schools, which were dominated by Hindu students and teachers, Hunter recommended a three-tier system of education geared toward the needs of the Muslim community. Classes would be conducted in Urdu, teach either Persian or Arabic as a language of prayer, and prepare the child for the performance of his religious duties. Because it was incumbent on every head of household to provide a religious education for his children, there could be no hope of luring the people into state-run or state-supported schools unless they offered such instruction. "We should thus at length have the Muhammadan youth educated upon our own plan. Without interfering in any way with their religion, and in the very process of enabling them to learn their religious duties, we should render that religion perhaps less sincere, but certainly less fanatical."[66]

Thinking of this sort was neither unique to colonial India nor exclusive to European officials. As Paul Sedra has argued in his study of education in nineteenth-century Egypt, the usefulness of religion to the preservation of civic order was a view shared by local elites as well. "British administrators and Egyptian landowners seized upon religion as they endeavored to transmit the values of discipline and productivity to Egyptians through the school—an Islam 'not of recited truth, but of behavioral guidelines.'"[67] Sedra's study recounts the degree to which colonial views toward religion as a fundamentally conservative force actually converged with those of local Coptic leaders. In the words of Akhnukh Fanus, a Coptic leader speaking before the 1911 Coptic Congress, "It is the most important consideration, both for humanity, and for Governments, that people should obey the commands of their religion, because a religious people is always the least inclined to crime, and the most careful of the rights of others, and a Government can always feel confidence in such a people."[68] It was a sentiment that would become widespread among colonial officials in Mandate Palestine: only through a new form of religious education could the masses be effectively controlled; that is, "proper" religious education was a political tool whose purpose was to undermine mass politics.

In sum, Britain carried administrative patterns into Palestine that were rooted in both domestic and other colonial settings and that granted a place of privilege to religious education. As I argue in Chapter 2, the ingrained reliance on volunteerism in the provision of education had serious ramifications for both Zionist and Arab public schools, mostly to the detriment of the latter, due to the greater level of autonomy given to the Hebrew Public System as a "religious" organization. More generally, this bias toward religious schooling—nurtured by both financial parsimony and ideological belief in the usefulness of religion in controlling the masses—obscured the fact that such an education might fuel the most militant nationalist movements. Crucial policy decisions related to education in Palestine were thus situated within a conceptual minefield concentrated around the contested nature of religion and the means by which education should express its values. What did it mean to call something or someone "religious" in Mandate Palestine, and what form of power is at work in making this determination—that is, in what material sense does it matter? I hope to show that far from being ancillary to the history of political turmoil of Mandate Palestine, the theoretical disputes raised here were at the heart of concrete policy decisions whose legacies we still confront.

2 EDUCATIONAL MODERNITY IN PALESTINE

"IN GENERAL IT MAY BE SAID that the public schools in the Turkish provinces were ill organised and that the methods of instruction were unsatisfactory." Taken from a report on educational developments in Palestine during the years 1920–29, this remark succinctly encapsulates the British attitude toward the system of schools they inherited from the Ottoman Empire. Indeed, officials often spoke of Palestine as a tabula rasa in which the Mandatory government was forced to construct a school system from the ground up. Like other self-serving imperial claims, the suggestion that educational innovation and modernization came to Palestine only in the wake of the British occupation ignored the significant shifts set in motion by public and private bodies during the late Ottoman period. The notion of a blank slate is misleading for another reason as well, conjuring up associations of starting something anew. In fact, being situated at the tail end of a long colonial history, Palestine offered British administrators an opportunity to apply certain "best practices" learned from other imperial geographies, most important in India, Egypt, and Nigeria. Informed by the mistakes of the past, these policies seemed to represent the tried-and-true methods for modulating the provision of education in furtherance of both economic and political goals. They included a commitment to the spirit of volunteerism (i.e., private financing) in education, the privileging of primary instruction over secondary schooling, and an ingrained association between "true" religion and obedience.

This chapter surveys these processes of educational change and modernization in Palestine, beginning in the mid-nineteenth century and continuing through the Mandate period. I argue that in many respects, the British educational administration was not nearly as revolutionary as it claimed; rather, key practices and institutions were in fact carried over from the late Ottoman period. Nevertheless, there was one important aspect of the Mandatory government's educational planning that departed from that of its predecessor: the extent to which officials refused to link schooling to a definite political program. Whereas Ottoman officials came to view public schools in the empire as a means to encourage intercommunal mixing and forge a new kind of imperial citizenship, their British successors approached education as a practice that could and should be insulated from politics. Though Ottoman schools fell short of truly becoming sites of acculturation, it is noteworthy that colonial administrators did not even begin by establishing such a goal. On the contrary, the notion of education as a neutral exercise in character formation contributed to a series of policy decisions whose long-term political consequences were either not considered or simply dismissed. This, too, was part of a politics of denial, in which the Mandatory government displayed remarkably little awareness of the link between discrete policies and the larger political future. Before turning our focus to the question of religious education in particular, we must first understand this broader context and how it shaped the Mandatory government's educational planning.

SEEDS OF CHANGE: EDUCATION REFORM IN THE OTTOMAN EMPIRE

Historians generally attribute the first steps toward creating a modern system of education in Ottoman lands to Muhammad 'Ali, the semiautonomous governor of Egypt who launched numerous educational initiatives in the wake of the Napoleonic retreat in 1801. He did so out of recognition of the superior military technologies and disciplines that enabled the French conquest and to further challenge the authority of Ottoman rulers in Istanbul. He dispatched student missions to European cities to study foreign languages and translate textbooks into Arabic. In Egypt, he opened professional schools for engineering (1816), medicine (1827), pharmaceutics (1929), mineralogy (1834), agriculture (1836), and translation (1836).[1] After such institutions had been erected, it quickly became apparent that a new system of primary schools was required to prepare students for study within them. Thus, he founded government preparatory schools that provided stipends, free clothing, and food to lure students away from *katātīb*. He still encountered much reluctance from parents who feared conscription and eventually resorted to recruiting by force. "It was obvious that all the new schools, whether military, ancillary or even civil, were geared to serve a military machine. None of them was for the purely intellectual or professional training of young Egyptians."[2]

Similarly, the Ottoman Empire first looked to appropriate European technical and scientific expertise in an attempt to modernize its outmoded military. In Istanbul as well as in Cairo, French advisers played a key role in proposing educational reforms and managing newly created schools.[3] The Ottoman leadership began the process of education reform slowly, in fits and starts over several decades during the mid-nineteenth century, and did not tackle the systematic reform of primary education until the 1860s.[4] Its first efforts were directed at integrating existing communal schools, such as the *kuttāb* and those managed by non-Muslim communities, into a single legal and administrative framework. However, the changes were limited in scope, with the primary goal being that schools produce literate candidates for the *rushdiyye* (secondary) schools in which government clerks were trained. The administrative structure attempted to build on existing forms of communal education rather than supersede them. Primary education was conceived of as rightfully belonging to the child's own religious community, whereas secondary schools would bring together different population groups as well as include a broader range of subjects.[5]

In contrast to these earlier attempts to weave the reformist project into existing social structures, by the late 1860s, the uneven nature of primary education at the communal level had transformed into a public liability. In 1869, the Regulation of Public Education was promulgated, prepared under the influence of the French minister of education, Jean Victor Duruy. It reflected an ambitious plan to introduce universal compulsory education and to transfer control of all schools within the empire's provinces to the Ottoman state. The regulation marked the abandonment of a more decentralized policy that would strategically employ existing forms of religious education; it envisioned instead a system of state primary schools with a utilitarian curriculum, supervised by a centralized bureaucracy and overseen by a professional class of teachers. While the Ottomans never achieved universal education as was hoped, they did open and manage a number of schools in Palestine: the administrative district (*sanjak*) of Jerusalem included 158 such schools in 1885, and another 35 existed in the nearby *kaza* (subdistrict) of Jenin.[6]

However impressive this may appear, there are indications that some Palestinian Muslims opposed the Ottoman government's attempts to open schools in the late nineteenth century, fearing that "the distinctly religious basis of education would be threatened, with consequent disturbances of the established social order."[7] Thus, it was in part because education was conceived of as an Islamic communal practice that attempts to organize new forms of state schooling were poorly received by the ulema. Within this framework, the creation of government primary schools served by a professional class of teachers represented yet another reduction in the scope of activities under their direct control. Another point of contention was the language of instruction in the Ottoman public schools, which was Turkish even in the empire's Arab provinces. By the first decade of the early twentieth century, Arab nationalists had seized on the primacy given to Turkish in both the educational and administrative realms as yet another instance of Turkish despotism stifling the renaissance of Arab culture, a discursive trope that also achieved some prominence in European circles.[8]

In short, far from representing the mere reform of communal schooling, the new system of education attempted—though did not necessarily achieve—a revolutionary break with the *katātīb* that preceded it. The curriculum in government primary schools still devoted much attention to reading, writing, and reciting the Qur'an, though upper grades also featured a smattering of arithmetic and "reading of passages on Morality, Geography, and Agriculture."[9] Secondary schools also included Persian, Arabic grammar and syntax, Islamic history, hygiene, and calligraphy, in addition to subjects like religious sciences (*ʿulum al-dīn*) that were typically taught in madrasas.[10] In some respects, the late Ottoman school system shared certain features with the Mandatory one that would replace it, including a curriculum divided into distinct religious and nonreligious components, uniform textbooks, and teachers that were—theoretically at least—graduates of specialized training schools.[11] Religious instruction formed a separate and important component of the Ottoman public school curriculum, one that arguably became even more pronounced toward the end of the nineteenth century as the state "tried to combat nationalist secession by stressing religious and authoritarian values in education."[12]

As a result of these developments, as well as the continued growth of private educational initiatives throughout the nineteenth century, late Ottoman Palestine featured a wide spectrum of schools, curricula, and pedagogical methods. The languages of instruction in schools varied and included Turkish, Arabic,

Greek, Armenian, German, Italian, French, Yiddish, and—after great effort on behalf of Zionist educators—Hebrew.[13] Religious minorities were free to maintain their own schools, though in theory the public schools were open to all Ottoman subjects. Local communities maintained dozens of schools, some of which were wholly autonomous and others of which depended on support from missionary or philanthropic bodies based abroad. For instance, the Alliance Israélite Universelle, an association of French Jews committed to "civilizing" their Eastern brethren through the spread of French education and culture, created Palestine's first modern agricultural school in 1870.[14]

In addition to these public and private ventures, numerous Christian missionary schools tried to lure children into the faith through the prospect of food, shelter, and a free education. They primarily attracted local Christian children, though they were still widely perceived by Jewish and Muslim leaders as a threat to the integrity of their respective communities. Even so, these schools offered a model of modern education that was widely adopted as local com-

FIGURE 2. Young schoolchildren at the Evelina de Rothschild School for Girls in Jerusalem (commonly called "Miss Landau's School" in honor of its longtime headmaster, Annie Landau), 1915. Supported by the Anglo-Jewish Association, the school was among the many privately funded educational institutions that operated in Ottoman Palestine. Courtesy of the Central Zionist Archives, PHG\1002820.

munities founded new schools to compete with missionary establishments.[15] Moreover, the fact that missionary schools often employed foreign languages rendered them suspect even among Arab Christian leaders, many of whom were at the forefront of the nationalist project. Exemplary in this regard was the Orthodox Christian educator Khalil al-Sakakini, who in 1909 founded the Dusturiyya school, which used Arabic (rather than Turkish) as the language of instruction and featured a largely humanistic curriculum.[16]

While Jewish communal schools remained commonplace in the urban centers of the Old Yishuv (Jerusalem, Sefad, Hebron, and Tiberias), new educational models found a foothold during the late nineteenth century in Palestine's coastal cities and agricultural settlements. These schools were not yet linked to a central Zionist administrative apparatus, though they shared many of the same educational goals and were usually conducted—or at least attempted—in Hebrew. In general, the schools associated with the First Aliyah, which sprang up during the final two decades of the nineteenth century, were not unified by a clear and coherent set of educational goals. This was reflective of the fact that Zionism itself was undergoing a contentious process of self-definition during these years, as Herzl's vision of a Jewish commonwealth along European lines came under intense scrutiny. Important thinkers like Ahad Ha'am argued that it was not enough to simply reproduce European values in a new place—Zionism required the spiritual renewal of the Jewish people, which could be achieved only through an engagement with the Hebrew language and Jewish culture more broadly. His views were influential among the pioneers who steered the Second Aliyah (which lasted from approximately from 1904 to 1914) and who opted to focus their energies on physically establishing a new form of Jewish life in Palestine rather than chasing a royal charter from the Ottoman sultan.

Education served as one of the crucial keys to creating a new Zionist society that would be organically rooted in the Palestinian landscape. The idealized product of this new educational effort was of course the sabra, that quasi-mythologized young man who tilled the fields by day and discussed questions of biblical ethics by night—in conversational Hebrew no doubt. Scholars of Zionism have often noted the oppositional quality inherent in the idea of the sabra, who served as the antidote to dominant constructions of Ashkenazi Jewish men as weak, effeminate, cowardly, and hostile to manual labor.[17] This "negation of the diaspora" found expression in other arenas as well, and it has often been assumed that religion—or, rather, the lack thereof—constituted an important site of Zionist self-differentiation. Yet it is important to note that, though the pioneers of the Second Aliyah are often associated with Zionism's golden age of secularism, many of them hailed from traditional religious backgrounds in central and eastern Europe. And as Arieh Saposnik has shown, the educational and cultural innovations of the period represented an attempt to appropriate and redefine Jewish religious traditions rather than merely negate or overcome them. Indeed, the national culture that emerged in these formative years did not arise "phoenixlike out of the ashes" of religious society but remained deeply, if ambivalently, embedded in religious structures of belief, custom, and ritual.[18]

The essential—and in many articulations, mystical—connection between the Jewish people, the Land of Israel, and the Hebrew language came to serve as Zionism's conceptual glue during the first decade of the twentieth century. The "language wars" of 1913, which began as a protest over the continued use of European languages at the Haifa Technion, offered the impetus to centralize the administration of Zionist schools. This factional squabble resulted in the resignation of numerous members of the Zionist Teachers' Association, while the remaining members created a *va'ad ha-ḥinuch* (board of education) that took control of twelve schools that were dedicated to teaching all subjects in Hebrew.[19] These schools formed the nucleus of the Zionist school system, and by 1918, they numbered nearly forty. After the British occupation, supervision by the Teachers' Association gave way to direct control by the Zionist Executive's newly formed Department of Education, with the former head of the Teachers' Association, Dr. Joseph Luria, as its director. The schools themselves were divided into three "trends," each corresponding to a Zionist political party—Labor, Mizraḥi (Religious Zionist), and General Zionists—and supervised by an inspectorate drawn from party members.[20]

This delicate social balance was forever altered when on October 29, 1914, the Ottoman Empire entered the First World War in alliance with the Central Powers—a decision whose long-term consequences can hardly be overstated.[21] In February 1915, Jamal Pasha established a notoriously brutal military government over Greater Syria, intent on rooting out (and hanging) Arab nationalists. From March to October, a plague of locusts descended on the region, decimating crops and contributing to a large-scale famine that killed an estimated five hundred thousand civilians.[22] And in April of the same year, the systematic murder and deportation of Armenian subjects began; many of those fortunate enough to survive became refugees in cities throughout Greater Syria. This was the country that the British inherited when they marched into Palestine in December 1917. Many welcomed them and regarded them as liberators, still knowing little of the Balfour Declaration and how irreconcilable Britain's various wartime promises would prove.

SQUARING THE CIRCLE: BRITISH EDUCATIONAL GOALS IN PALESTINE

Beginning in 1918, the military government reopened Ottoman public schools that had been closed during the war and changed the language of instruction to Arabic. It established teachers' training colleges for men and women and began a school expansion campaign in both towns and villages, opening approximately seventy-five schools a year. The civilian government that assumed the reins of power in 1920 continued this expansion program through 1922, when it was suspended due to financial stringency.[23] Expansion moved at a much slower pace throughout the remainder of the period, leading Abdul Latif Tibawi to note, "Future historians . . . will not fail to observe that a *de facto* military administration was able to open within two years, comparatively more schools than a *de jure* government could open within more than a quarter of a century, and that while the action of the former was guided by a well conceived plan, the action of the latter was guided by little or no long-range planning."[24]

Adopting the status quo ante bellum, the nascent Department of Education of the Government of Palestine also assumed nominal control of schools maintained by Zionist and other private organizations. Like its Ottoman predecessors, the Department of Education would never gain true supervisory powers over nongovernment schools, which greatly outnumbered public schools throughout the Mandate period.[25] Yet unlike the Ottoman regime, the Government of Palestine recognized the schools maintained by the Zionist Organization as part of the public school system. This made these schools, dubbed the Hebrew Public System, eligible for public financing and theoretically subjected them to a greater level of government scrutiny. In reality, the Zionist educational system was granted almost complete autonomy.[26] This disparity stemmed both from the dual status of Zionist schools as public and religious institutions and the fact that they were largely self-financed at the outset of the Mandate.[27] This classificatory scheme engendered as much confusion as it did bitterness: from government inspectors, whose role was thereby curtailed; from members of the Old Yishuv, who found themselves outside Palestine's official "Jewish community" and thus ineligible for the public funds dedicated to Jewish education; and from Palestinian Arabs, who lamented the discrepancy between educational autonomy granted by the government to the Arab and Hebrew Public Systems.

After assuming control of public education in Palestine, the Mandatory government articulated two interrelated goals: first, to expand access to primary education among the Arab population, which officials hoped would increase literacy rates, rationalize agricultural production, and encourage technical and vocational training. This initiative was part and parcel of the second goal, the policy of "equalization." Effectively, this policy stated that it was undesirable for "two races" of radically different educational levels to inhabit the same land. Whereas education among Jews was nearly universal, only a fraction of the Arab population received any form of schooling. In the words of the director of education, "It would be difficult to exaggerate the cumulative seriousness of the situation which has been gradually created and is still being created by the inadequacy of the educational provision made by the Government since the Occupation. . . . The natural result of this disparity between the educational facilities offered to Arabs and Jews is to widen the cultural gulf between the two races, to prevent social intermixture on equal terms and to tend to reduce the Arabs to a position of permanent inferiority."[28]

FIGURE 3. A carpentry lesson at the Government Boys' School in Jaffa, 1924. Courtesy of the Library of the Institute for Palestine Studies, PC82/8.

However, the Department of Education was forced to work within the boundaries demarcated by the Mandate for Palestine and the financial stringency of the British Treasury. As a rule, colonies were expected to be self-sustaining and finance their own social services. As in other colonial settings, because police and "security" spending was disproportionately high, few resources remained for education. The immediate consequence was that public education was consistently and dramatically underfinanced. Consequently, the government was unable to offer any educational services to the majority of the Arab population throughout the Mandate period. In 1936, the Peel Commission expressed dismay that schools existed in only 293 of Palestine's 780 villages, and that the 42 percent of applicants rejected annually by rural schools due to lack of accommodation did "not include all the children in all the other villages where there are no schools, who may be panting for education."[29] In 1945–46, the last year for which there are complete estimates, there were approximately 124,000 Arab children in public or private schools out of an estimated school-age population of 300,000.[30] Thus, after twenty-five years of British rule, nearly 60 percent of Palestinian Arab children were still without access to public education.

The government education budget never reached more than 7 percent of annual expenditures, and for most years it was less than 5 percent.[31] The funds available for education and other social services were destined to remain paltry as long as the top financial priority was security. This spending category, which financed the British colonial administration, the police force, and the prison system—all the tools necessary to overpower opposition to the Mandate by sheer force—accounted for 15 to 20 percent of all government expenditures.[32] In sum, a vast amount of funds available to the Government of Palestine, derived primarily from local taxation, went toward maintaining the British occupation. The meager public funds earmarked for education went hand in hand with an attempt to decentralize school funding and "empower" local communities to open and finance their own institutions. While the Department of Education consistently maintained that financial decentralization was a form of empowerment, in reality it was too heavy a burden to bear for most fellahin, who were in an almost permanent state of financial crisis.

Moreover, unlike towns, where schools were built or rented and maintained entirely by the government, villages were initially required to provide the school building and furnishings and later to provide LP (Palestinian liras) 75 toward the construction of the building. The government would then appoint a teacher and pay his salary.[33] "Afterwards," Bowman stated regarding this policy, "there might be a measure of decentralization, both of finance and control." He "felt sure that the members of the [Advisory] Council would agree with him that the more education was decentralized the more likely it is to succeed and the greater the interest the inhabitants will take in it."[34] Though the administration was well aware of the heavy indebtedness of most villagers, they defended this policy before skeptical members of the Palestine Royal Commission (PRC), who asked if "in the expansion of your rural schools . . . villages have found real difficulty in producing the money?" Bowman noted that "some villages find difficulty in doing so; other villages are more ready to come forward with their contribution," thereby implying the education scheme was not hindered by the ability of peasants to shoulder the cost of opening schools but by their unwillingness to do so. Still skeptical, the PRC again asked Bowman if it was "true to say the expansion of rural schools has been checked by the incapacity of the villages to do their share?" And yet again he denied any link between government frugality, village indebtedness, and the stalled expansion of rural education.[35]

The decentralization of education was not, however, uniformly applied. Rather, it was the financial burden associated with schools—not their actual curricula or administration—that the Mandatory government tried to delegate to local communities. The Education Ordinance of 1933 included a provision that would transfer partial responsibility for education finance to local education authorities (LEAs) established at the local level. In many ways LEAs in Palestine resembled those in Great Britain itself, with the crucial exception that they were granted financial responsibility without any corresponding measure of administrative control. This selective nature of educational decentralization did not escape the notice of the municipalities. The Jerusalem council, perhaps one of the few public bodies that included both Jews and Arabs, submitted a memorandum detailing its objections on this front:

> While the Director of Education is empowered to deal with all administrative questions, such as the opening of schools, registration of schools, appointment of teachers, registration and licensing of teachers, determination of their qualifications, closing of schools, rejecting their registration, refusing the applications made for the registration of teachers, inspection of schools, preparation of the syllabus, issue of licenses, cancellation of licenses, examination of candidates for appointment of teachers; while all these powers are vested in the Director of Education, the local education authorities are only executive implements in the hands of the Director in order to meet all the required expenses which cannot be estimated.[36]

In addition to trying to offload some of its financial burden to local communities, the Government of Palestine, because of the limited funds earmarked for education, had to depend heavily on private, missionary, and Zionist organizations to supplement public social services, schools in particular. In fact, the Department of Education conceived of an educational structure wherein government and nongovernment schools would jointly constitute the public school system. In this way, the British pursued a policy that was strikingly similar to that of the French in Mandatory Lebanon and Syria, also regions with a high concentration of foreign and missionary schools. As Elizabeth Thompson has argued in her insightful study of gender and colonial citizenship, "the highly privatized delivery of social services" mediated through missionary and other private bodies was a direct by-product of French budgetary constraints throughout the Mandate period. Such an administrative arrangement took full advantage of the presence of missionary schools "where nuns worked for a pittance" to minimize government expenditure on necessary social services.[37]

It is within this context that we must approach a policy decision that would prove decisive for the future of Palestine: to recognize Zionist schools as "public" entities. In particular, the elevation of a separate system of schools supervised by the Zionist Organization to the same status as those maintained by the Government of Palestine legitimized a view of the country divided into distinct public spaces, each with its own language, administrative system, and official status.[38] This represented a radical departure from the nature of educational separatism under the Ottoman Empire, in which numerous private realms surrounded and interacted with a common public sphere. In contrast, the educational history of Mandate Palestine testifies to the eradication of any shared notion of the public as the country and its institutions became fragmented into competing private spheres—each of which, of course, claimed the "public" mantel. These dueling school systems no doubt contributed to what Bernard Wasserstein described as the "hollowness of the concept of a political community" that characterized the period—a civic fragmentation from which the land has not yet recovered.[39]

SEPARATE AND UNEQUAL: EDUCATION FINANCE AND PALESTINE'S "PUBLICS"

Given the limited public resources directed toward education, Palestine's various communities vied to secure as much of this small pie as possible by lobbying local administrators and officials in London regarding the distribution of funds among private, Zionist, and Arab public schools. While the Palestinian Arab community, across confessional lines, pushed for an increase in overall expenditure on education and a greater share of control over the Arab Public System, the Zionist Education Department waged a more limited (though no less heated) battle related to the public financing of Zionist schools. Until 1927, Zionist schools were regarded as private entities, and they therefore received the same per capita grants as those extended to schools maintained by ecclesiastical, missionary, or philanthropic organizations—a fact that generated no little discontent. In response, the Palestine government introduced a contentious formula that was designed to apportion public funds between Jewish and Arab schools.

To understand the formula and its complicated history, it is necessary to return to the early days of British rule. Offered the prospect of being absorbed into the government public school system, with the corresponding level of oversight, the Zionist Executive opted to safeguard its educational autonomy by forgoing government funding.[40] Then when faced with a severe budgetary crisis during the mid-1920s, Zionist leaders appealed to the government for a larger share of funding in proportion to the Jewish community's percentage of the total population. The issue reached the Permanent Mandates Commission in 1925, to which the British government responded that it was "unable to accept the contention that the Palestine government are under any obligation to ensure that in any head of expenditure of the Palestine Estimates the amount of money devoted to the needs and services of a particular part of the people in Palestine should be proportionate to the size of that part."[41] The Permanent Mandates Commission deemed this response adequate, but the Zionist Organization continued to press for a greater measure of government support within a structure that would not compromise its educational autonomy.

Leaders found a friend in Lord Plumer (high commissioner, 1925–28), who in 1927 wrote to the secretary of state for the colonies requesting to rectify a "long-standing grievance" of the Zionist Organization: "that it has not hitherto received benefit from Government expenditures on Education commensurate with its size and importance." Plumer argued that it was improper to treat Zionist schools as private institutions, as they in fact represented a parallel public system. He echoed the opinion of officials in the Department of Education in arguing that it was impossible for Jewish students to attend government public schools because the latter employed Arabic as the language of instruction. The conclusion, supported by a committee formed to investigate the matter, was as follows:

> The Arabic system of schools established by the Government and the Hebrew system supported by the Zionist Organization should be promoted along parallel lines and entitled to receive proportional assistance from public funds, whether from general revenue or local rates. A new Education Ordinance to make legal provision for the practical application of these conclusions has been drafted and will be submitted to you at an early date.[42]

The high commissioner was anxious to satisfy Zionist demands and proposed that the government provide an annual grant, "proportionate to their numerical strength," to the Zionist school system. Given that "the proportion at present between the Hebrew and Arabic sections of the population is one to five," he proposed granting the Zionist schools LP 20,000 annually, approximately one-fifth of the sum spent on Arab education after shared administrative expenses were deducted.[43]

Lord Plumer's letter introduced into the realm of policy making a number of assumptions that had never before received official sanction and, indeed, that had been previously contested. The first was that the system of schools maintained by the Zionist Organization for the exclusive use of Palestinian Jews should be regarded as a public institution on par with that maintained by the government itself. Officials in the Colonial Office questioned how the high commissioner had reached this conclusion, but nevertheless, such recognition was granted.[44] The 1927–28 Department of Education's annual report reflects this change by making reference to "the Zionist Public School System"; soon after, the term "Hebrew Public System" was adopted. Neither officials in Palestine nor those in the Colonial Office drew any attention to the difficulties raised by equating the total Jewish population—on which basis the block grant was calculated—with the Zionist community, which would receive the entire sum. The theoretical eliding between Zionist and Jew was widespread; however, it is harder to comprehend at a time when one-third of Jewish children did not attend Zionist schools.[45] These calculations would continue to serve as a point of intra-Jewish tension throughout the Mandate period.[46]

Lord Plumer supported his position by arguing that language marked an unbridgeable gap between Jews and Arabs in Palestine, a point augmented by educational administrators' insistence that it was pedagogically unsound to employ a foreign language as the language of instruction. In many ways, this was an essentially conservative position that grew out of imperial anxieties lest the peasantry learn English, migrate to cities, and upset the social balance. Yet the argument came gift-wrapped in the language of progressive pedagogy by education officials such as Jerome Farrell. He defended the decision to use Arabic as the sole language of instruction in public schools, even at the secondary level, by relying on contemporary European arguments regarding the harm of multilingualism to the child's intellectual and psychological development. For instance, when the PRC of 1936 began its task of studying the crisis in Palestine, members questioned whether more might be done to foster communal integration through schooling. Farrell retorted, "On purely educational grounds the proposals can hardly be justified. No elementary or secondary pupil whose native language is of literary and cultural value should be encouraged to seek instruction through a foreign medium."[47] Similarly, Humphrey Bowman spoke of the difficulties involved in fostering a common educational space as primarily linguistic rather than political in nature: "The language of Arabs is Arabic; the language of the Jews is Hebrew. Both races attach very great importance to the education in elementary schools through their own language. It would be impossible in my opinion to have Arabs and Jews in one school as long as the language difficulty exists and I see no possibility of that language difficulty being solved."[48] The fact that Hebrew itself was a foreign language to most Zionist immigrants, or that Palestine was a multilingual society in which children often attended European-language schools, did not seem to complicate this "natural" link between language and community.

Further complicating matters was that monolingual education in one's "native" language also happened to be one of the few policies that earned the unequivocal approval of Palestinian and Zionist nationalist forces. For Zionists, multilingualism was deeply associated with diasporic existence, *galutiyut*, and thereby ran counter to the aims of Jewish national "normalization" in Palestine. While never without its points of ambivalence, analyzed recently by Liora Halperin, the Zionist promotion of communal separatism through the exclusive use of Hebrew remained a central part of creating a new and unified generation that would shed diasporic identities in favor of a reconstructed Hebrew nationalism.[49] Within the *yishuv*, leaders such as Menahem Ussishkin argued that "the multiplicity of languages is unnatural," while educators like Itzhac Epstein warned of the psychological damage of multilingualism, drawing on the latest in pedagogic research from European countries.[50] Palestinian nationalists welcomed the elevation of Arabic as the language of instruction in government public schools, a change effected soon after the British occupation. During the late Ottoman period, the use of Turkish in public schools had been a chief complaint of imperial decentralists, who promoted the use of Arabic as an administrative and educational language within regions of the empire with an Arab majority.[51] Simultaneously, educators and political leaders decried the influence of missionary schools that educated Arab children in foreign languages and supposedly led to estrangement from the national tongue. Palestine thus evolved over the course of a few decades from a place in which it was not uncommon to find the same individual fluent in Arabic, Turkish, and French into a society that was multilingual not because it had a cosmopolitan character but because each community was meant to know only a single tongue.[52]

In their discussion of Lord Plumer's request, officials in the Colonial Office expressed dismay at how far afield such calculations were from the principles on which the distribution of state services should be based. In a minute "that raises an important issue of principle," T. I. K. Lloyd of the Colonial Office summarized the problem:

> The Jews have shown little desire to enter Government schools, or hospitals, or to comply with the conditions on which Government grants are made to private schools, with the result that the expenditure of the Palestine Government on social services generally, and perhaps educational services in particular, has hitherto been mainly for the benefit of the Arabs. . . . Lord Plumer now proposes a further increase to the grant bringing it to LP 20,000 per annum, i.e., an amount which bears the same proportion to other Government expenditures on education (after deducting administrative charges) as the Jewish population bears to the remainder of the population of Palestine.[53]

Lloyd opposed Lord Plumer's proposal for two reasons. The first was that the increased grant represented an additional expense at a time of budget shortfalls, making it "urgently necessary to restrict recurrent expenditure of all sorts." But more important, he reiterated the objection British officials voiced before the Permanent Mandates Commission in 1925: "If expenditure on education is to be apportioned between Jews and Arabs," Lloyd asked, "why should not expenditure on health, on police and on other Departments be similarly apportioned? Police expenditure, on the other hand, is incurred for the protection of the Jewish community out of all proportion to their numbers and the Zionist executive would be the first to object if the Palestine Government decided to reduce police expenditure in mixed population areas to what one may call 'a proportionate basis.' "[54]

Lloyd concluded by stating that while an increased grant to the Zionist schools might be desirable for political reasons, "the contention cannot be accepted that the Palestine Government are under any obligation to apportion between Jews and Arabs, according to their population, Government expenditure on education or on any other service," adding that "this point of view was accepted by the Mandates Commission and the Council of the League of Nations at the end of 1925."[55] The secretary of state for the colonies, Lord Amery, advised the Colonial Office to draft a reply agreeing to the increased grant-in-aid without offering a position on the principle of proportionality. He stated only that he "should prefer to abstain from comment on the principles laid down in Lord Plumer's dispatch until I receive the proposals of the Palestine Government with regard to education."[56] The Colonial Office's ensuing silence on this question of principle was interpreted by all parties as tacit consent. After many years of administering the LP 20,000 block grant, clearly based on the population ratio of Jews to Arabs, officials found themselves committed to the policy of proportionate funding "even if it should appear to lack justification."[57]

The Zionist Organization repeatedly insisted that the grant-in-aid should actually be based on the number of Jews as a percentage of children enrolled in school.[58] Due to the widespread system of Zionist education—funded in large part by the Zionist Organization and donors abroad—and the fact that public schooling was available to only a minority of Palestinian Arabs, a formula calculated on such basis would have entitled Zionist schools to claim approximately 42 percent of the education budget at a time when Jews represented less than 20 percent of the population.[59] The Mandate government rejected this proposal and used instead the Jewish percentage of the total school-age population, thereby accounting for the thousands of Arab children for whom no educational services were yet provided. Finally, the treasurer suggested "an ingenious, but very complicated scheme" based on "the extent of the potential liability for Government for Jewish schools if private funds for the maintenance of such schools were not available."[60] The amount of the grant was therefore fixed at the amount that the state would incur if it educated the same percentage of the Jewish population as it did the Arab and at the same price per pupil.

Confusion stemming from the legal status of Zionist schools and the distribution of government financing among Palestine's communities reflected a larger set of questions regarding who exactly constituted the public. The Zionist

Organization could legitimately claim to be administering a public school system as long as its view of the public did not extend beyond the boundary of the Jewish community. Within this zone, it desired universal and compulsory education under strong centralized control, funded by tax revenue distributed on a progressive basis. Zionist officials admitted as much in conversations with the Colonial Office during which they expressed anxiety that groups dissatisfied with the Va'ad Leumi's administration might found their own schools, effectively meaning that "the more wealthy section of a Jewish community might object to paying for the education of the poorer sections."[61] However, in regard to Palestine as a whole, the Zionist Organization requested that revenue derived from Jewish taxation be used to fund only Jewish education, a demand that was partially met by the Colonial Office and incorporated into the Education Ordinance of 1933.[62] Thus, with regard to the internal world of the Jewish community, the Zionist Organization jealously guarded the principles of universal access to education and progressive taxation to finance it; externally, it rejected both premises.

Lurking behind this rejection was, of course, the unwillingness to see the Palestinian Arab as part of the polity-in-formation. This feeling was not exclusive to the Zionist community; the opposite view found widespread acceptance in Arab circles, as the battle for control over Palestine undermined any concept of shared citizenship. Given the political climate of the period and the asymmetric recognition of national rights on which the Mandate was based, it is hard to see how the situation could have been otherwise. Yet, as Michelle Campos has recently shown in her study of the Ottoman constitutional period, it would be wrong to assume that this was the natural or inevitable state of affairs stemming from the reality of multiple ethno-religious groups inhabiting a single territory. Separatism had to be produced at numerous levels, and the administrative means devised to accommodate this fragmentation should not be overlooked.

MANAGING EDUCATION: POLICY AND POLITICS

Having agreed to leave the management of Zionist schools chiefly in Jewish hands, the Department of Education directed the bulk of its energy toward administering the Arab public school system. Palestinian nationalists frequently criticized the Department of Education for maintaining almost total control of public education. Here, the case of Palestine offered a striking contrast with other Class A Mandates in which education was among the first portfolios handed over to local leaders.[63] Moreover, critics claimed that the centralization of control in the hands of the directorate actually overturned the status quo by eliminating the active participation of local education councils that helped manage Ottoman public schools. There was no Arab Agency with parallel functions and status to those given to the Jewish Agency that could lobby for similar powers of consultation in issues affecting Arab schools, nor was the Supreme Muslim Council a true parallel to the Va'ad Leumi, which came to serve as the local representative body of the Zionist community.[64] The Palestinian educator Khalil Totah famously gave voice to these frustrations in his testimony before the PRC in 1936. "The major grievance of the Arabs as regards education, is that they have no control over it," he stated. "It would seem that Arab education is either designed to reconcile the Arabs to this policy [of creating a Jewish national home] or to make that education so colourless as to make it harmless and not endanger the carrying out of that policy."[65]

In managing Arab education, the Department of Education prioritized primary education over secondary instruction and sought to provide the maximum number of children with the minimum amount of schooling necessary to guarantee permanent literacy. In towns the elementary cycle was five years, and in villages, four; limited higher elementary or secondary opportunities existed, and no publicly funded secondary school offered a full four-year course with the exception of the Government Arab College (the men's teacher training school). A handful of private secondary schools existed in urban areas and primarily served the upper social classes who were able to pay their fees. In his testimony before the PRC, Bowman explained this policy as one designed to maximize access to minimal education—"with a limited budget it has always seemed to me much more necessary to provide elementary education as far as one could rather than provide secondary schools"—while at the same time providing for a small number of exceptional students to continue their studies at the secondary and postsecondary levels at government expense.[66]

Village schools were designed around an "agricultural bias"—intended to provide enough knowledge to improve cultivation techniques but not so much as to make the peasant discontent with his lot—and were thus quite distinct from those in urban areas, in which the period of schooling was longer and the curriculum broadened to include subjects like foreign languages.[67] Experience in Egypt and India had fueled British anxieties over the destabilizing economic and political effects of "literary education," and thus the primary goal in Palestine was to keep the fellahin on the land and prevent their migration to urban areas, where it was feared they would become unemployable vagabonds or, worse yet, communists. Lord Cromer had offered the paradigmatic condemnation of literary education in his *Modern Egypt*, which Humphrey Bowman quoted approvingly in his own memoir:

> The great mistake in the education of the poor has in general been that it has been too largely and too ambitiously literary. Primary education should . . . teach the poor to write well and to count well; but for the rest it should be much more technical and industrial than literary, and should be more concerned with the observation of facts than with any form of speculative reasoning or opinions. There is much evidence to support the conclusion that the kinds of popular education which have proved morally, as well as intellectually, the most beneficial have been those in which a very moderate amount of purely mental instruction has been combined with physical or industrial training.[68]

Though educational opportunities were generally more abundant in cities, the average Palestinian schoolboy's prospects for securing an education in urban areas were also quite low. Due to the high level of demand, lack of teachers, and insufficient accommodations, the rejection rate for applicants to public schools in urban areas averaged more than 50 percent. For the 1929–30 school year, the rejection rate for boys applying to Jerusalem public schools was 63 percent. The situation improved only slightly throughout the Mandate, and the average rejection rate for town schools remained above 50 percent for the 1945–46 school year.[69] The contrast with Jewish education draws these figures into even sharper relief. For instance, in 1943 the city of Haifa had approximately 9,000 Jewish and 7,200 Arab children enrolled in schools; conversely, there were between 500 and 1,000 Jewish and 7,000 Arab children without access to formal schooling.[70]

With regard to Jewish education, the Government of Palestine's initial satisfaction with its private (i.e., cheap from the perspective of public financing) character morphed, by the close of the Mandate period, into extreme frustration regarding its administrative inefficiencies, political character, and excessive centralization. The principle of volunteerism, so central to the development of educational thinking in nineteenth- and twentieth-century England, produced nothing but exasperation among education officials who had essentially forfeited control over a large share of Palestine's schools. In terms of the provision of education, the basic course of schooling in the Hebrew Public System was eight years. The Zionist Department of Education also oversaw numerous secondary and vocational schools, in addition to teachers' seminaries, which offered another four years of education. Modeled on the European Gymnasium, secondary schools were largely financed by school fees and thus served primarily the upper classes. By the 1929–30 school year, at a time when Jews represented less than 20 percent of the population, the Hebrew Public System included 1,465 pupils in secondary and approximately 1,200 more in training or commercial schools; there were 353 pupils enrolled in Arab secondary schools.[71] By 1943, there were approximately 9,000 pupils enrolled in Zionist secondary education, including vocational schools and the teachers' seminaries.[72]

It is unclear whether the Department of Education grasped the degree to which primary and secondary schooling were codependent operations. When the Advisory Committee on Education in the Colonies, together with the Department of Education, drafted a plan in the early 1940s to extend elementary schooling to all Palestinian Arab children living in villages with populations greater than three hundred, they did not account for this mutual dependency. This incongruity prompted the education adviser to the secretary of state for the colonies to state he was "at a loss" to understand how an additional seven hundred schools were to be opened without any dramatic increase in the number of graduates from the teaching training colleges. Moreover, he wrote, the extremely restrictive nature of secondary education provided by the government could in no way prepare Palestinian Arabs for the future:

> The Committee's Report appears to envisage that, at the end of the ten year period, the annual output of Arab boys with a full secondary education will still only be about 25, of whom about 15 will be earmarked as future teachers. I very much doubt whether the Arab will have been given a reasonable chance of holding his own in the proposed independent state if, apart from teachers, only 10 young men are to be turned out annually with a full secondary education.[73]

The situation was even direr with regard to female education. Bowman agreed with members of the PRC that "in these days particularly, the education of girls is almost, if not quite, as important as the education of boys,"[74] yet the majority of Arab girls remained illiterate throughout the Mandate period. During the 1945–46 school year, 35 town schools and 55 village schools were open to girls, in contrast with 47 town and 377 village schools for boys.[75] The curriculum in girls' schools was specifically tailored to the presumed educational needs of women inside the home. A typical syllabus would include subjects like housewifery, infant welfare, and sewing. British educationalists laid special emphasis on the development of domestic science in schools, generally reflecting the professionalization of household labor that occurred in early twentieth-century England. Purely academic subjects were thought to be of little value in girls' schools, as the proper educational goals for Palestinian girls should be to "understand the value of a good home, where cleanliness, sanitation and above all the care of children are to be regarded as the aim of every woman."[76] The dreaded literary education was to be avoided if possible, and administrators therefore stipulated that little time should be "wasted" on subjects like history, geography, or classical Arabic.[77]

The Department of Education frequently noted that the demand for female education was strong but that it was unable to meet this need due to the lack of qualified female teachers. The government maintained a women teachers' training college in Jerusalem and opened a rural training center in Ramallah in 1935, but the combined annual graduates from these institutions numbered approximately twenty-five. Administrators did not entertain the possibility of male teachers working in a girls' school, though the practice of male sheikhs teaching girls in *katātīb* was not unknown prior to the British occupation. Furthermore, the government required female teachers to resign their posts upon marriage; thus, the replacement rate for female teachers was much higher than that for their male counterparts.[78] "The trained women teachers are apt to marry as soon as they may, since they are specially prized by Arab husbands who want educated wives, and the result is we have a continual wastage of trained teachers," Bowman explained.[79] The prohibition of married women continuing their work in the civil service, according to another high-ranking official, stemmed from the greater amount of sick leave (presumably, maternity leave) required and "the embarrassment caused to other members of the staff and to the members of the public by their presence in a certain condition."[80] The presumed unacceptability of married women in the workforce seems to be yet another example of the enforcement of "harem conditions" by a colonial power eager to demonstrate its commitment to "tradition," whether real or invented.[81]

Not surprisingly, these policies led to a permanent shortage of teachers in girls' schools and an ongoing lament within the Department of Education that the expansion of female education was therefore delayed. This excuse appears, on examination of the archival record, completely baseless. Despite its rhetorical support for female education and lament over the shortage of qualified teachers, the Government of Palestine consistently pursued policies that dramatically limited the applicant pool. As in other realms of educational planning, a disconnect existed between officials' stated goals and the reality engendered by the policies they pursued. For instance, the Department of Education narrowed the pool of qualified female teachers by severely restricting class sizes at the training colleges. Of 1,022 applicants to the Women's Teacher College (WTC) from 1925 to 1936, the school accepted only 209.[82] The small number of applicants accepted to the WTC annually meant no substantive expansion of girls' education could occur. The dearth of female teachers was sometimes blamed on Muslim cultural biases, though even administrators were forced to admit that this explanation was lacking. Writing in 1927, the principal of the WTC noted,

> When we began in 1919, we could obtain Christian girls in numbers, for they led freer lives, and the attendance at mission schools had accustomed them to leave the seclusion of the home. Moslem girls, however, were very difficult to secure, only the daughters of the poorest classes or destitute orphans could be persuaded to enter a boarding school, and trained to earn their own living by teaching. In such cases the prospect of a salary was the deciding factor, and no call to a vocation. This prejudice is gradually weakening, and in the entrance examination held a month ago, we had 96 applications for 21 vacant places, nearly two-thirds of these from Moslems.[83]

Furthermore, the government actually *decreased* the number of female teachers available by suspending scholarships to girls entering the WTC. Thus, the school's enrollment during the 1920s was on average double that of the 1930s. The "fall off in the number of entries after 1930," explained the principal of the college, "is due to the fact that no scholarships are now given until the first two years have been completed, i.e. all pay the boarding fee of LP 24 p.a. [per annum]."[84] Here, as elsewhere, the desirability of certain educational policies was not enough to maintain even the most meager streams of funding. It is indeed difficult to escape the rather cynical conclusion that education for girls was systematically neglected based on gendered and colonial assumptions about the superfluous nature of education for Palestinian women. That this occurred precisely at the time when an Arab women's movement had emerged and female education had gained widespread acceptance even in Palestinian villages is but one of the many ironies that characterized Britain's supposedly enlightened rule.[85]

The government's choice to privilege Arab primary education at the expense of secondary training therefore had very real consequences in terms of exacerbating the educational gulf between Palestine's population groups. This was but one example of the impact wrought by policy decisions that were supposedly designed to serve the pragmatic and psychological needs of a peasant population not naturally inclined toward abstract thinking or political concerns. The reality, of course, was that politics was all around, with the introduction into Palestine of a large, well-organized, and well-funded Zionist movement that set its sights on demographic, cultural, and political dominance. Viewing education as a force to preserve the status quo rather than transform it, the Government of Palestine thus inadvertently laid the foundation for a discrepancy in Jewish and Arab educational access that still looms large today.

EDUCATION AND THE RIGHT TO POLITICS

These policy decisions related to educational administration and financing were linked to the material and political reengineering of Palestine in ways that, with the benefit of hindsight, seem almost obvious. Yet it is one of the overarching claims of this book that such political effects were routinely denied by British officials, who regarded it their professional duty to insulate schoolchildren from the surrounding political tension. Questions regarding the political nature of education arose frequently in Mandate Palestine yet were almost always accompanied by a sense of the invisible, often transgressed, but nevertheless very real conceptual boundary that separated the state's practices from those of Arab and Jewish communities. Colonial administrators thus went to great lengths to distinguish *their* project—dictated by pedagogic necessity, managed through benign administrative channels, and devoted to character formation—from education as a form of political indoctrination. Humphrey Bowman saw no contradiction, for instance, in stressing the virtues of citizenship to a population thoroughly subjected to colonial rule, as if civic duty and responsibility were somehow separable from political control of one's country. Writing in his diary in 1929, he stated that " 'public service' is what I preach everywhere now, and though it does not meet with much response, I believe gradually the people must realize that the leaders must do something for their own youth, for the blind, for the infirm, for the halfwitted. They expect government to do everything and of course government can't. Partly because there is not the money and partly because, chiefly because, there are some things which are so much better done by private . . . enterprise."[86] Noting this tendency to separate "the concepts of citizenship and character from their cultural base," Ylana Miller has argued that British officials "sought to use education . . . to maintain a stable social order and to transmit what seemed to them universal values," thereby immunizing "the population against nationalist emotions."[87]

Indeed, we find a continual refrain that colonial educational practices merely reflected the application of value-neutral, scientifically sound best practices. This had the discursive effect of separating pedagogic concerns from political ones, even when the political impact of educational decisions was clearly apparent. Such was the nature of policies like educational monolingualism, which were justified on pedagogic grounds yet undoubtedly contributed to the segregation of Palestine into two linguistically isolated communities.

This unease regarding politics peaked at times of domestic upheaval, such as during the school strikes that accompanied Lord Balfour's 1925 visit and the riots in 1929.[88] Following the 1925 strikes, the government forbade teachers in the Arab Public System from membership in any political organizations and required teachers to sign the following oath:

> I, ____________________ hereby give a solemn undertaking that so long as I am a teacher under the Department of Education I will not introduce any political considerations into my duties as a teacher, nor will I take any active part in any movement or in any meeting or demonstration which has a political character or purpose, or engage in any form of political propaganda.[89]

Conjuring up the idea of an educational utopia set apart from the question of Palestine's political future—a scenario that, in theory, would not foster foment against its British rulers—the teachers' oath demonstrates how the "politics of denial" could become a tool of genuine power. Moreover, while teachers were no longer free to belong to popular Muslim-Christian associations, which were at the forefront of the Palestinian national movement, they were still able to belong to the presumably neutral Young Men's Christian Association (YMCA).[90] This was but one instance in which English, and more broadly, Christian, organizations were regarded as disinterested parties in the unraveling of Palestine into warring Semitic factions.

However futile the attempts to prevent politics from entering the classroom would eventually prove,[91] for many years officials maintained faith that the right curriculum could help neutralize the threat. An exchange between High Commissioner Wauchope and Susan Lawrence, a British Parliament member, is instructive in this regard. Following a visit to Arab public schools in Palestine, Lawrence expressed a mixture of admiration and alarm at what she had witnessed:

> I cannot tell you how impressed and touched I was that the first demand of these bitterly poor people was for education. I don't believe that any European peasants would have done the same.
>
> But when I have talked to my Jewish friends, I find they look on the Arab schools with a great deal of alarm. They say that they teach race-hatred and that the teachers everywhere are the very centre of the agitation against them.
>
> I mention this—for if it is true—it would be comparatively easy for you by means of private or public utterances to your inspectors, the training schools, or the teachers to impress upon these servants of the Government the correct view that the schools must take no part in current politics.[92]

In his response, the high commissioner assured Lawrence that a combination of suitable textbooks and detailed syllabi was an effective barrier against the politicization of schools. For potentially contentious subjects such as history, for which no textbook "in Arabic suitable for pupils in Palestine schools at present exists," the detailed nature of the syllabus ensured that this absence was "not necessarily an encouragement to undesirable propaganda by teachers." To the contrary, "the syllabus for history, as for all other subjects, is clearly laid down by the Department, and may not be altered by the teacher, whose notes of lessons are always available to the Head of his school and to Inspectors."[93]

Writing a decade after Lawrence's visit, Humphrey Bowman recounted his growing recognition that schools could not be effectively isolated from the forces of politics. Describing his tenure as education director, he wrote, "As the political situation gradually worsened, we were faced by another danger. This was the effect of politics on teachers and pupils. In the neighboring Egypt, school strikes and demonstrations had had a disastrous effect on discipline, and had seriously reacted on educational progress. Once this virus entered the schools of Palestine, I knew we were doomed."[94] Interestingly, Bowman characterized his attempt to shield Palestinian schools from politics, "in so far as this was humanly possible," as largely successful up until the outbreak of the Arab Revolt in 1936. He attributed this success in part to the department's contacts with Hajj Amin al-Husseini and other Muslim leaders: "We never tired of stressing the disastrous results on character and upbringing of political agitation in the schools."[95] Government schools were only sporadically operational during the years of the Arab Revolt, which ended in 1939 after the intervention of approximately fifty-thousand British troops. In the years following the rebellion, which coincided with the onset of World War II and a period of relative quiet and prosperity in Palestine, Jerome Farrell pursued the separation of education from mass politics with renewed vigor. His efforts were almost certainly aided by the fact that most of Palestine's Arab leadership was now in exile, but Farrell preferred to attribute the government's success in combating "a violent nationalism" within the Arab Public System to the department's "directing the syllabus in accordance with true pedagogic values rather than by the demands of an artificial and hysterical racial pride."

In making the claim that politics entered the classroom only at the hands of unruly nationalist subjects, Bowman and Farrell belied the fact that state-sponsored education is an inherently political venture, and indeed there was almost no facet of life in Palestine that was as closely supervised by the government as education. Schools were funded largely by public tax dollars, centrally administered and inspected, and the curriculum was designed to achieve explicit political and economic goals. The problem with politics was a problem of transgression, of education being used to articulate interests at odds with the colonial order. The seepage of nationalist concerns into the schoolroom therefore constituted nothing less than an *intrusion* that compromised the nature of education itself. While children were to be educated in their "native" language and preserve their "national" culture, administrators nevertheless held that education should never veer into contemporary nationalist politics. In Farrell's terms, although Arabic was the language of instruction in government schools and the curriculum even devoted some attention to the Arab *nahḍa*, "the aim has been the formation of individual character" rather than the creation of budding Arab nationalists.[96]

It is noteworthy that, in contrast to the dreaded creep of politics into the classroom, the Government of Palestine hoped that religious education could establish the foundation for shared moral principles that remained aloof from this political turmoil. This is not to say that educators found the existing models of religious education particularly worthy of preservation. As I argue in the next chapter, the goal was to reconstitute existing forms of religious education to accommodate the contradictory demands that schooling both nurture the traditional order and support the introduction of new technical skills geared for Palestine's changing economy. Yet it is nonetheless striking that a government that continually fretted regarding the politicization of Palestine's schools was so unwavering in its support for religious education. Not only did colonial officials express confidence that religious education represented an efficient way to nurture common ethical norms, but they also feared that its absence threatened to undermine Palestine's fragile political and social fabric. Nowhere was this discomfort more evident than in the Department of Education's attitudes toward Zionist education, whose molding of Judaism into the basis of political identity seemed to signal its moral bankruptcy as a "real" religion. For officials like Farrell, this sense was no doubt exacerbated by the eastern European origins and socialist leanings of many Zionist leaders. It was this group that had not been "long, widely and intimately subjected to civilising influences either at home or in Palestine and, having abandoned religious practices, [was] without any basis for the development of moral principle.[97] With regard to the education offered within the Hebrew Public System, Farrell compared the Zionist abandonment of traditional religious observance unfavorably to the situation within Arab public schools:

> Religion is a full subject in the curriculum and thus the ultimate basis of ethical values in the Government schools is common to Islam and Christianity, for both accept a theology and moral principles based largely on Greek philosophy, while Islam regards Christ as at least a prophet. But "unassimilated" Judaism after rejecting successively both Hellenism and Christ is now reducing its own traditional faith, so far as it still survives at all as a religion, from monotheism to the older henotheism which leads to that racial self-worship which Albert Rosenberg [*sic*] borrowed from the Jews for Nordic ends.[98]

Farrell was in all likelihood referring to Alfred Rosenberg, one of the Nazi Party's chief ideologues. It was one of several instances in which the education director likened Zionist education to Nazi indoctrination. Beyond its naked anti-Semitism, Farrell's comparison of Zionist schooling with that of totalitarian states is telling. The latter offered the clearest example of using education as a form of social engineering, a practice that was supposedly foreign to Britain's own "politically neutral" approach to schooling both at home and in the colonies. Yet what makes Farrell's comments most fascinating for our purposes is the view of religion found therein. In his telling, having turned away from all possible sources of civilization—Christianity and Hellenism—Zionism was found guilty of further reducing the remnants of Judaism into a form of militant national chauvinism.

Obviously the religion that Jerome Farrell had in mind, and that was supposed to serve such a formative role in the moral formation of Palestine's children, was not that which found expression in Zionist schools. So what were the contents and purpose of this religion, and what forms did it assume in Palestine's schools? In the chapters that follow, we gain a better sense about how the various parties involved answered this question in radically different ways. To better frame this conceptual discussion, the following chapter attends to the centrality of religion in structuring Palestine's educational system as a whole as we consider how disagreements about the nature of religion became meaningful in material terms.

3 EDUCATION AND COMMUNITY UNDER SECTARIAN RULE

IN RECENT YEARS, scholars from multiple disciplines have turned their attention to the politics of sectarianism, its discursive characteristics, and historical consequences.[1] Scholars of British colonialism in particular have noted the late imperial preference for governing territories through structures of religious authority, which, by the end of the nineteenth century, were widely perceived as bulwarks against popular discontent. By demonstrating their support for "tradition"—as they understood and constructed it—colonial administrators hoped to quell anxieties about the British destruction of native culture and affirm their support for the presumed centrality of religious leaders therein. In the Palestinian context, Nicholas Roberts has pointed to the establishment of the Supreme Muslim Council (SMC) to argue that the British viewed the country as naturally divided along religious-communal lines, even though this type of segregation was historically far less pervasive than imagined.[2] Roberts argues that the creation of the SMC must be understood as a reflection of this view, which considered religion the central organizing principle of Palestinian society and which sought to control the Muslim masses through their "natural" leaders. In a similar vein, Laura Robson has argued that the sectarian structure adopted by the British in Palestine turned religious categories into legal ones—a process that served to marginalize Christians, transform the Muslim majority into a *millet*, and discourage cross-communal Arab national organization.[3] Both works highlight how, despite claims that it was doing nothing contrary to tradition, the Mandatory government created an administrative structure wherein religious affiliation became more determinative of political identity than it was during the preceding period.

Important as these recent studies have been, they do not fully register the fact that a great deal of ambiguity and debate actually existed over what precisely constituted "religious" practices, institutions, or communities. This applies not only to developments in Palestine itself—such as which groups were regarded as religious communities and what criteria were used to judge—but to broader interpretive patterns through which we envision a clear division between the religious and the political. When, for instance, Roberts asserts that the British conquest of Palestine was chiefly driven by imperial rather than religious feeling, he—perhaps unwittingly—reaffirms the idea that the latter can be neatly cordoned off from economics, politics, or culture.[4] I find such designations much harder to sustain and prefer to view British imperial politics and Christian theology as mutually constitutive rather than distinctive facets of colonial life.[5] The notion, still so prevalent in contemporary polemics, that *our* politics are rationally guided and easily distinguishable from religion in a way in which *others'* are not is a central feature of what I have coined the "politics of denial." That we might all exist within a muddled mixed-up state despite our best attempts at purification—or in Latour's terms, that we might never have been modern—is a critical potentiality lost in the process of taking religion for granted. Our attempt to attend to the role of religion in structuring Palestine's educational system must therefore begin by appreciating the ambiguity inherent in religion as either an analytic or administrative category.

In this chapter, I argue that Palestine's educational structure offers a productive vector on which to chart the sectarian governance of the country, but it also offers an opportunity to appreciate the points of tension inherent within this style of rule. In particular, I argue that ambiguity surrounding the religious proved particularly advantageous for Zionist education, as this definitional confusion allowed the Jewish state-in-the-making a degree of educational autonomy wholly unavailable to Palestinian Arabs. This privileged position was of course rooted in the League of Nations' Mandate—which famously recognized Jews alone as a national group—but it became meaningful only through discrete policies that the Government of Palestine adopted regarding the provision of education by religious communities.[6] Analyzing these policies in greater detail not only directs our attention to the points of tension within sectarian rule but also demonstrates why and how the conceptual fuzziness surrounding religion became meaningful.

"COMMUNITY" AND THE SECTARIAN ORDER

On February 18, 1926, the Jewish Telegraphic Agency (JTA) announced that the Government of Palestine had taken "a step toward the organization of the Jewish communities in Palestine on the basis of self-government." The act in question was the promulgation of the Religious Communities Organization Ordinance, which provided that "each Religious Community recognized by the Government shall enjoy autonomy for the internal affairs of the Community" and conferred on the community the right to hold property, enter into contracts, and levee taxes on its members.[7] It was not until the next month that the JTA published the full text of the ordinance, but its initial communiqué from February is quite telling when we consider that the Zionist Organization was the only political group that ever applied for statutory recognition under its terms.[8] In the words of the JTA, "The ordinance gives the power to the High Commissioner to issue a special Jewish communities ordinance. The general ordinance grants the rights of a juridical person to the communities and the right of self-taxation for the needs of the communities. The ordinance bases the existence of the communities on a religious principle."[9] Yet as was so often the case, the ordinance did not specify what made a community religious, how this classification intersected with the categories of race or nation, or what religious principles (to use the JTA's terms) actually entailed.

Before delving into the legal framework that was devised to structure education in Palestine, we must first understand the nature of the Religious Communities Organization Ordinance. The ordinance served as the legal basis for recognizing the Jewish population of Palestine as a *religious* community, and this classification became particularly significant in regard to the provision of education. Through the ordinance, the government recognized a representative body called Knesset Israel as the organ of Palestine's official Jewish community; the Va'ad Leumi served as its executive committee. As the political center of gravity within the Zionist movement migrated to the *yishuv* in the 1930s, the Va'ad Leumi would come to serve a central role in the organization of Jewish life in Palestine.[10] Reflecting this broader shift, in 1932 the Jewish Agency transferred administrative control over Zionist schools to Knesset Israel. These were crucial developments with regard to the centralization of Zionist education under a single entity based not in London but in Palestine. Unless they opted out (which a number of Orthodox Jews did), all Jews above the age of eighteen were automatically included in Knesset Israel. It was therefore the Zionist community, its representative body, and even its system of religious courts that gained statutory recognition under the Religious Communities Organization Ordinance.

Numerous representatives of the Old Yishuv protested this arrangement throughout the late 1920s, with the most active among them, Agudat Israel, going as far as to request official recognition as a separate Jewish community.[11] Such recognition would theoretically restore their communal rights in issues of personal status (heretofore handled by the Zionist religious courts) and enable their schools to receive a portion of local education taxes. The issue was still not resolved by 1934, when the Palestine *Annual Report* noted that the government, acting as an intermediary, had convened negotiations between representatives from Agudat Israel and the Va'ad Leumi in the hope of absorbing the former into the community represented by the latter. The heart of the compromise involved dividing Jewish affairs into religious and lay categories overseen by distinct committees. If it had succeeded, such a compromise would have effectively left secular matters in the hands of the Va'ad Leumi, whose political standing derived from its status as a religious community. The attempted reconciliation of Jewish interests was challenging to enact, however, chiefly because the parties involved had divergent ideas about the boundaries (or the existence of a boundary at all) between religious and lay matters. The Va'ad Leumi's representatives proposed to cede supervision of the Rabbinate, *shechita* (ritual slaughter), and burial services to a board "consisting of persons with a sympathetic attitude to religion," while retaining for itself control of "all economic, social and political affairs."[12] Agudat Israel defined religious affairs in a far more expansive fashion, encompassing "the Rabbinate, Shechita, burial, education, maintenance of orphans, treatment of the sick, etc."[13] In an era when "religious" and "secular" were still very much categories in formation, a compromise of the type envisioned by the government was all but impossible to achieve.

Moreover, it is noteworthy that the Mandatory government cast itself as an objective party attempting to reconcile a petty squabble between warring Jewish factions.[14] The Palestine *Annual Report* stated that incorporating Agudat Israel into the official Jewish community was preferable over the recognition of it as a second community, lest a schism emerge among Palestinian Jews: "The hope and intention of the Government are by this means to satisfy the legitimate requirements of the Agudath Israel without perpetuating the schism in the Jewish population of Palestine which separate recognition of the Agudath Israel as a community under the Religious Communities Organization Ordinance, 1926, might involve."[15] The irony, of course, was that this schism was largely the by-product of government legislation that bestowed official recognition on one portion of the Jewish community and granted it quasi-ecclesiastical powers over all others. That these religious powers were granted to the Va'ad Leumi at a time when many Zionist immigrants were avowedly secular or even atheists—while Jews who maintained the highest level of *halachic* (Jewish legal) observance were not recognized as part of the Jewish community—was but one of the many points of tension.

While the high commissioner was adamant to bridge the schism between Agudat Israel and the Va'ad Leumi, his correspondence with the Colonial Office also demonstrates that he misunderstood the nature of their conflict. For instance, when representatives from Agudat Israel proposed the creation of a second *beit din* (rabbinical court) so its members did not have to submit to the authority of Zionist courts, the high commissioner greeted the proposal with apprehension.[16] At the most basic level, he could not comprehend the resistance to a unified religious authority given that members of Agudat Israel were "not in any fundamental respect in theory or in practice at variance" with the Orthodox Jews within the Zionist fold. What is important about this claim for our purposes is the high commissioner's extreme reluctance to recognize the Jewish community as a heterogeneous entity, indeed, as multiple Jewish communities. He may have been correct in stating that many Zionist Jews were as observant as those within Agudat Israel; however, he did not grasp that disagreements related to observance were of lesser importance than the larger dispute: the replacement of numerous communities and religious courts bearing distinct *minhagim* (customs that can assume the status of law) with a single religious authority under Zionist control.[17] The fact that a single *beit din* had never exercised juridical authority over the whole of Palestinian Jewry since the time of the Sanhedrin was apparently unimportant.[18]

In commenting on the high commissioner's dispatch, the Foreign Office noted, "The Government are clearly prejudiced against the Agudath Israel, which is doubtless explained by their reluctance to allow a schism to develop in the official organization of the Jewish community, with its resultant administrative inconveniences."[19] Perhaps needless to say, there was little awareness that such "administrative inconveniences" were not merely the product of intra-Jewish squabbles but the result of government policies. Of course, substantive divisions between the Zionist Organization and Agudat Israel existed and certainly predated the Mandate. However, they assumed the form of a dispute over the right to act as the exclusive representative of the Jewish community—with the corresponding privileges—only within the context of British rule.

THE MECHANICS OF SECTARIANISM: THE PALESTINE EDUCATION ORDINANCE

During the same years in which Agudat Israel was protesting against the Religious Communities Organization Ordinance, the Government of Palestine was engaged in drafting a new education law that would in many ways build on the ordinance's frame. It was first published as a draft in October 1927, but it would take six years for administrators in Palestine and officials in the Colonial Office to produce a piece of legislation that appeased its critics, though it still failed to satisfy them.[20] Not only was such legislation much delayed, but it was finally published as an emaciated version of its former self, largely due to the difficulties the Government of Palestine encountered in attempting to extend its powers of supervision over those schools maintained by Catholic bodies. While it is clear that the resulting compromise was designed to accommodate the privileged position of Catholic and other Christian missionary schools in Palestine, it created legal and administrative structures that had far-reaching implications for education as a whole.

British officials dealt with the storm of diplomatic protests to the proposed legislation by designating religious education as a category of exception that was largely removed from state supervision. As politically expedient as this compromise was, it was possible only due to an understanding of religion as a conservative force that functioned—or at least was supposed to function—to augment the social and political status quo. While the exemption of religious education from the ordinance's provisions may seem to constitute its removal from the political space, it in fact marked an attempt to encourage the "appropriate" form of political organization at the sectarian level. Thus, the ordinance rendered religious organization through a singular and monolithic community as the only means through which to attain educational autonomy. Those who opted out of such communities, or those who wished to organize schooling on a nonsectarian basis, were left to support their endeavors without official sanction or government support.

The question regarding how to best organize and supervise education in a country featuring such a wide variety of schools—ranging from former Ottoman public schools to a plethora of private ones, including those of the

Zionist Organization, teaching in no fewer than seven languages and often maintained by political, philanthropic, or missionary groups abroad—proved a particularly difficult one. Overseeing such a motley crew was a tall order in and of itself, but it was made even more so by the peculiar terms of the League of Nations' Mandate for Palestine. Article 15 guaranteed "the right of each community to maintain its own schools for the education of its own members in its own language, while conforming to such educational requirements of a general nature as the Administration may impose."[21] The Mandate did not specify what precisely counted as a "community," though the provision was undoubtedly intended to offer a sense of continuity with the Ottoman *millet* system, in which religious minorities maintained a large degree of autonomy in educational affairs. However, as Laura Robson has recently argued, rather than simply preserve the *millet* system as a continuation of the status quo, the Mandatory government actually expanded its scope and codified it in a legal system that rendered sectarian identity a prerequisite for political participation.[22] For our purposes, the ambiguities over what constituted a community are of particular importance. Palestinian leaders who leaned on Article 15 to lobby for greater educational autonomy, for instance, were denied it on the grounds that theirs was not a (religious) community. Meanwhile, the Zionist Organization was able to secure statutory recognition of its local political organ, Knesset Israel/Va'ad Leumi, under the Religious Communities Organization Ordinance of 1926. Zionist schools thereafter became recognized as those belonging to an official religious community, a position that came with numerous advantages.

Until the Government of Palestine adopted its own Education Ordinance in 1933, Ottoman laws were in theory still enforceable. The Ottoman Education Act of 1913 reserved for government the right to supervise the curriculum, teaching staff, hygiene, and general administration of all schools in Palestine, whether public or private. In not distinguishing between types of schools, the Ottoman law reflected a view of education as a central concern of the modernizing state. In his critique of British educational policy in Palestine, Abdul Latif Tibawi placed blame on the British for not exercising closer supervision of private schools as a continuation of this status quo ante bellum.[23] However, he overlooked the fact that the Ottomans' control of private educational institutions was in most cases purely nominal.[24] In practice, the Sublime Porte's concessions to European powers often included a pledge not to interfere in the affairs of Christian or Jewish schools. Thus, both Christian missionary groups and the Zionist Organization would protest that the Mandatory government's attempt to supervise their schools represented a drastic departure from the status quo. "It has been said that some of the requirements (e.g. registration of schools) merely maintain the Turkish law," the Latin patriarch wrote to the Colonial Office in response to the proposed regulations. "The fact is shown . . . that the Porte has granted many privileges, and what are privileges, if not suspensions from the law?"[25]

The laissez-faire approach to supervision of private schools provided a sharp contrast with that of public schools, over which the director of education assumed complete control. "If the English reader can imagine one single person who combines the powers and functions of Parliament, the Minister of Education, the local education authorities and the National Union of Teachers, he will have an approximate picture of the powers and functions of the Director of Education in Palestine."[26] Given the anomalous case of Palestine—where the government was charged with facilitating the Jewish national home project despite opposition from the country's majority population—officials felt that the administration of Arab education must remain concentrated in British hands, lest schools become swept up in the surrounding nationalist agitation. A robust education law that would enable school surveillance was therefore viewed as both a political and pedagogic necessity.

The ordinance itself was based on a combination of former Ottoman law and education legislation taken from Great Britain and Nigeria.[27] The latter served as the immediate colonial model for the more draconian aspects of the Palestinian legislation. Meanwhile, provisions that were particularly sensitive for religious schools—including the licensing of teachers, inspection of schools, and the role of LEAs—can be traced to England's own education reforms at the turn of the twentieth century, particularly to Conservative attempts to strengthen the position of Anglican schools at a time when many were seeking public alternatives.[28] Interestingly, even groups that explicitly opposed the Mandate argued that the proposed legislation was contrary to its terms. Christian and Jewish groups claimed that the government's attempts to register and inspect their schools violated Article 15, which guaranteed communities the right to maintain their own schools. Meanwhile, Palestinian leaders asserted that Article 15 should also be read to ensure the educational autonomy of the Arab *national* community and therefore demanded a greater role in the administration of the Arab Public System. I deal with each of these protests in turn, as the form each assumed tells us a great deal about differing conceptions of governance and the legitimate location of authority within a fragmented political and social space.

The first draft of the ordinance gave the Department of Education and its director complete power of supervision over all schools irrespective of type. This control encompassed matters of curriculum, school syllabi and textbooks, licensing, appointment and dismissal of teachers, registration, opening and closing of schools, health and medical inspections, and general oversight to protect against "morally or politically corrupt" teachings. Importantly, the regulations were to be applied to all categories of school without exception, effectively granting the director of education the same inspection rights in missionary and Zionist schools as he enjoyed in those maintained by the government.[29] This was in fact the goal. Humphrey Bowman, who drafted the ordinance along with Lord Plumer, expressed hope that it would provide the legal means for extending government supervision over private schools, which had previously proved impossible to control. After the first draft of the ordinance was published, he noted with satisfaction that the new legislation might provide the statutory basis for such supervision: "It will be a great help with bringing into line the non-government schools."[30] Bowman expected the ordinance to take effect within months, and in this he greatly underestimated the storm of controversy the draft legislation would generate.

At least initially, the loudest voices of protest came from France, Italy, and the Vatican and were chiefly concerned that the draft ordinance represented a direct challenge to the autonomy that Catholic schools historically enjoyed. In response, Lord Plumer argued that the educational freedoms granted by Article 15 of the Mandate were tempered by Article 16, which gave the Mandatory supervisory rights over religious or missionary bodies "as may be required for the maintenance of public order and good Government." The high commissioner held that it was therefore possible to impose requirements on schools maintained by religious bodies "which are educational in nature."[31] Generally speaking, the high commissioner and the director of education sought to bestow on the Government of Palestine far greater powers of educational supervision than the Colonial Office—faced with a flurry of complaints—was willing to allow. Part of the dispute stemmed from the fact that local administrators had substantial experience in colonial settings and expected similar regulations to be enacted in Palestine. Officials in the Colonial Office, on the other hand, were preoccupied by the novelty of a Mandate under international control and unsure of what legal limitations it entailed. Regarding the Education Ordinance, the latter group was unconvinced that the legislation as drafted was consistent with the terms of the Mandate and noted that "the mere fact that the question is one of interpretation, that the whole subject of education in Palestine is so controversial and that neither the Turkish nor the Palestine governments have in the past interfered in any way with religious schools, clearly makes it desirable to proceed with utmost circumspection."[32]

Officials in London also feared that robust legislation would create barriers to private educational initiatives, which would consequently place a larger financial burden on the Palestine government. At the most basic level, the more children who were enrolled in Zionist, missionary, and other private schools, the more the government's own responsibility for education would diminish. This approach was not at all surprising given that England had left the education of its own population primarily in the hands of the Anglican Church and other private organizations until the end of the nineteenth century.[33] Thus, ever conscious of their dependence on private bodies to supplement state social services, officials in the Colonial Office deemed certain proposed regulations "badly drafted" and "characteristically meddlesome." In the words of T. I. K. Lloyd, writing in 1928, "To the need for the development/spread of education, which in present financial crisis must be left largely to non-governmental agencies, the regulations as a whole would appear to be far too restrictive in character."[34] As in the Indian context, this "attitude of practical non-interference in regard to private enterprise" depended on a laissez-faire framework to posit that less government intervention would result in more privately funded ventures.[35]

Thus, while the Government of Palestine initially sought to extend its powers of supervision, the Colonial Office argued that any substantive measure of control would discourage private initiative and thereby undermine the financial strategy for delivering social services. It is noteworthy that even by the late 1940s, far more children continued to be educated in Zionist and private religious schools than in the government-run Arab Public System. For instance, the *Annual Report* for 1945–46 estimated that there were 81,042 students attending Arab public schools, 87,287 in the Hebrew Public System, and 64,523 in private schools.[36]

Eager to encourage this spirit of volunteerism, the Government of Palestine was alarmed by the barrage of diplomatic protests from European powers anxious to exempt missionary schools from the proposed legislation. Catholic powers, for instance, found fault with clauses requiring all schools to register and all teachers to secure licenses from the Department of Education and took further issue with the broad powers of inspection given to government officials. In response, the high commissioner recommended amending the legislation to exempt religious schools from certain clauses. Because of "apprehension on the part of religious bodies . . . that the draft gave possibilities of inquisitions by officers not properly qualified to inspect schools," the high commissioner limited powers of "general inspection" to the director of education. He agreed to exempt from the ordinance schools imparting religious education exclusively and to not interfere with matters of religious curriculum in private schools, even those receiving government aid. Finally, he offered assurance that any teacher's license "signed by the Religious Head of the Communion to which the teacher belongs" would be recognized as valid.[37]

An amended draft of the ordinance was published in July 1928, though critics still found it far from satisfactory. A particularly scathing rebuttal arrived in the form of a twenty-one-page missive from the Latin patriarch of Jerusalem, Louis Barlassina. The patriarch objected to the draft ordinance on the basis of prior assurances given by the British government not to interfere in the affairs of Catholic schools. As a matter of precedent, he wrote, France (acting in its self-appointed role as "Protector of Catholics in the Ottoman Empire") had secured an arrangement with the Sublime Porte "which secured the liberty of teaching in Catholic schools without let or hindrance from the officers of the Ottoman Government." After the war, Great Britain agreed "to recognize all the rights obtained by France from the Ottoman Government, including those of schools." He continued, "Although the Ottoman Law has some regulations and restrictions with regard to private schools, which are found in the Ottoman Code, nevertheless, if on one side the Turkish Government has inserted them as a sign of its authority, on the other it was conscious of the inconvenience of putting them into force."[38]

The patriarch sought to communicate that any British attempts to supervise Catholic schools would prove equally inconvenient. Some of the most vociferous responses to the legislation came from Christians, such as the patriarch, who displayed no greater enthusiasm for British rulers than he did for the former Ottoman variety. Furthermore, he argued that by adopting legislation from colonial settings, the Mandate government's laws were actually far more meddlesome than any he had faced in the past. "Palestine is not a COLONY and cannot be treated as such," he stated with characteristic frankness.[39] The patriarch offered the domestic British model in place of a colonial one and proposed that private schools in Palestine should be given the complete autonomy they enjoyed in England, where they operated unregistered and did not submit to government inspections.

Though the Palestine government did not attempt to dictate what could be taught in schools maintained by religious orders, the draft ordinance stipulated under what conditions schools could open or continue to operate and thus affected their capacity to teach at all. Barlassina regarded these regulations, cloaked in the language of public order and sanitation, as of equal danger as those that would have interfered in curricular matters. He objected, for example, to the school registration forms the department required and viewed furnishing the government with data on attendance numbers as "only a matter of courtesy" rather than a legal requirement.[40] Unable to secure the patriarch's cooperation, the Department of Education tried to establish direct contact with individual priests and the European consuls that supported them, which in turn generated even more outrage.

Faced with such attacks on the proposed legislation, Lord Plumer appealed to the Colonial Office that the British government should "make Catholic opinion in Europe realize that the Mandatory for Palestine has no intention to seek to exercise, under the cloak of legislations, any interference with Catholic instruction to adherents of that confession inconsistent with the provisions of the Mandate." However, the Colonial Office refused to launch such a publicity campaign, stating that, in effect, "they ask that H.M.G. should instruct Catholic opinion in Europe and the Vatican, that . . . it is not the intention of the Palestine Government fully to use the powers which in the draft Ordinance they propose to take." In short, Plumer's proposed solution to the controversy was to communicate that the Palestine government was officially substituting its own Education Ordinance in place of the old Ottoman one, but that in practice, enforcement would be just as lax. Instead, the Colonial Office pushed the Palestine government to whittle down its powers of supervision, not just de facto but de jure. "An alternative . . . is to redraft the Ordinance and Regulations so as to define clearly and exactly the powers which the legislation confers on the Palestine Government in respect of religious non-assisted schools."[41] One official recommended the following course of action:

> I should therefore prefer definitely to abandon the claim that the Mandate entitles the Palestine Government to enforce on religious schools "educational requirements of a general nature." If it is possible in practice to distinguish between schools of *religious bodies* and schools of *national bodies* . . . I see no rea-

> son why educational requirements of a general character should not be imposed on the latter class of schools. . . . The position would then be that, in the case of schools of religious bodies (not necessarily schools imparting only religious instruction), the Palestine Government would take the minimum powers necessary to ensure public order and good government.[42]

The maintenance of "public order and good government" would enable the Palestine Government only to demand "the dismissal of any teacher convicted of an offense involving moral turpitude" and to ensure the hygienic and sanitary conditions of the school were adequate. Schools maintained by religious bodies would be exempted from all other regulations. We should note the willingness reflected here to exempt religious schools from oversight, while arguing that control should be maintained over purely national ones. Of equal importance is that the practical difficulties involved in distinguishing between the two categories proved insurmountable, and the Colonial Office therefore recommended that concessions be granted to both types of schools. A minute dated December 24, 1928, noted, "Mr. Lloyd discussed amended draft with [Humphrey] Bowman on Friday morning. He was rather reluctant to see the powers taken in the draft Ordinance whittled down, but we at last induced him to agree to the memo."[43]

In the end, the following categories of private religious schools were finally adopted: (1) assisted schools in receipt of public aid, (2) non-assisted schools in which religious instruction exclusively was given, and (3) non-assisted schools maintained by religious bodies in which some secular instruction was given. The first category of schools would be subject to the whole of the ordinance, with the exception that the government had no rights of supervision over religious curriculum or teachers of religious subjects. It was agreed that schools in which religious instruction exclusively was given should be exempt from the ordinance, save for sanitary requirements deemed necessary for the sake of public health. The third category of schools—which included most Catholic and missionary schools—proved the most difficult to address. After much discussion, the Colonial Office recommended exempting these schools from provisions related to registration and teacher licensing and deleted a clause reserving for the high commissioner the right to "require the dismissal of any teacher who has been convicted of any criminal offence, or who has been shown . . . to have imparted teaching of a seditious, disloyal or otherwise harmful character." The director of education and his immediate deputy would have the authority to visit schools, but not inspect them, and this only after "due notice" was given. In the end, the only provisions that fully applied to schools maintained by religious bodies were those related to sanitation and hygiene. T. I. K. Lloyd noted that while "it would perhaps be open to the Palestine Government to impose educational requirements of a more stringent character" on schools maintained by religious bodies, "the subject of education in Palestine is complicated by the presence of so many communities and religions it is desirable to proceed with the utmost circumspection."[44]

Before concluding this discussion of the ordinance, we should pause to consider the willingness evident here to grant religious schools, curricula, and instructors a large degree of autonomy. In my view, this reflected not only a pragmatic accommodation with European powers, on whom the Government of Palestine depended to educate thousands of the country's children, but also a conceptual order in which religion was both distinct from, and less threatening than, politics. As Nicholas Roberts has argued, the intense policing by British officials of Palestine's "political sphere" did not extend to the religious realm, "where the adoption of political positions that opposed the Palestine government (such as sermonizing against the legislative council elections of 1923) were seen as regrettable but not nearly as dangerous as an unchecked political sphere."[45] Making sense of the privileged treatment of religious education requires that we recognize these conceptual links to a much older and longer history in which religion was associated with obedience, moral fashioning, and the large-scale preservation of tradition.

Yet there were also difficulties that stemmed from the fact that the religious realm was notoriously hard to demarcate, which occasionally came to the fore among officials in Palestine. For instance, Jerome Farrell, acting in his capacity as Bowman's deputy, argued that the Education Ordinance relied on terms that "require very careful definition" in a setting where "such definitions are neither possible nor desirable." Pointing to these ambiguities, Farrell remarked,

> It is not always easy to distinguish schools giving only religious instruction from schools of a religious character giving also some secular instruction. Strictly regarded, no school, except for adults, can come under 1. at all, but Moslem schools teaching reading and writing from the Quran, and teaching law, logic, etc., might claim to be exclusively religious, since Islam touches every human activity. Such schools are precisely those which require most moral supervision, and possibly political supervision too.[46]

Farrell was unique among administrators in identifying religious schools as potential political actors, though even his understanding of this possibility remained limited. Thus, in the previous passage, it is primarily "moral supervision" that such schools required, a sentiment that was wholly consistent with the emphasis on religious education as an exercise in character formation.

This is not to claim that administrators were blind to the fact that religion, and Islam in particular, could incite the public into action. Throughout the nineteenth century, Muslim leaders and reformers—ranging from Syed Ahmed Barelvi in India's Northwest Provinces to Muhammad Ahmad bin ʿAbdallah, the self-proclaimed Mahdi of the Sudan whose revolt ended the life of General Charles George Gordon—had demonstrated the mobilizing power of Islam in battles against British forces.[47] More recently, the disturbances that accompanied the annual Nebi Musa festival in 1920, in which Arab rioters attacked the Jewish Quarter of Jerusalem's Old City, made the alliance between Islam and popular politics seem all the more menacing.[48] Yet, rather than view instances of popular revolt as manifestations of authentic religious feeling or actions directed toward real political ends, colonial officials usually understood them as examples of mass fanaticism that should be distinguished from "real" religion. For example, in describing "the Mahdist Avatar" of the Sudan, Lord Cromer argued it was "enlightened self-interest, more especially in acquisition of wealth," that drove his revolt and "may be traced in the stage tricks by which it was sought to strengthen the faith of a credulous and fanatical population."[49] This was a far cry from the austere and decidedly apolitical virtues of hospitality, monotheism, and honesty that Cromer identifies as the "original grandeur" of Islam. Indeed, Cromer claimed, because Muhammad was driven "to do more than found a religion" and "endeavored to found a social system," Muslim societies became so backward. Quoting the British Orientalist Stanley Lane-Poole with approval, Cromer wrote, "As a religion, Islam is great; it has taught men to worship one God with a pure worship who formerly worshipped many gods impurely. As a social system, it is a complete failure."[50]

As a religion, then, Islam was respectable and even enviable in certain regards. Yet when it crossed the boundaries into the civic and material worlds—when it broke the mold of what a religion was supposed to be—the result was disastrous. Widespread sentiment of this type contributed to the view that the masses needed to be ruled through structures of religious authority like the SMC, which could presumably redirect their passions and prevent them from spilling over into the public sphere. As Roberts has argued, "Most importantly, as shown in the appointment of Hajj Amin [al-Husseini], religion was considered by British officials to be a check on the political impulse. According to this point of view Hajj Amin's concentration of power was not obviously dangerous; instead it might be useful in creating a strong institution in the Palestinian Arab community that would divert Palestinian attention away from politics."[51] Within such a context, the need for "proper" religious education seemed all the more obvious, as genuine religion was thought to lead schoolchildren toward obedience and industriousness rather than toward political agitation. As it turned out, these purported distinctions between the religious, the political, and the national were far less stable than the British had hoped, and this fact would continue to complicate the sectarian scheme for governing Palestine.

AUTONOMY AND AUTHORITY: JEWISH AND MUSLIM RESPONSES

Having addressed the reactions from Catholic powers to the proposed legislation and traced their impact on the ordinance's eventual shape, we now turn to the rather different responses from Palestine's Jewish and Muslim communities. These responses, I suggest, are particularly interesting for what they convey about various parties' views of the Mandatory government and the legitimate scope of its authority. Generally speaking, the Zionist response to the proposed legislation was to advocate two, somewhat contradictory, courses of action. On the one hand, the Zionist Organization lobbied the Palestine government and the Colonial Office for explicit recognition of an autonomous Zionist school system: "The special position of the Jewish Agency under the Mandate should be recognized in the Ordinance, and . . . express provision should be made for the special treatment . . . of schools maintained by the Jewish Agency."[52] The Zionist Organization argued that its schools represented a public school system that paralleled that maintained by the Department of Education, thereby casting itself as an equal party to the Mandatory government. As discussed earlier, after their classification as "public" entities, Zionist schools were entitled to a share of government funds based on the percentage of Jews in the total population, paid in the form of an annual block grant. Yet the Zionist Organization argued that the schools were also "community schools," those maintained by a religious community recognized under the Religious Communities Organization Ordinance. This was significant because British officials, borrowing from an English law that made Anglican schools eligible for a portion of any taxes levied by LEAs, inserted a similar provision into the Palestine Education Ordinance. This clause stipulated that any school maintained by a community recognized by the Religious Communities Organization Ordinance was eligible for a portion of education funds raised by LEAs. In this regard, the Va'ad Leumi schools gained a similar legal status as that granted in England to schools maintained by the Anglican Church. Such classification guaranteed Zionist education a substantial measure of autonomy and also required the government's director of education to consult with the Zionist Education Department in any matter related to these schools.[53]

On the other hand, this classification scheme adversely affected Jewish schools that were not part of the Va'ad Leumi system, which found themselves suddenly ineligible for the privileges that accompanied membership in Palestine's official Jewish community. In fact, those who refused to participate in the Zionist political organization sacrificed the two chief streams of public financing for education: the annual block grant for Jewish education, based on the total number of Jews as a percentage of Palestine's total population, but given to the Va'ad Leumi exclusively; and tax revenue collected by LEAs, which only public and community (i.e., Zionist) schools were eligible to receive. As one official in the Colonial Office characterized the situation, with regard to "schools of Jews who find themselves outside the recognized Jewish Community, it was alleged that there was unfair discrimination, since they would not be eligible for those financial benefits which might be anticipated for the schools of the recognized Jewish Community."[54] Non-Zionist Orthodox groups therefore requested exemption from the requirement to pay taxes levied by LEAs since their schools were not community schools and were therefore ineligible for any portion of these funds.[55] However, British officials did not consent either to exempt members of the Old Yishuv from the education rate or to amend the ordinance so that schools outside the recognized Jewish community could apply for assistance.

Alongside its push for official recognition of the Jewish Agency's "special position" and the corresponding status of its schools, the Zionist Organization lobbied the Palestine government to delegate the vast portion of its educational authority to officials in the former's Board of Education (*va'ad ha-ḥinuch*) and Department of Education (*maḥleket ha-ḥinuch*). The basis of this request represented nothing less than an all-out assault on the expertise of British administrators, who, after centuries of experience with imperial governance, were nonetheless deigned unqualified to oversee Jewish education:

> Seeing that it is admittedly impossible for any non-Jewish authority to execute the technical duties involved in the direction of the National Hebrew Educa-

> tional system, it is proposed that the same article [that recognized the Jewish Agency] should invest the Director of the Jewish public school system of education with the necessary powers, while reserving for the Director of the Department of Education full powers in all such matters as should properly be subject to governmental control.[56]

Officials in the Palestine government rejected the suggestion that managing the Zionist school system was somehow beyond their capacity, though they did agree to consult closely with education leaders within the Zionist Organization.[57] However, the contention that Jews, unlike Palestinian Arabs, were inappropriate subjects for colonial tutelage would continue throughout the period. Thus, when an attempt was made in the early 1940s to expand government supervision over Va'ad Leumi schools, Sir Luke recounted,

> When I saw Mr. Ben Gurion recently he discussed at length the usual Zionist contention that a Jewish community is unsuited to Crown Colony administration, and produced as an illustration of what he regarded as the extraordinary impertinence of the Palestine Government in assuming that they could profitably interfere in the administration of the Jewish community's educational organization. In his view, Jews of Palestine are far too cultivated and experienced to be prepared to subordinate their organization to the directions of a Palestine Colonial government."[58]

Any Zionist claims of superiority did not sit well with Jerome Farrell either, who later noted, "Until little more than a century ago the Jews . . . had like the Arabs a markedly medieval form of oriental culture."[59]

Consequently, controls that the Zionist Organization thought appropriate for the Arab Public System were dismissed as unsuitable when applied to their schools, though both were technically public bodies. For example, the Zionist Organization objected that the Education Ordinance would provide the high commissioner with power over curriculum in public schools, including those of the Hebrew Public System. Leaders expressed their alarm that such curricular powers even extended to religious instruction, which—while certainly not objectionable in the Arab Public System—was out of the question for the Zionist schools. "It is not thought that this is a power which it is intended that the Government should actually exercise," the Zionist Organization wrote, as "it does not follow that it is necessary or desirable that the Government should take the initiative in laying down regulations as to the syllabus . . . in schools which are not Government schools."[60] In sum, the Zionist Organization desired official recognition of its schools as public entities without the corresponding measure of supervision, at least from the Government of Palestine.

Conversely, these letters display a great deal of anxiety about centralizing control of Jewish education in the hands of the quasi-state apparatus administered first by the Zionist Organization and, after 1932, the Va'ad Leumi. For instance, when the first draft of the ordinance effectively put LEAs in charge of all schools in their district, including Zionist ones, the Zionist Organization petitioned the government to allow for separate subcommittees in districts with mixed populations, for Jewish and Arab schools, respectively. The government complied and, furthermore, stipulated that in mixed areas, the LEA would include two nominees of the Zionist Organization. The latter, however, deemed these measures inadequate, as "the proposed new regulation is to apply only in mixed areas, so that there would apparently be no representatives of the Zionist Organization on the Committee dealing with the Hebrew schools in a Jewish area." The result, they feared, was "that the unity of the Hebrew school system is not ensured by the new legislation."[61] Thus, it was not just government or Arab control of their schools that the Zionist Organization feared, but any decentralized control, even by Jews themselves.

On issue after issue, the refrain remained the same. The recognition of Zionist schools as public entities was of vital importance, but any corresponding supervision should reside in the hands of Zionist leaders. Centralized control was essential, but the Government of Palestine was not the legitimate entity to exercise it. In short, the Zionist Organization requested official recognition from an entity whose authority it constantly called into question. This mix of audacity and insecurity was not unique to Zionist education but emblematic of a larger dynamic whereby the Jewish state-in-the-making wavered between bold political assertions and recognition of its own weakness. In education, as elsewhere, the Zionist Organization did not want government control but still needed its support.

As it turned out, the Zionist Organization got much less than it asked for, at least as far as the letter of the law was concerned. "The Zionists have had their say in the matter," wrote Sir John Shuckburg of the Colonial Office, "but . . . it is not possible to accept most of their suggestions." Writing after the Passerfield White Paper of 1930—which recommended new restrictions on Jewish immigration and land purchases—Shuckburg was aware that "in the present agitated state of Jewish feeling, that the promulgation of the Ordinance will be greeted as another deathblow to Zionist aspirations in Palestine. I submit that we must face that."[62] The final draft of the ordinance made no mention of the Jewish Agency or any other Zionist body, though it did attach a schedule of schools that were to be recognized as the nucleus of the Hebrew Public System. Similarly, no mention was made of the Zionist Education Department or its director, and the ordinance granted them no powers. It did, however, stipulate that in his dealings with schools maintained by a communal association, "the Director shall consult with such authority or association."[63] Moreover, officials in the Department of Education promised the Zionist Organization that the Hebrew Public System would not be subjected to the full regulatory scope of the ordinance, and in practice the legislation never posed a threat to the autonomy of these schools.[64]

In comparison, the protests that emerged from Palestinian Arab quarters were generally milder than those raised by either Jewish or Catholic bodies, even as their schools were most subject to supervision and surveillance. Though they expressed concern at certain provisions, the principle of government supervision was not actively disputed. This, I believe, stemmed partially from the immediate historical past, in which the Ottoman Empire exercised similar educational oversight. The overriding cause, however, was that Palestinian Arabs had no other government to which to turn and, indeed, no reason to contemplate building a state within a state akin to that created by the Jewish Agency/Va'ad Leumi. While Zionists generally viewed the Mandatory government as a transitory structure that would soon be replaced by the "real" (i.e., Jewish) government, Palestinians assumed that they would gradually assume control over the existing administration as was occurring in neighboring Arab countries. Despite their consistent opposition to the terms of the Mandate and the refusal to accept its legitimacy, on the whole, Palestinian Arabs lobbied for greater participation within the Mandatory government, not the depletion of its powers.

Perhaps because of this fundamentally different relationship to the public realm represented by the government and its schools, the Education Committee of the SMC's protest against the ordinance deviated from that put forward by the Zionist Organization. For example, the committee complained that the ordinance enabled education or medical officials the right to inspect schools at any time, so "with no definite procedure . . . inspection will be unnecessarily repeated." They suggested that the provision be amended to "regularize the inspection of schools whether for education or medical purposes."[65] The council neither questioned the need for such inspection nor nominated an outside party to complete it. Similarly, the committee took umbrage with the provision requiring all teachers to register with the Department of Education, which was thought would "impose an undue restriction on private and communal schools, which may be obliged from time to time to engage teachers from outside Palestine." Once again, however, the committee offered a measured compromise that the emergency license usually granted to unregistered teachers for a duration of three months be extended to a full academic year.

The SMC did protest more forcefully against the provision that granted the high commissioner the authority to close any school he deemed was being conducted "in a manner contrary to good order and morals." The council noted that "there is no doubt that differing meanings and interpretations may be given to the term 'good order and morals,' which differ according to the locality, religion and sex. . . . It is believed that the interpretation of the term and the issue for closing of schools should be vested in the Courts."[66] This remark was consistent with the general tenor of Palestinian protests over education: it was not that the government did not have the prerogative to exercise certain powers but that it should do so in concert with local bodies. In the same vein, the memo from the committee reiterated its suggestion that an education council be recognized by the ordinance, "in which the inhabitants would be represented and whose members should participate in the proper enforcement of the Ordinance and the regulations issued thereunder." Such a council was of special importance in Palestine "in view of the non-existence in this country of any legislative body representing the inhabitants which would take into consideration the wishes and needs of the population."[67]

Absent such a representative body, Palestinian leaders hoped to at least expand the role of LEAs. As mentioned previously, LEAs were created primarily to levy rates to supplement central funding for education but given no real administrative powers. While the Jewish Agency lobbied the government to transfer much of the Department of Education's authority to the Zionist Organization's internal education department, Palestinian protests sought the delegation of certain powers to LEAs. For instance, in the memorandum submitted by the SMC, the latter wrote, "The Local Education Committee should be vested with powers wider than those provided for in the Regulations so long as such Committee is the responsible body for the maintenance of the school. The Local Education Committee should be given exclusive jurisdiction in licensing teachers and in matters referred to in Articles 18, 19, 22 and 24 of the Regulations; and therefore should have power to withdraw, transfer or cancel licenses."[68] Similarly, a letter from the Jerusalem Municipal Council recommended the following course of action:

> More powers should be allowed to the local education authority in that all the powers given to the Director of Education be now vested in them as from the administrative point of view. These authorities will cooperate with the Director of Education in all the administration on condition that the latter will have no right to take action on any administrative matter before the Local Authority gives its decision.[69]

In what must have been a shock for colonial administrators, the Municipal Council demanded the creation of a "General Education Authority" composed of "representatives elected from the local authorities [LEAs] to supervise the work of the Department of Education in Palestine."[70]

As we can see from these petitions, the general tenor of Palestinian objections and recommendations was quite distinct from that expressed by Zionist leaders. Both political factions found fault with the Department of Education's attempts to supervise schools and regulate the conditions under which they operated, yet the way in which each party responded to these attempts revealed a great deal about differing views of the Mandatory government as the legitimate bearer of sovereignty. The Zionist Organization lobbied for the recognition of a distinct Hebrew public space that was represented by its own quasi-state apparatus and supervised by its own education administrators. Fiercely protective of its autonomy and anxious to extend its control over *all* Jewish education in Palestine, officials pressured the government's director of education to delegate many of his powers to Zionist administrative bodies. These demands advanced a single agenda: to gain recognition from the Government of Palestine that its authority over Jewish education was at best partial and, correspondingly, that power should be centralized in the parallel state apparatus being constructed under Zionist auspices. The greater participation of Jews in the management of their education therefore went hand in hand with the erosion of their presence in a general Palestinian public space inhabited by multiple groups and overseen, however contentiously, by the Mandatory government.

In contrast, at least during the first decade of the Mandate when debates over the Education Ordinance occurred, Palestinian leaders responded to the legislation with a greater willingness to compromise with the government and the Department of Education. They largely acquiesced to the principle of government supervision and attempted to reach a modus vivendi with education administrators regarding concrete points such as sanitary inspection and the licensing of teachers. Above all, they demanded a seat at the government's table, not a separate administrative structure. Likewise, both the SMC and the Jerusalem Municipal Council lobbied for the expanded role of local administrative bodies, like the LEAs, which were regarded, importantly, as *extensions* of the central government rather than rival institutions. These proposed forays into the realm of school administration were unacceptable to the Department of Education, which argued that Arabs who petitioned for such powers were welcome to found and oversee independent communal institutions for Muslim and Christian students, respectively. In the end, Palestinian Arabs were faced with a catch-22: the government public schools afforded them no say in educational matters, and the prospect of gaining greater educational autonomy by organizing on a religious basis entailed the dissolution of national unity.

Writing in the early 1940s, one American observer noted this difficulty and the important role of sectarian legislation like the ordinances discussed here in producing it:

> Though in name the Jewish governmental organization was that of a religious community, in fact it was that of a non-territorial, semi-autonomous state, and for such a position the Arabs showed no desire to apply. In the face of Zionism, every effort was being made to reduce the gulf between Moslem and Christian, and the leaders wanted no self-government which would be based upon religious lines and which would tacitly recognize Arab community life as something apart from that of the territorial state of Palestine.[71]

Given this context, the SMC occupied a somewhat awkward position within Palestine's educational landscape. As Rashid Khalidi has argued, the council and the office of grand mufti of Palestine were primarily designed to divide the Arab populace on religious lines and, by bestowing some element of prestige to the officeholders, co-opt the notable class into cooperation with the government. The council's creation also represented an attempt to divert Arab political energies toward communal matters of religious significance, such as the management of *awqaf* (charitable endowments) and the appointment of judges to the sharia courts.[72] However, much to the government's chagrin, the SMC did not provide the desired outlet for Palestinian Arab political frustrations, nor did the SMC embrace the divide between religious and political affairs that the British envisioned. Instead, as Laura Robson has argued, the Mandate government "unwittingly assisted the emergence of religious nationalism" that drew heavily on Islamic symbolism and rhetoric. Rather than redirect energies toward a clearly delineated religious sphere, the SMC infused the political one with a religious sensibility.[73]

Education, however, occupied a somewhat anomalous space within this framework. Because Muslims were the numerical majority in Palestine and therefore the primary beneficiary of government public schools, they had no reason to contemplate building a parallel school system akin to the Zionist one. The SMC did maintain its own system of private schools;[74] however, the vast majority of Muslim children attended either government public schools or private *katātīb*.[75] Furthermore, while many in late Ottoman Palestine still viewed education as a communal affair, the expansion of government public schools with secularized curricula functioned to remove them from the religious realm in which the SMC could claim jurisdiction. The result of these crosscurrents was that the Palestinian Muslim community was, on the one hand, part of the majority population that depended on government social services, as in Ottoman times, and on the other, a religious community, whose autonomy hinged on private initiative. The Government of Palestine thus presided over a shrinking public sphere that forbade political participation within its boundaries while suggesting that Arab management of education could occur only within the context of Muslim and Christian communal organization. Had this suggestion been fully followed, "the Department of Education in Palestine would have suddenly found itself in a position with no schools to control and no education to direct."[76] Conversely, the Zionist Organization sought to secure official recognition of its schools as both public and communal entities, a demand that the sectarian nature of Palestine's legal structure was able to confer. The erasure of a common sense of the public was thus not an unfortunate by-product of the Mandate educational system but one of its essential characteristics.

In conclusion, the Palestine Education Ordinance was far from a perfect mechanism for policing the country's schools. Nevertheless, the enactment of this legislation is significant not only for its role in accelerating the division between Arab and Jewish communities but for the creation of a legal structure that privileged religious education over nonsectarian national models. Whereas the structure of education financing helped constitute dual publics based on linguistic difference, the Education Ordinance envisioned the country's schools as divided among and managed by religious communities, the only groups eligible to petition for educational autonomy under its terms. Underlying these policy choices was a particular conceptual orientation toward religion and the role of religious education in shaping individuals at both the civic and economic levels. The following chapter analyzes this process in detail as we examine the Government of Palestine's attempts to reform Muslim and, to a lesser extent, Jewish religious education in accordance with these goals.

4 NEW SCHOOLING FOR AN "OLD" ORDER

THUS FAR, this study has surveyed the points of tension surrounding the provision of education during the Mandate period and, in particular, conflicts regarding the autonomy of schools in the emerging Arab and Jewish nationalist communities. The intense nature of these disputes renders it all the more noteworthy that there was one point about which British administrators found themselves largely in agreement with Zionist and Palestinian intellectuals and leaders: the ineptitude of "old-fashioned" religious schools such as the *ḥeder* and *kuttāb*. All parties in question believed that the transformation of these schools, and of religious education more broadly, represented a political necessity. Yet there was no more agreement on the precise nature of that transformation than on the political future of Palestine as a whole. Was religious education a stabilizing force or a revolutionary one? Should religious instruction be more concerned with the moral formation of the individual or the social and political welfare of the community? And in what ways should religious knowledge, increasingly defined as lacking in utility, intersect with the "practical" training geared toward navigating Palestine's integration into the modern economy?

Having looked thus far at the ideological and legal underpinnings of religious education as an analytic category, we begin to explore the concrete means by which the Mandatory government tried to alter the nature of Jewish and Islamic schooling in Palestine. One of the more interesting things about this process was the degree to which customary forms of schooling like the *ḥeder* and *kuttāb* became targets of overlapping colonial and communal reform efforts.

Indeed, as detailed in Chapter 1, the backwardness of these schools and their association with political and social stagnation had appeared as a key trope in the writings of Jewish and Arab modernists, reformers, and "enlighteners" throughout the nineteenth century. In what follows, I examine the Mandatory government's policies toward rural schooling among Palestinian Arabs and the ways in which the reformist urge was tempered by late imperial thinking regarding the preservation of tradition. Finally, this chapter highlights the unexpected points of overlap that linked the government's reform of rural schooling among Palestinian Muslims to its attempts to modernize Jewish education in the Old Yishuv, a fact that should make us reconsider the historiographical tendency to treat Arab and Jewish education as unrelated entities. In institutional terms, they clearly represented separate realms; however, we should not take this to mean that these school systems existed without intersections at either the discursive or material level. Rather, many leaders within both communities shared the Department of Education's assumption that cultural and religious authenticity was something that could be imparted only away from the family and the customary paths of transmission. Only then could modern schools become vehicles for transmitting a traditional education free from the adverse influence of the actual communities they served.

MUSTY ROOMS AND MEDIEVAL MASTERS

If education was to become the germ of social transformation, as modernists argued it should, the first line of attack involved discrediting existing modes of religious learning as backward and socially debilitating. Literature served as one of the primary vehicles for advancing such critiques, and depictions of the *ḥeder*, *talmud torah*, and *kuttāb* assumed a remarkably similar form in writings of Jewish and Arab intellectuals despite their otherwise distinct milieu: the schoolroom is dark, musty, and dirty, lacking in the necessary furnishings; the teacher is foolish and abusive; rote memorization is promoted over real understanding; the texts studied are inappropriate for young children; the language is corrupted, either by the Yiddish of the *melamed* (teacher) or the vulgarities of colloquial Arabic.

The portrayal of the *ḥeder* as a "schoolroom of hell" was a recurring trope in *Haskalah* literature aimed at discrediting the old social order, so much so that any positive aspect of this education was forcibly repressed in furtherance of the *maskilim*'s ideological agenda.[1] The paradigmatic condemnation of the *ḥeder* came in Shelomo Maimon's autobiography, in which he stated that "the defective approach to teaching, deriving from the ignorance of the teacher, prevented the student from attaining systematic knowledge of either the Hebrew language or the Bible."[2] In other words, the deficiencies of the *ḥeder* were responsible for depriving the child of an intimate connection to his authentic Jewish heritage. In addition to its pedagogic shortcomings, *maskilim* often depicted the *ḥeder* as a place of physical violence directed against young children by the teacher and his assistant. In Avraham Bar Gottlober's memoirs, for instance, the *ozer* (assistant) is so abusive that children perish from his beatings.[3] Similarly, In Yehuda Lieb Levine's autobiography, a stick-wielding *melamed* kills the writer's brother at the tender age of six. Even more astoundingly, the author recounts that he himself is nonetheless sent to the same *ḥeder* with the same savage teacher, until his father relents and agrees to hire private tutors instead.[4] Within this literature, the abuses of the teacher are mirrored by the filthy conditions of the school, which is almost without exception portrayed as dark, dirty, and lacking space—both physical and psychological—for children to develop freely and flourish. If the Enlightenment marked a high point in the concern for the individual as an autonomous, self-fashioning agent, the *ḥeder* represented the narrowness of the corporate Jewish community in which collective welfare was continually privileged over individual growth.

Yet, as Avraham Holtzman has shown, the *ḥeder* was not without possible redemption. Rather, for Zionist writers, it could serve as a vehicle for the preservation and further development of the Hebrew language and culture but only on the condition that it be drastically transformed. The clearest articulation of this latent potential appears in Hayyim Nahman Bialik's short story "Safiaḥ" (Aftergrowth), in which the protagonist attends two different *ḥederim*. The first is characterized by the usual darkness, *yiddishkeit*, and physical filth, while the second offers a manifestation of what the *ḥeder* could be: still steeped in classical Jewish texts, but now conducted in Hebrew, often outdoors, and absorbed in tales of biblical heroism rather than with the ritual laws stemming from Leviticus. This impulse to reconstitute an institution—or an entire tradition—by returning to core texts, languages, and ideas was not unique to Zionists but emblematic of a larger modernist phenomenon that stressed the primacy of one's roots. While interest in this project, which placed renewed emphasis on the Hebrew language and the Hebrew Bible (i.e., Old Testament), began with European *maskilim*, these interests grew more critical among Zionist thinkers and activists. The more-committed ideologues among the latter tended to view the diasporic existence of the Jews and its trademark cultural artifacts—chief among them the Talmud, Yiddish, and other "foreign" languages—as a blip in historical time and ultimately insignificant to a national past and future rooted in the Land of Israel.[5]

Likewise, critiques of the *kuttāb* among Arab-Muslim intellectuals in the late nineteenth and early twentieth centuries were part of a larger movement of *nahḍa*, which focused considerable attention on social reform through a return to Islam's essential core.[6] The *kuttāb*, associated with the backward masses and the sheikhs who taught them, who were themselves often ignorant of "true" Islam, served as a favorite target of scorn. This was not necessarily a modernist trope, as the Arabic language has no shortage of proverbs dedicated to the supposed foolishness of the *kuttāb* teacher—"stupider than a *kuttāb* teacher" being a frequent insult. Such claims were already being countered in the ninth century CE when the famed writer al-Jāḥiẓ defended the lowly *kuttāb* teachers, who "like any other class of men" included "the superior and the inferior" alike.[7] Yet these critiques assumed a sharper quality in the writings of *nahḍa* intellectuals, many of whom began their education within *katātīb*, pursued advanced studies in European cities, and returned to their native lands with a

FIGURE 4. The *kuttāb*'s antithesis: a Palestinian school in Hebron of the ideal type, 1935. Courtesy of the Central Zionist Archives, PH\1013992.

passion for political and social reform.[8] These writers were not just criticizing the *kuttāb* in the abstract but measuring its deficiencies in comparison to contemporary European models and linking its shortcomings to the political and cultural status of the nation as a whole. In this regard, the modernist critique of the *kuttāb* was not a mere continuation of medieval jesting.

One of the more famous—and entertaining—treatments of the subject can be found in *al-Ayyam* (The days), the autobiography of Taha Hussein. His account references the physical violence often found within *katātīb*, but the teacher (mockingly referred to as "Our Master") and his assistant ("the *'Arif*" or "knowing one") are primarily faulted for their dishonesty, corruption, and blatant opportunism. The teachers are seen as benefiting from a well-established bribery ring, wherein children offer dates, sugar, and money to secure their teachers' favor or, at the very least, to mitigate their blows. The teacher treats young Taha with benign neglect—purchased through such bribes—and allows him the freedom to play and converse with other children while almost completely ignoring his studies. His abiding interest remains his own financial gain in the form of school fees, food, drinks, clothing, and other gifts given after a child's memorization of the Qur'an. This "capacity for falsehood" is what remains with the author even after the Qur'anic verses dim from his memory.[9]

During the Mandate period, Taha Hussein's autobiography became required reading in one of Palestine's most prominent nationalist schools, al-Najāḥ in Nablus. The modernist critique of the "vile *kuttāb*" reached a fevered pitch within institutions like al-Najāḥ, which positioned itself as its enlightened antithesis. Textbooks authored by the school's headmaster, Muhammad 'Izzat Darwaza, reflected a heightened awareness of the link between traditional schooling, public ignorance, and political weakness. For instance, writing of the waning days of the Ottoman Empire, Darwaza singled out its educational failures as one of the government's key offenses:

> The (Ottoman) government was not interested in opening schools and educating the country's children, because education opens people's minds, makes them aware of their rights, and spurs them to demand them. Pupils would learn reading and writing in the vile *katātīb* . . . sitting on the earth, and the teachers who taught them did not know much of anything. And their salaries did not come from the government, but [they] would rather take bread from every child.
>
> The situation of governments in Europe was much better than this state because they convened representatives of the people, created assemblies out of

> them, and consulted [*tashāwara*] them in everything they wanted to do. They took an interest in the country's condition and improved schools and roads, while no citizen dared to accept a bribe. As a result of this the countries of Europe progressed, while the Ottoman countries became degenerate and weak.[10]

As we have seen, the Ottomans *did* open many public schools in Palestine in the decades prior to the First World War, making this characterization more significant in terms of what it tells us about contemporary Arab nationalist thinking than the Ottoman education record itself. In particular, it is worth noting the attention Darwaza draws to the lack of furnishings and other school equipment and the fact that the teacher was paid not by the state—as would befit a truly modern country—but in the form of bread from each student.

A further element of the modernist critique sprang from the association of communal schools with popular forms of religiosity, particularly with mysticism. Anxiety over the influence of Hasidism in European Jewish communities was widespread among the rationalist proponents of the *Haskalah*, who charged the movement with fostering a culture of illogic and superstition.[11] Eager to find a place for Jews within the emerging social and political order promised by legal emancipation, Hasidism represented a major obstacle that threatened the attainment of a pluralistic accord founded on reason. Conversely, it was the medieval figure Maimonides and his famed adoption of Aristotelian logic that *maskilim* looked to as a source of inspiration for the modern Jewish renaissance.[12] Within the spectrum of communal figures that undermined the Enlightenment sensibility, the *ḥeder* teacher was among the worst offenders. A recurring trope in this literature charged him with provoking superstition and anxiety within children who, so afraid of ghosts, would recoil from their own shadows. Furthermore, this educational culture of irrationalism was thought to represent the source of the (male) Jew's supposed physical and spiritual degeneration. It is within its walls and at the hands of its cruel teachers that the Jew emerges as weak, uncultured, and disconnected from nature.[13]

In a similar fashion, Sufism functioned within the metanarrative of Islamic modernism as a barrier that separated Arab Muslims from "authentic" Islam. Sufism and popular customs like visits to the tombs of local saints were derided as sources of unlawful innovation (*bid'a*) that had corrupted Islam's rationalistic foundations. The fact that Sufi practices were closely tied to local and popular forms of piety similarly undermined the idea that true Islam existed in a singular form that was textually determined. Reformers held that mysticism must be forcibly rooted out from Muslim communities—beginning, of course, with schoolteachers—to combat the interconnected slides toward popular ignorance and political subjugation. In his autobiography, for instance, Taha Hussein explicitly identified Sufism as the premier source of social backwardness, noting that "the country people, including their old men, youths, lads and women, have a particular mentality in which is simplicity, mysticism and ignorance. And those who have had the greatest share in producing this mentality are the Sufis."[14]

Despite these failings, the old and corrupt could become the basis of the new and noble if tradition could be stripped down to its elemental core. Though initiated earlier by Jewish and Muslim reformers themselves, this was a process in which the Government of Palestine also became an active participant. But how could such a transformation be enacted? As I argue, the government's reform efforts operated on two planes that may at first seem contradictory. On the one hand, education administrators supported the introduction of "practical" education within communal schools as a means of inculcating the economic values of industriousness and self-sufficiency. On the other, they insisted that any curricular or pedagogic reforms be in the best interest of preserving tradition itself. Thus, rather than upend customary forms of Jewish and Islamic schooling, officials in the Department of Education viewed themselves as chipping away at the ossified crust of custom to allow the light of religious authenticity to shine through.

TOWARD A NEW KIND OF TRADITIONAL LIFE

Situated at the tail end of a long imperial history, Palestine offered educational administrators the unique opportunity to apply the lessons learned from India, Egypt, and elsewhere. When articulating the types of reforms the government felt worthwhile, particularly with regard to the transformation of old-fashioned schools such as *katātīb*, officials were influenced by late imperial ideologies that stressed the unbridgeable cultural differences that rendered Western forms of life deeply destabilizing for native peoples. This ideology, most often associated with the development of indirect rule as a theory of colonial governance, represented a departure from the liberal models of imperialism, which tended to be universalist, reform minded, and assimilatory in aspiration. Karuna Mantena describes this ideological shift:

> The strategic abandonment of the liberal agenda in this case implied the turn to a very different philosophy of imperial governance, one in which the native

> was thought to be best ruled through his/her own institutions and structures of authority. Ruling was thought to require a more precise knowledge of the dynamics of native society, and an adjustment to the supposedly natural and traditional foundations of native society. As an ostensibly less intrusive and less disruptive mode of power, *indirect rule*, the rule through native institutions, was often championed as both more efficient and more fruitful for stabilizing the imperial order.[15]

Yet it would be a mistake to argue that colonial administrators in Palestine embraced indirect rule and its ideological scaffolding without any reservations. At the most basic administrative level, implementing the Zionist national home project against the wishes of Palestine's majority population meant that key functions had to remain in British hands, and thus Palestine was something of an exception in the late imperial constellation. However, the creation of and rule through traditional institutions like the SMC pointed to a view of native society that was wholly consistent with late imperial ideologies of empire. In Mantena's words,

> For the concept of traditional society to have the impact it was to have, it needed to be tied to a new account of the sources of instability, specifically a theoretical outlook that saw the protection of native society as a prerequisite to imperial order. It was the portrayal of native society as simultaneously *intact* and *vulnerable* that underpinned the paternalistic impulse of indirect rule.[16]

The Government of Palestine's approach to education reform reflected this ambiguity, as administrators argued that it was only through the introduction of new types of education that tradition could be saved. Moreover, officials viewed their cultivation of tradition—represented by the triumvirate of Arabic, Islam, and agriculture—as representing a modern, progressive departure from older forms of rule, including both the assimilatory model of liberal imperialism and the cynicism toward native improvement that accompanied the doctrine of indirect rule. Understanding these nuances is crucial to grasping the ways in which a modernized education came to serve as the paradoxical guarantor of the traditional order. In what follows, I briefly consider the government's policy toward Arab rural schooling and begin to examine the function of religious education within this old/new framework.

In March 1939, in a speech given to the Royal Central Asian Society soon after his retirement, Humphrey Bowman reflected with satisfaction on his seventeen years as education director in Palestine. Within colonial and Orientalist circles, Bowman had come to be regarded as something of an educational expert who had successfully avoided the pitfalls that undermined his predecessors elsewhere in the empire. Commenting on Bowman's career in Palestine, the chairman of the Royal Central Asian Society offered the following words of praise:

> Mr. Bowman arrived in Palestine before Lord Macaulay. That is the point. In India it was not really Lord Macaulay but his followers who were at fault; but Mr. Bowman was in Palestine first. Rural minds might have been there first in India, but they were not, and consequently we have a hundred years of leeway to make up. The minds of people are imbued with the idea that what you have to do is to be a white-collared clerk.[17]

Lord Macaulay was a Whig politician and colonial administrator who became well known for his role in education reform in India. Undoubtedly, his most influential act was to advocate that English should serve as the language of instruction in secondary schools. In his *Minute on Indian Education* of 1835, Macaulay stated that the goal of education in India was to create "a class who may be interpreters between us and the millions whom we govern; a class of persons, Indian in blood and colour, but English in taste, in opinions, in morals, and in intellect."[18] Little attention, therefore, should be devoted to expanding the system of primary schools, as the government operated on the assumption that a newly formed hybrid class of Indian civil servants would serve as intermediaries between it and the uneducated masses.

However, in light of the Indian Mutiny in 1857 and later experience in Egypt, a new educational orthodoxy began to emerge. Henry Maine's late nineteenth-century writings on customary law bore practical fruit in the early twentieth-century doctrine of development along native lines, which argued that an overemphasis on literary education would only lead the natives into revolt.[19] Rather than try to reform colonial subjects in the likeness of their British overlords, the emphasis shifted to the preservation of "traditional" structures of authority that could be ruled indirectly.[20] The gospel of indirect rule was articulated most forcefully by Lord Lugard, the former governor of Nigeria who held that "the education afforded to that section of the population who intend to lead the lives which their forefathers led should enlarge their outlook, increase their efficiency and standard of comfort, and bring them into closer sympathy with the Government, instead of making them unsuited to and ill-contented with their mode of life."[21]

Lord Lugard later served as Britain's representative to the League of Nation's Permanent Mandates Commission and as a member of the Advisory Committee on Education in the Colonies, which convened numerous meetings to discuss educational affairs in Palestine. Administrators in Palestine were therefore well acquainted with Lugard's approach but modified it in key ways. As precisely the type of "rural mind" that should have been in India, Bowman was positioned to offer an alternative vision that neither promoted the potentially destabilizing literary education nor fell into the cynicism that advocated restricting access to education to all but the most gifted. Instead, he argued that something new was required to maintain the old, that only through the proper type of modern education could traditional life remain viable. In his speech before the Royal Central Asian Society, Bowman gave voice to this position:

> There are those who say: "Why teach the agriculturalist at all? You will only spoil him, make him discontented with his lot, and turn him into an agitator." These critics may speak the truth if the schooling provided is of the wrong kind. But if it is of the right kind you will make the peasant more, not less, contented; you will save him from his eternal enemy, the moneylender; and you will give him a new pride—a pride in himself and in his village. And you will keep him on the land.[22]

While the first lines of this passage reflect the wariness toward native education that had taken root among many colonial administrators, Bowman's response is to offer a different solution that nonetheless fulfills the same political function of keeping the peasantry on the land. He argued that education with a rural, agricultural bias—the right type of schooling—was crucially important to maintain the structure of traditional society and prevent the dreaded rural drift to urban areas. This was explicitly opposed to the old way of doing things "in both Egypt and India," where "we had colleges and universities before rural schools; in both education began at the wrong end."[23] Thus, it is no surprise that the Department of Education privileged primary education at the expense of secondary schooling in Palestine and that the institution charged with training primary school teachers offered the only complete course of public secondary education throughout the Mandate period.

There were two immediate consequences of this policy: first, secondary education was much more widespread among Jews, particularly Zionist immigrants, which could only exacerbate the gulf between them and the Palestinian Arabs;[24] second, limited access to secondary education meant a permanent shortage of teachers and, consequently, yet another limitation on the pace at which new elementary schools could be opened. Though the men and women's training colleges remained the primary source of new teachers for the Arab public schools, little was done to expand their class sizes. Thus, the number of pupils in the Government Arab College in 1945–46 was barely larger than the number in 1925–26, though the population had nearly doubled.[25] Approximately twenty men entered the teaching field annually, which was hardly adequate to replace retiring teachers, to say nothing of providing personnel for new schools.

Despite these notable shortcomings, the emphasis on primary education was routinely cast as an improvement on both the Indian and Egyptian models: moral education that was practically directed toward the village economy. To better illustrate what this entailed in material terms, we examine Humphrey Bowman's description of an idyllic rural school in southern Palestine:

> I would invite you to visit with me in imagination a model rural school in the wild hill-country of Southern Palestine. . . . The villagers, who are all cultivators, paid themselves for the greater part of it, with some help from the Government. The buildings are divided into three sections: one for classroom work, one for carpentry, ironwork, and boot-making, and one for weaving. . . .
>
> Below the buildings, which command a magnificent view over the surrounding country, and from which the Mediterranean can be seen fifty kilometers away, is the garden, where vegetables, flowers and fruit-trees grow, well watered by irrigation from a cistern. Goats are kept out by a stone wall. Poultry and rabbits of various kinds are kept, while bees provide the best honey I have ever tasted.
>
> The time of the boys is divided between lessons in the classroom and practical work in the garden or the workshops. One of the older boys is responsible for the cleanliness and the feeding of the poultry, another for that of the rabbits, a third looks after the beehives. Others are engaged in the cultivation of the garden, the pruning of fruit-trees, or the irrigation of plants. There is a radio in the teachers' room, and the clock, which is regulated daily by wireless, gives the correct time to the village.[26]

Bowman's rural school has all the features of an ideal type: It was built by empowered villagers with little government help; it introduces children to modern agricultural practices and teaches them how to tend to a range of domestic animals, who presumably produced the best meat and eggs alongside the sweetest of honey. And finally, a well-regulated clock ensures that villagers conduct their lives according to "correct time." The school was to serve as a modernizing agent that would transform every element of village life through the production of hygienic, literate, and, above all, industrious children.

The village teacher played a central role in the Department of Education's rural improvement scheme.[27] Bowman often stressed that the village teacher's duties extended far beyond the school itself to tasks like adult education, agricultural demonstrations, and disease prevention. In his lecture before the Royal Central Asian Society, he described the headmaster of the model school as "a Moslem Arab wearing native dress, trained in agriculture and in several crafts, an excellent teacher, though without a word of English, an enlightened, loyal and devoted servant of his village and of his country." He was a man of the village, still cloaked in the familiar garb of tradition—signified here by the markers of Islam, the Arabic language, and agriculture—but nonetheless bearing all the tools necessary to rationalize the economic basis of rural life. It was the latter skill set that most distinguished this teacher from his predecessor in the "inefficient" *kuttāb*, who did not dispense any "practical" instruction and whose pedagogical standards remained "rather low."[28] Bowman continued:

> With village welfare as a primary duty of the teacher, the enthusiasm will spread to all who dwell there, and conditions will be so changed as to make life not only bearable, but enviable. Improved cultivation will increase prosperity; malaria and eye disease will diminish and gradually disappear; infant mortality will decrease; literacy will spread; the burden of debt will vanish. Livelihood and contentment will take the place of poverty and misery; the peasant, instead of being lethargic and despairing, will become active and hopeful.[29]

However poetic Bowman's vision, it hardly corresponded to the material experience of Palestine's fellahin. As Amos Nadan has shown in his study of the Palestinian peasant economy under Mandate rule, the period from 1922 to 1939 was in fact associated with a *decrease* in per capita income among the peasantry.[30] Actual government expenditure on agricultural education remained paltry and was hardly adequate to make a significant impact in terms of rationalizing agricultural production. Moreover, large-scale projects that could have dramatically increased productivity, such as irrigation, were never undertaken.[31] Here, as in other realms of colonial management, such self-serving claims corresponded poorly with a material reality shaped by land insecurity, generational debt, and market policies that favored the Jewish agricultural economy.[32]

A TEMPLATE FOR TRANSFORMATION

If Palestine's rural schools were to be transformed into the model type just discussed, they would first and foremost require a new, uniform curriculum. The Government of Palestine's official syllabus for town and village schools, based largely on an Egyptian model, was first published in 1921. It included detailed instructions regarding the number of hours devoted to each subject in each grade, the topics to be covered therein, and additional directions to teachers regarding the proper conduct of students. For instance, "During the intervals between classes, boys should be encouraged to run about as much as possible, or take part in easily-organised games. Books should not be taken into the playground."[33] While a syllabus cannot reflect the reality of lived experience within schools, it is nonetheless worth examining in some detail because such curricular planning does offer a window into the way that the Mandatory government conceived of Palestine's "new" educational order and the role of religious education therein.

Within the context of mobilizing the new to preserve the old, Islamic education—albeit of a reformed variety—formed an essential part of village schooling. In rural schools, religious instruction commanded between 17 and 23 percent of the total school hours, exceeded only by Arabic.[34] In contrast to schools in urban areas, which devoted scarcely any attention to religious instruction,[35] rural schools were anchored by subjects that were commonly found in the *katātīb* they were meant to replace: the Qur'an, Arabic, and basic arithmetic. This is not surprising given that many rural public schools were in fact former *katātīb* that were absorbed into the Arab Public System through the extension of grants-in-aid during the early years of the Mandate.[36] Even with the growth in public schooling, the number of *katātīb* actually increased throughout the period to peak at 191 during the 1940–41 school year. By the end of the Mandate, more than fourteen thousand pupils were still educated in 131 private *katātīb*; the relative decline in their number can be explained in part by the expansion of public schooling over the same period (from 402 to 478 schools), "as some of the private schools were taken over by the government."[37] The government's policy of absorbing these schools into the Arab Public System as part of expansion programs suggests that the total availability of educational opportunities was even smaller than usually appreciated since many new schools were actually preexisting *katātīb*.

According to the claims of the Mandatory government, village public schools differed substantively from their former selves in terms of both pedagogy and curriculum. There was much about customary forms of Islamic schooling that were deemed archaic, misdirected, or pedagogically unsound, and *katātīb* were a favorite target of colonial administrators and Palestinian reformers alike. Even before the First World War, letters in Palestine's burgeoning Arabic press lamented that the village teacher was "more ignorant than Hubnaqa" and "the germ of every evil and the source of all corruption."[38] For educators like Khalil Totah and 'Izzat Darwaza, such teachers represented not merely the backwardness of the old social order but a political threat that hindered Palestinians' ability to achieve independence. The new syllabus directed teachers to avoid memorization as a pedagogic method, echoing the widespread sentiment that the traditional reliance on the practice came at the expense of true comprehension. Education officials aimed to develop in its place the child's "facility for and a habit of rapid silent reading."[39] Oral recitation and memorization were to be used only sparingly in teaching religious subjects and expunged from all other parts of the new curriculum. An assortment of classroom materials accompanied these new pedagogic guidelines, not only blackboards and other furniture but attendance registries and standardized texts.

Another way of distinguishing the new rural school from the *kuttāb* was through the introduction of new subjects of study. For many, the subjects traditionally learned in the *kuttāb* were seemingly devoid of practical application, and an overexposure to religious texts was thought to produce children who were alienated from the necessities of village life. The Palestinian educator Khalil Totah offered the anecdote of overhearing a peasant exclaim, "What! Do you expect my son to work—he can read!" Echoing the viewpoint of the British administrators, Totah identified this alleged distaste for practical education to be at "the crux of the educational problem in the Holy Land, where education, elementary as it is, seems incompatible with manual work."[40] Without addressing the agricultural basis of village life, the customary curriculum would do nothing to remedy the economic hardship that propelled urban drift. Thus, to the usual subjects were added geography, nature study, history, hygiene, drawing, and agricultural and manual work.[41] Many of these new subjects in fact represented the professionalization of everyday rural activities so that farming and raising poultry—or in the case of girls, children—were transformed into forms of knowledge that were acquired only by removing the child from the home in which they were usually learned.[42] This is no doubt why Humphrey Bowman insisted that the village school be physically separated from the village it was meant to serve, "away from the dust, noise and (may I add?) smells, which are invariable concomitants to the Eastern village."[43] According to this schema, we might say that only by shielding the next generation from traditional modes of rural life could tradition be saved in Palestine.

Attempts to realize this idealized traditional life faced no lack of hurdles, chief among them the shortage of trained teachers. In reality, village imams were known to maintain their posts even after their *katātīb* became absorbed into the Arab Public System. The example of Hassan al-Siba'i sheds light on the pragmatic compromises that the Department of Education made as a result of the teacher shortage. He had no formal training as a teacher but was a village imam and *kuttāb* teacher in Majd al-Kurum prior to the Mandate period. His application for employment indicated he was able to teach Islamic religious instruction, Arabic, history, geography, hygiene, writing, nature, and physical education,[44] though inspection reports were lukewarm at best. Inspectors noted that he was hardworking, energetic, and respected in the village but described his teaching methods as at best "fair" and at worst "primitive." One report, from January 1926, made note of his limited knowledge but suggested he was fit to retain his post in "a simple village school."[45] He was urged to sit for the Teachers' Licensing Certificate exam, which he failed twice, meaning he remained an "unclassified" (i.e., uncertified) teacher throughout most of his tenure.

By the late 1920s, inspectors began to lose patience with Hassan al-Siba'i. In February 1928, the district inspector wrote, "This teacher is not fit to be retained in the service. He has very limited knowledge and a very primitive method. His school has never been found progressing."[46] When al-Siba'i was still employed in his post in July 1930, the inspector lamented, "His work is not so much satisfactory." The report continued by stating that, if he did not show improvement by the next term, "he should be discharged from the service."[47] The next term arrived, during which al-Siba'i assumed a new post in the Tarbikha village school. Inspectors remained underwhelmed by his performance, again denouncing his method of teaching as "primitive" and noting he "had to be reprimanded for very bad work in arithmetic in 2nd class and for bad work in history in all classes." The inspection reports for the following two years observed that he "has not yet shown the desired improvement in his work" and that "his appointment should be terminated unless he shows improvement."[48] However, it does not seem that he was fired from his post but merely transferred back to his old position at the Majd al-Kurum village school in 1933.

He retained this position until 1938, when he was transferred to the Ja'uneh village school in the district of Sefad. Here his performance improved, at least according to the headmaster of the school, who continually praised his method of teaching as *ḥasana wa jaīda* (good).[49] However, this was not an assessment with which the government inspector could agree. He sent a sternly worded letter to the school's headmaster, dated October 30, 1943:

> The teaching situation in your school during its inspection on October 20, 1943, was not satisfactory in some of the lessons and classes that were observed, and in particular the students in the fourth class are weak in multiplication and long division, while the students in the third class are weak in geography, subtraction, dictation, and writing, and their notebooks are filthy and disorganized. Students in the second class are weak in spelling, writing, subtraction, and geography, and they memorize their lessons by heart without understanding. I therefore demand you and your assistant Mr. Hassan al-Saba'i devote greater effort to raising the level of the school.[50]

Subsequent reports showed more promise, and in March 1947, the Department of Education finally agreed to promote Hassan to the position of classified teacher.[51]

A number of points surface from these documents. First, they demonstrate that not every teacher corresponded to Bowman's ideal, but these teachers were nevertheless retained, transferred to different schools, and even promoted. Hassan al-Siba'i served the Department of Education for twenty-five years despite his lukewarm performance and repeated recommendations that he be dismissed.[52] Moreover, the reports gesture at certain traces of his former life as a *kuttāb* teacher who "does not use the necessary apparatus for illustrations sufficiently," "does not take sufficient care of letters received . . . as instructed by the Department," and "relies on memory work."[53] Thus, while the Department of Education clearly intended rural schools to differ in substantive ways from the *katātīb* they replaced, in practice certain vestiges of the old style inevitably survived in teachers like Hassan al-Siba'i.

Using the rural school as a case study, we can discern that colonial administrators introduced a number of subjects and administrative practices that were, paradoxically, linked to the preservation of traditional village life. Thus, it was only through access to modern agricultural training and courses on housewifery that young boys and girls could battle the misery, poverty, and disease that fueled rural migration to the cities. In short, we might say that modernity was required to make traditional life bearable and thus represented the sole hope for its continuation. This tradition, as numerous scholars have indicated, had the tendency to crystallize into less dynamic forms amid the state's attempts to classify, codify, and govern through it. Postcolonial scholars who have analyzed this turn to tradition have often characterized it as part of a larger transition in British colonial policy away from liberal attempts to remake the native toward a conservative project that created absolute boundaries between the colonizer and colonized. There is no doubt much to be said in support of such a diagnosis, yet, at least with regard to education policies in Palestine, this explanation falls a bit short. On the most basic level, it fails to capture the extent to which the respect for tradition was self-consciously understood as a progressive departure from colonial norms, that is, as doing something undeniably new that was justified not merely on political grounds but through arguments about pedagogic and psychological necessity. What we encounter, in sum, is neither the replacement of the old by the new nor the mere privileging of the former at the expense of the latter. The dialectical interplay between the traditional and the modern points to the ways by which the old and new were in fact co-constitutive.

EDUCATION AT THE CROSSROADS OF AUTHENTICITY AND REVOLUTION

While the Arab Public System was the most immediate object of the Mandatory government's reform efforts, it was not the only one. Officials in the Department of Education routinely expressed their dissatisfaction with the state of Jewish education in Palestine, which seemed to be divided between the "national chauvinism" (to use Jerome Farrell's term) of the Zionist schools and the narrow religious curriculum found in *ḥederim* and *yeshivot*. More frustrating from the government's perspective, the large share of autonomy granted to Zionist education left little room to mold these schools in accordance to its wishes. Thus, with approximately two-thirds of Palestine's Jewish children in schools under Zionist administration, the Department of Education explored other means to impact the character of Jewish education. In this regard, numerous initiatives began in the early 1940s that offered financial assistance to Orthodox schools that were often at political or ideological odds with the Zionist schools managed by the Va'ad Leumi. These included not only the schools maintained by Agudat Israel but a number of private *talmudei-torah* and schools that served Jews from Sephardic or Middle Eastern Jewish communities. This was, in many ways, a curious development, and we should ask which goals the Department of Education hoped to achieve by supporting

Orthodox Jewish education in Palestine. This is all the more necessary because little scholarly attention has been paid to the relationship between the Department of Education and Orthodox schools, while a review of this relationship challenges many of the commonly held assumptions about Jewish education during this period.

The surviving papers from the Department of Education illustrate that the government grew increasingly involved in the support of Orthodox religious schools during the final decade of Mandatory rule. It is also evident that this policy was not advanced only by Farrell or the Colonial Office but largely embraced by the Department's Jewish inspectorate as well. This is significant, as these inspectors were influential educators in their own right. They included Joseph Bentwich, Shlomo Dov Goitein, and the honorary secretary of the Jewish Scouts in Palestine, J. L. Bloom. In addition to their regular responsibilities, Jewish inspectors oversaw a separate body, the Jerusalem Orthodox Schools Committee, which distributed more than LP 14,000 in direct grants to Orthodox schools from 1942 to 1947.[54] This was apart from a separate grant-giving initiative to aid schools in centers of the Old Yishuv, which awarded between LP 3,000 and 10,000 annually to Orthodox schools unaffiliated with the Va'ad Leumi.[55]

Members of the Jewish inspectorate tended to hold ideological positions that differed in important ways from dominant strains of Zionist thought. According to Humphrey Bowman, "The Jewish inspectors in the Department did much to raise the general level [of Zionist schools]. One of them was of British birth and upbringing; the rest were Palestinians, born and bred. They had all distinguished themselves at British Universities. While comprehending and sympathising with the Jewish standpoint, they were imbued with British ideals."[56] In a similar vein, it was likely men of their ilk whom Farrell had in mind when praising the small minority of Jewish teachers who were "influenced by a modernist and more living religious sentiment."[57]

Among the Jewish inspectors was Joseph Bentwich, who hailed from a prominent British Zionist family that included his older brother Norman, Mandate Palestine's first attorney general.[58] Both men greatly admired the British liberalism and were alienated by the extreme nationalism expressed by the Eastern European Zionist leadership. And judging by his activism following Israel's independence, Joseph was also dissatisfied both with contemporary forms of Orthodox Judaism and with secular Zionism, and this dissatisfaction may hint at why he was able to remain in Farrell's good graces.[59] Another inspector, Shlomo Dov Goitein, was similarly out of step with the Zionist mainstream. He received a doctorate from the University of Frankfurt, where he wrote a dissertation on Islamic prayer under Joseph Horovitz.[60] After immigrating to Palestine in 1923 (with his close friend Gershom Scholem), he served as a teacher at the Reali School in Haifa and became one of the first lecturers at the Hebrew University. Goitein's Zionism was distinctive in that it stressed the Semitic origins of the Jewish people and held that the success of the national revival hinged on the extent to which Jews were willing to embrace this patrimony. He encouraged Jews to study Arabic and stressed the Arabian context of ancient Israel.[61] Perhaps as an extension of this view, he performed ethnographic work on the Jews of Yemen, whom he viewed as vessels for the preservation of Judaism in its most authentic form.[62]

Goitein also wrote extensively on Jewish education, both historically and prescriptively, publishing several articles in the leading education journal of the *yishuv*, *Hed ha-ḥinuch*. During his time as an education inspector, he also authored a full-length book, *Hora'at ha-tanakh*, on teaching the Hebrew Bible, to which he often referred Jewish educators.[63] In managing his own children's education, Goitein stressed the centrality of the Torah and personally devoted attention to preparing his son for his bar mitzvah. Goitein's religious practice seems to have been largely private: he prayed at home every morning and with his family on the Sabbath.[64] Perhaps most important, Goitein maintained a distance from overt political activism and never affiliated himself with a Zionist party, despite being friendly with Judah Magnes and members of Brit Shalom. In this regard, it is telling that Goitein's political worldview is disputed: while his daughter, Ayala, believes he generally sympathized with the Labor Party,[65] a former student of Goitein's, Eric Ormsby, has characterized him as politically right wing.[66]

Pivoting back to the archival record, it appears that the impetus to aid Orthodox Jewish schools outside the Zionist system came from two directions: first, the refusal by the Va'ad Leumi to undertake certain administrative reforms, which resulted in the Government of Palestine withholding a portion of its annual block grant; and second, the desire to improve the status of Orthodox religious education as a potential alternative to Zionist schools. It is likely that the financial stress on schools whose funding sources were disrupted by World War II also contributed to the department's decision, though the notoriously parsimonious Mandatory government was unlikely to extend its resources based on financial need alone. Summarizing the government's position in a dispatch to the Colonial Office, High Commissioner MacMichael noted that, "after due warning," the Department of Education had withheld a portion of the annual block grant given to the Va'ad Leumi for the financial years 1938–41. These funds were then redirected toward the "large number of Jewish schools" that existed "outside the Vaad Leumi system which for various reasons they are unwilling or unable to enter."[67] The causes of the present predicament were "not simple," MacMichael stressed, and were ironically the products of the government's preference for administering Palestine on sectarian lines. "In the first place the Vaad Leumi though it is the council of the Jewish Religious Community in Palestine as established by Religious Communities (Organization) Ordinance is not essentially a religious body and discourages religious education except in a minority group of Vaad Leumi schools known as Mizrachi." However, he noted, "Mizrachi itself is a political body and does not commend itself to all orthodox Jews. Complaints are frequent that the Vaad is swayed by political rather than educational considerations and that the progress of schools is hindered thereby."[68]

As argued in the previous chapter, the sectarian management of Palestine was a complicated and often contradictory enterprise precisely due to the sorts of difficulties that the high commissioner notes here. What resulted in the 1940s was a sense of befuddlement that Palestine's official Jewish religious community discouraged religious education while numerous Orthodox schools from the Old Yishuv were ineligible for government support because they were not part of that community. One official from the Colonial Office summarized the situation following a meeting with members of Agudat Israel: "It was inequitable that in the Holy Land the Community of Orthodox Jews were, by reason of their religious convictions, treated as of less importance than the large immigrant population introduced into Palestine by the Zionist movement."[69] We should also note here the ease with which the high commissioner distinguishes between political and pedagogic considerations as if the separation between the two were self-evident. Distinctions of this sort were central to what I have termed the "politics of denial" in that they functioned to elide the routine transgression of the boundary between politics and pedagogy by the state itself.

As a solution, MacMichael proposed to extend direct aid to the schools of Agudat Israel and those serving "Oriental Jews" who were underserved by the Va'ad Leumi. For the 1941–42 school year, the government distributed LP 4,200 in direct aid to schools maintained by the Alliance Israélite Universelle, Agudat Israel, and local committees in Jerusalem, Tel Aviv, Tiberias, and Yavneh.

Though the sum in question was relatively small, the high commissioner voiced support for increasing these grants in coming years in pursuance of a policy whose main aim was "to secure secular efficiency in the religious schools and a more religious spirit in the secular schools. A single Jewish system of public education may then be gradually formed under a more unified but more tolerant and varied control than the Vaad Leumi has yet learnt to exercise."[70] Responding to the dispatch, the Colonial Office noted satisfaction with the Mandatory government's approach and voiced full support of its attempt to evolve a single system of Jewish education with a more "religious spirit."[71]

MacMichael was merely putting into action the education director's longstanding desire to combat the secularism of the Hebrew Public System as a means of reform. Thus, for example, in a 1939 letter to the Department of Education of the Va'ad Leumi, Jerome Farrell stressed the rights of "parents of strong religious sentiment" to secure for their children "not only proper instruction in faith, morals and ritual, but also secular teaching in a religious atmosphere." Furthermore, "the gap between the denominational [i.e., Mizraḥi] and the general schools should be closed by the encouragement of religious instruction in these latter schools too. This instruction may follow a more modern syllabus than that of the denominational schools but will accept the religious basis for conduct."[72] An editorial in the *Palestine Review* published in response to the letter cheered: "The religious authorities should rejoice that they have found so doughty a champion outside their own ranks."[73] And indeed, Farrell was a firm believer that a more robust religious education could help restrain the overtly nationalist character of Zionist schools.

While grants to schools maintained by Agudat Israel may have been in part politically motivated, there is evidence that the department sought more than simply to strengthen the position of the Va'ad Leumi's rival. For instance, the department rejected Agudat Israel's attempt to act as an intermediary in distributing grants to a number of private *ḥederim* and *talmudei-torah*. Deploying the language of administrative efficiency the department was known to favor, Rabbi Blau of Agudat Yisrael argued in a letter to Farrell that "such centralization [of Orthodox education] would no doubt improve education itself, and would also most probably be welcomed by yourself, Sir, as they would serve to centralize the control of the schools concerned through the cooperation between your Department and the Education Department of Agudath Israel."[74] In response to the request, S. D. Goitein noted that a number of the schools Agudat Israel proposed to include in its network were "*talmudei torah* for *Oriental children*" with "no spiritual connection" to Agudat Israel. Goitein rebuffed Agudat Israel's attempt to represent schools of this type in a newly centralized scheme, noting, "It would be more beneficial to consider these schools in connection with the other institutions for Oriental children assisted by us so far in Jerusalem, than to tie them up with Aguda, which would involve unnecessary obstacles to reform."[75]

If the primary purpose of extending government aid was to encourage educational reform, what were the features of this reformist agenda? In a fashion that mirrored their efforts to transform *katātīb* into public elementary schools, the Department of Education seized on the *ḥederim* and *talmudei-torah* of the Old Yishuv as sites for hygienic, pedagogic, and curricular transformation. "Is there no way of compelling the man to improve conditions at least insofar as this can be done without expenses, such as keeping the rooms, the latrine, himself, and the children clean and doing something useful with them?"[76] The question, posed by one government inspector after visiting the *talmud-torah* of Rabbi Ovadya Eliahu, was illustrative of prevailing attitudes toward the old-fashioned Orthodox schools, which, similar to the *katātīb*, were regarded as filthy, poorly staffed, and pedagogically backward. As was the case with the latter, the Department of Education aimed not at the eradication of religious schools but their transformation into clean, rationally administered institutions that would retain the centrality of religious instruction while introducing additional subjects to encourage the embrace of "productive" professions.

Schools that were located within private dwellings, had insufficient ventilation, and lacked drinking taps, working toilets, playgrounds, or furnishings were bound to clash with the Department of Education, whose authority over private (unassisted) religious schools was limited to ensuring they registered with the government and met its hygienic standards. The latter were ideally conceived and had little relation to the realities of the Palestinian schoolhouse, particularly among the poverty-stricken Orthodox Jews who made up the Old Yishuv. In extreme cases, the director of education ordered the closure of noncompliant schools, preferring no education to one conducted in unsavory conditions. Though the majority of interactions between the department and Orthodox schools related to sanitary requirements, the government was equally interested in promoting curricular and pedagogic reforms. Many of the suggested reforms complemented Zionist critiques of the old educational model, such as the insistence that lessons focus on those sections of the Hebrew Bible deemed appropriate for a child's sensibility. Secular subjects were not meant to challenge the primacy of religious instruction but to prepare children to be economically useful members of modern society. As earlier suggested in our discussion of *katātīb*, we must distinguish between the utilitarian use of secular education and secularism; while the former was to be heartily embraced, the latter represented a moral danger to be avoided if possible. A few case studies help elucidate the patterns that characterized the Department of Education's interactions with Orthodox schools.

MODEL STUDENTS AND REPEAT OFFENDERS

There are notably few instances of praise for (non-Zionist) Orthodox schools in the Department of Education's records. On the whole, the director and the Jewish inspectorate agreed with the prevailing view of them as sorely in need of hygienic and pedagogic reform. Similarly, the Va'ad Leumi characterized the vast majority of *talmudei-torah* and *ḥederim* as existing in "lowly condition, both in the context of the sanitary conditions that prevail within them and the educational status."[77] Echoing this sentiment, an editorial in the Hebrew daily *Ha-aretz* lamented the continued survival of such antiquated schools, which offered "an education that is insufficient for the general good, and particularly the national good."[78] While these characterizations suggest a certain sense of uniformity, it is important to note that there were in fact internal attempts to reform Orthodox schools during the first decades of the twentieth century and that the landscape in Palestine was far more varied than these polemics suggest. For example, the Bais Ya'akov network of schools for girls, which was founded in Krakow in 1917 but also maintained schools in Palestine, could be understood as a case of radical innovation wrapped in the garb of tradition. The schools offered a rigorous Jewish religious education to girls, which generated no little controversy in light of the widespread acceptance of a *halachic* prohibition against women learning Torah. Up until the school's establishment, the only formal education available to Jewish girls was found in Polish public schools, which were widely regarded as incubators of assimilation. Bais Ya'akov's founder, Sarah Schenirer, therefore justified her innovative enterprise as a necessary step to ensure the continuity of Orthodox Jewish life.[79]

In Palestine, too, there were notable exceptions to the "backward model of Orthodox schooling, which the Department of Education eagerly supported as a means of promoting a new form of traditional Jewish education. Such was the case of the Jerusalem girls' school founded by Rabbi Altschuler, which began receiving government aid in the late 1920s. Though it catered to Orthodox families, the school of Rabbi Altschuler "differs from the old traditional girls' school" in "curriculum, method and school organization." Described as very clean and orderly, the school displayed the other hallmarks of modernization: "there is a definite time-table; attendance registries are properly kept; recesses are well arranged." Though a government inspection report noted that teachers were largely lacking in higher education or pedagogic training, the department nevertheless looked favorably on the school and viewed the government's support as a means to implement further reforms: "Though the school falls slightly below the general elementary standard and is not entirely efficient I would strongly recommend that it be given a grant-in-aid. The school, being perhaps the only one of this very desirable type, deserves encouragement, and the more control we can exercise over it the better."[80] As occurred in Europe, the historical lack of formal education for girls often meant that schools that catered to them had greater leeway to innovate; and while girls did learn Torah, the prohibition on studying Talmud afforded them more school hours to dedicate to general subjects.

Similarly, the inspectorate offered qualified praise to the *talmud-torah* maintained by the Federation of Haredi Jews, "one of the best talmud torahs," and deemed it worthy of both government and municipal aid.[81] Housed in a large, modern building, it was among the few schools of this type to pass inspection by the Palestine Health Department. Moreover, the Department of Education approved of its curriculum, which included Hebrew, arithmetic, geography, science, history, and English among its "lay subjects." The school even devoted three to four hours weekly to the prophetic writings, undoubtedly "as a sop to those of 'modern' views on education."[82] This represented a departure from the custom in most *talmudei-torah*, in which the Torah was the only portion of the Hebrew Bible studied in some detail, and this only as a stepping-stone to more advanced legal commentaries. While such a curriculum was undoubtedly a relative novelty in historical terms, the Federation of Haredi Jews labeled itself as nothing other than "the voice of true, pure Judaism [*ha-yahadut ha-amitit ve ha-tzerufah*]."[83]

On the opposite end of the spectrum were schools that served children from *edot ha-mizraḥ*, Jewish communities from Sephardic, North African, Middle Eastern, or Central Asian origin. From the outset of the Mandate, education among *edot ha-mizraḥ* had proved a thorn in the side of Zionist educators, who explicitly aimed at creating a *dor aḥid*, a uniform generation of schoolchildren whose homogenization was essential to the national project. "The Jews who are returning to Palestine come, literally, from the four corners of the earth and speak many diverse languages," wrote the director of the Zionist Department of Education in 1930. "The restoration of Hebrew," in which the new schools played so central a role, was thus "not only a romantic venture." It was also "the instrument of Jewish unification."[84] While communities from *edot ha-mizraḥ* did not typically express the same ideological opposition as the Ashkenazi Old Yishuv to the inclusion of secular subjects in school curricula, they nevertheless desired to maintain their native languages and a distinct sense of communal identity rather than assimilate to the "universal" Zionist model.[85] As a result of extreme neglect from Zionist educational bodies and a lack of donations from communities abroad similar to those that supported Ashkenazi institutions, schools serving children from *edot ha-mizraḥ* were among the poorest in Mandate Palestine. Reflecting this fact, the vast majority of Jewish children without access to *any* formal education came from these communities.[86]

Thus, depending on one's perspective, Jews from Eastern communities were either the living embodiment of ancient Judaism or a force that destabilized the Zionist attempt to render Jews modern (i.e., white, European, secular). S. D. Goitein was a member of the former camp. In a 1953 article, he argued that Yemenite Jews "remain very much the same as they had been at the end of the Talmudic period" and contrasted the Yemenite Jew as a member of "Homo Religiosus" to modern man. Thus, while "we belong to the type of 'Homo Economicus,' whose aim it is to achieve a good life for himself and the greatest possible number of his fellowmen, the Yemenite represents 'Homo Religiosus' who is preoccupied with the salvation of his soul and the souls of those for whom he feels responsible." In this he was not unlike Jews, even European ones, from generations past: "If we disregard outward appearances, we shall find that the personality of the Yemenite Jew does not essentially differ from that of the Jew of Eastern Europe, Hungary or Southern Germany generations ago. What makes the Yemenite seem 'strange' to us is the fact that he has remained true to the ancient Jewish tradition."[87]

Conversely, Zionist teachers and headmasters expressed concern at the corrupting influences of Jews from Eastern communities. Letters to the Department of Education of the Jewish Agency, and later, the Va'ad Leumi, about the "Yemenite problem" or the "Kurdish question" were not uncommon. For instance, one headmaster complained about "a bothersome question, the problem of the Kurdish children," in his school:

> This problem is an obstacle that hinders our work in the school. Their lack of education in the home and their dwelling in an Arab village appears to damage their virtues [*midot*] and corrupt the rest of the students in the school who play [with them], and who are fed the poor values that they introduce into the school. . . . We strive to treat them in a special manner and we hope we will succeed. But our success will increase only when they move out of the village and come dwell close to Jews.[88]

In this instance, the Kurdish Jews did not represent a more authentic or primitive form of Judaism, but rather, by existing in uncomfortable proximity to Palestinian Arabs, they constituted a seed of corruption that threatened to undermine the Zionist endeavor.

The case of Yemenite schools, which were notoriously underserved during both the Ottoman and British periods, offers a particularly compelling example of how certain groups became situated on the receiving end of overlapping British and Zionist reform efforts. Immediately following the First World War, petitions lamented the indifference of Zionist leaders to Yemenite education, despite the high value the Yemenite community itself seemed to place on the education of their children.[89] Several years later, the material conditions of Yemenite schools had hardly improved:

> On 26th October, 1926, I paid a casual visit to the Yemenite Talmud-Torah "Torah-Or." . . . The school is of the usual Yemenite kuttab type, where only religious subjects are taught, and very old-fashioned methods employed. The sanitary conditions are unsatisfactory. The rooms are badly ventilated and lighted, and were found dirty. No drinking water arrangements at all, latrines not sufficient; no furniture of any description, except for some very bad benches.[90]

At the time of the inspector's visit, the school was not registered with the Department of Education and operated under the auspices of Agudat Israel. Numerous letters demanding that the latter body register the school and arrange for its inspection by a medical officer yielded no results, until finally the Yemenite community registered it as an independent entity.[91]

Unsurprisingly, the government medical officer found the school "unfit from a sanitary point of view," based on various deficiencies, including the lack of toilets, running water, and a playground. Humphrey Bowman ordered the deputy district commissioner of Jerusalem to close the school.[92] In response to the pleas from Yemenite community leaders—and a promise that they would work in earnest to locate a more suitable building—the department allowed the school to reopen for a two-week period. Two months passed before it was discovered that "the Yemenite Community have not kept their promise," and Bowman ordered the school closed yet again.[93] These two closures over a three-month period, with the corresponding bargaining between representatives from the Yemenite community and the Department of Education, marked the beginning of a recurring pattern that would characterize relations between the two parties for years to come.

The assumption that education could occur only under specific sanitary conditions, and in a place specifically designated as a school, underpinned the Department of Education's sanitary policies. In one instance, the senior medical officer rejected a possible location for the Yemenite school because the landlord's living quarters were within the same dwelling.[94] Synagogues, which had frequently housed schools, were also suspect. After inspecting a synagogue that was the proposed space in which to reopen Torah-Or, the medical officer noted that "the pillows or cushions on the benches, used by the congregation, will

FIGURE 5. A school for Yemenite Jewish children in Silwan (Kfar ha-Shiloah), now part of East Jerusalem, 1926. Courtesy of the Central Zionist Archives, PHKH\1291703.

have to be removed when the school functions, as they are liable to carry vermin." Latrines were also needed, both "as being the only way of introducing a little order and cleanliness in this dirty and unwholesome spot" and as a means of bureaucratic training: "the people really must be taught not to transgress P.H.D. [Palestine Health Department] orders."[95]

Meanwhile, the leaders of Torah-Or engaged in a number of tactics to prevent school closures or at least mitigate their effects. When, for example, the original school was closed in the spring of 1927, the community seems to have simply reopened it in a different quarter without informing the government. Similarly, letters from the Yemenite community promising to undertake sanitary repairs at some future date proved effective, at least temporarily. The community also deployed language that almost certainly capitalized on British anxiety about unsupervised youth, noting in one petition that were it not for the school, scores of Yemenite children would wander the streets without purpose.[96]

Government inspectors criticized the old-fashioned teachers and narrow curriculum. As a partial remedy, the Department of Education looked favorably on negotiations in 1937 to absorb the school into the Mizraḥi system:

> This Talmud Torah . . . used to be maintained by the Committee of the Yemenite Community in Jerusalem. The Talmud-Torah was then conducted on the lines of the old fashioned Talmudi-Torah, in which nothing but religious subjects are taught. Negotiations were recently conducted between the Mizrachi and the Yemenite Committee with a view of absorbing the two branches of the school. . . . The Yemenites agreed to the teaching of certain secular subjects, and the Mizrachi had to put with up the teaching of certain religious subjects by old fashioned Yemenite teachers. The result is a good step forward in transforming the old-fashioned and extremely orthodox Talmud-Torah into a more or less regular Talmud-Torah of the Mizrachi type. . . . The experiment deserves encouragement in as much as the pupils now attending the Talmud-Torah will get some secular education, whereas in the old Talmud-Torah they had no chance of getting any at all.[97]

School attendance forms for later years confirm that the *talmud-torah* was subsequently administered by Mizraḥi, and from this point forward teachers appointed by the Va'ad Leumi oversaw a revised curriculum that included Hebrew, arithmetic, drawing, and singing. Physical training and nature study were "not tolerated at all, but the teachers are attempting to touch some of the subject matter in the Hebrew and other lessons."[98]

A similar series of events occurred in numerous schools serving children from *edot ha-mizraḥ*, and in many of these instances the Department of Education facilitated the eventual absorption of schools into the Mizraḥi system. Such was the case for *talmudei-torah* serving Iraqi, Assyrian, and Anatolian Jewish communities. They were often deemed pedagogically backward institutions and likened to *katātīb*—"The teacher . . . does not know Hebrew. He teaches letters with vowels according to the method [used in] kuttabs"—and were purportedly supervised by school committees that were "obstinate and incompetent."[99] In each instance the solution was the same: "I see no possibility for further development if they do not get substantial help from the Va'ad Leumi Dept. in the future."[100] More specifically, the Department of Education's Jewish inspectorate felt that "only a supervisory authority like Mizrachi is able to bridge the ethnic factionalism," that is, to help assimilate communities from *edot ha-mizraḥ* into a "standard" form of Jewish identity.[101]

In a similar vein, S. D. Goitein grew frustrated with the rabbis who supervised *talmud-torah* Torat Aharon, which served Jerusalem's Iraqi-Jewish community. The rabbis rebuffed Goitein's suggestion that the school employ a married woman as a teacher for the first grade, stating that Maimonides had forbidden such a practice. Goitein attempted to counter this argument by stating that Maimonides also forbade a bachelor from teaching boys, yet the school employed no shortage of the latter. The rabbis claimed that the legal ruling itself, the *halacha*, was beside the point; the community would not consent to a female teacher in the school. Exasperated, Goitein could only conclude his minute by stating that, in his opinion, "Mizrachi will have greater power to safeguard the religious character," cast here as an adherence to *halachic* textualism rather than the customary practices of different Jewish communities.[102] As Goitein's letter suggests, it was precisely by abandoning the customs of the *edah* that these communities could come to represent Judaism in a more authentic form. These efforts on behalf of the Department of Education found corollaries in Zionist educators' tendency to view the education of children from *edot ha-mizraḥ* as a means of separating them from the languages and manners of the home. As Rachel Elboim-Dror's work on Hebrew education following World War I has shown, the newly empowered Zionist Organization struggled to deal with pupils whose home environment was "foreign in wisdom and spirit" to that of the school. "What the school repairs, the home removes."[103] There are discursive parallels between these efforts and those developed in the Department of Education's dealings with rural Arab society, which, as I suggested, could be preserved only in its "traditional" form by removing children from the usual sites of cultural transmission.

Regarding curricular reform, the Department of Education's inspectors frequently advised teachers and administrators of Orthodox schools regarding subject matter and pedagogic practices. Here, government officials pursued a path that complemented the modernist revolt against an education wholly devoted to religious subjects. While the Department of Education did not endorse any Zionist educational stream, administrators seemed to have the most sympathy with Mizraḥi's attempt to create a dual curriculum that included both religious and general subjects. Certainly, the attempt to channel schools from eastern communities into the Mizraḥi system suggests that the latter was regarded as the lesser of many evils.[104] In this respect, it is useful to consider a 1942 report by the inspector J. L. Bloom, in which he relayed the details of his meeting with the chief rabbi of Tel Aviv and a Mizraḥi representative of the Jewish Agency. The report suggested an ambitious plan that was illustrative of the department's goal of achieving "secular efficiency" in Orthodox schools. Describing an "argument of importance" relayed to him with which "we all agree," Bloom asserted that "the study of Talmud to be of value has to be done after say the age of 12." It followed, therefore, that

> Talmud Torahs, which are differentiated from other schools by the amount of Talmud taught, are not justifiable for children under 13. Children under that age should attend decent religious schools, where the religious element would be represented by Pentat. [Pentateuch] with Rashi, Bible, Mishnah and beginnings of Talmud. After that, the gifted boys should transfer to decent talmud torahs or "small" yeshivas.[105]

These "small yeshivas" were "to be run on lines consonant with present day requirements," effectively meaning that they would feature a basic general curriculum alongside the usual sacred texts and commentaries. Bloom noted that S. D. Goitein also advocated this line of action and concluded his memo on a hopeful note: "The grant at our disposal may serve as a lever in bringing about a reform in religious education."[106]

At the same time that Bloom envisioned reformed *yeshivot* with diversified curricula, he also supported the extension of more rigorous religious studies into General Zionist schools. Told of an existing program that dispatched members of the Organization of Talmudic Education to teach Talmud in Mizraḥi schools, Bloom responded that "it would be more to the point if they were sent to General [Zionist] schools" and promised to investigate whether the Department of Education would be willing to extend a grant to further these efforts.[107] While it is unclear from the records if this plan reached fruition, the willingness to recommend government funding for Talmudic studies in a memorandum addressed to the director of education is noteworthy in its own right. In sum, the report expresses the two pillars of the department's reform agenda: "to secure secular efficiency in the religious schools and a more religious spirit in the secular schools."[108]

Finally, administrators attempted to transform the way that religious subjects themselves were taught, though here they had admittedly less leverage. The payment of government grants depended on the adoption of a minimal secular curriculum, and suggestions regarding pedagogic practices were merely advisory. Nevertheless, the nature of these suggestions is useful in understanding the type of reforms that the department envisioned and the extent to which they overlapped with ongoing attempts within Zionist circles. Of primary importance here was an expanded place for the Hebrew Bible in school curricula. The customary educational order had used the Torah as a pedagogic tool for acquiring knowledge of the Hebrew language and devoted little if any attention to the other books in the Bible. Within such a setting, familiarity with the Torah served as a stepping-stone to learning the oral traditions recorded in the Talmud, which formed the true center of the curriculum.

The revolt against the Talmud in favor of renewed attention to the Hebrew Bible began with the *Haskalah*, continued through the scholarly ventures associated with the rise of Jewish studies as an academic discipline (*Wissenschaft des Judentums*) in Germany, and reached a fevered pitch in the Zionist embrace of the Hebrew Bible as a textbook of Jewish political and cultural history. The relative neglect of legal commentaries was thus the other side of the embrace of the Hebrew language and the Hebrew Bible as the true foundations of the Jewish nation, the vessels that had preserved its ancient *kultur* and that united Jews from across political and geographic spectrums: "We have one language and one Tanakh [Hebrew Bible], one history and one homeland."[109] Conversely, Zionist educators held that extensive Talmudic study "created an atmosphere of diasporic inertia in the midst of a period that was distinguished precisely by national and ideological independence."[110] Even the commentary of Rabbi Shelomo Yitzhaki (known as Rashi), which had long served as an indispensable aid in reading the Torah, was fair game for those who desired an unmediated relationship with the ancient text. In the words of Eliezer Riger (who was among the founders of the socialist Zionist organization *ha-shomer ha-tza'ir* [the Young Guard] and who later served in the Department of Education of the Va'ad Leumi), however impressive from an intellectual perspective, Rashi's commentary nevertheless "serves as a barrier [*meḥitza*] that separates our children from the Torah, this at the time that they have a direct and natural relationship to the Torah and what is written there."[111]

What was unique about the Department of Education's recommendations regarding the reform of Orthodox educational models was not their content but the harnessing of them to a professional language that claimed to speak in the name of pedagogic necessity. Discrediting educational traditions that had evolved over several centuries, department officials scoffed at the use of "incorrect" Hebrew, the reading of the Torah out of order, neglect of the prophetic writings, and the inclusion of subject matter deemed inappropriate for immature sensibilities.[112] Such efforts found parallels in Zionist schools, where "the portions of Tanakh that include things that are unsuitable for children's spirit will dropped."[113] What connected these points—both to one another and to the larger reform effort undertaken by the department—was the sense that, in order to gain access to Judaism's essential core, religious education must be carried out in a novel fashion. Connecting the child with this Jewish authenticity was thereby dependent on a number of departures from customary educational practices.

Finally, this attitude toward Orthodox Jewish schools was not something that existed in a vacuum. However unexpected—particularly given the prevalence of studying Palestine through the "dual society" model—these policies found corollaries in the approach we examined to rural Arab education. In particular, administrators attempted to preserve the central place of religious education—again of a "reformed" type—while introducing new subjects that were deemed more economically useful given "present day requirements." In both contexts the Government of Palestine found points of ideological convergence with Jewish and Palestinian intellectuals and educators, whether it was their distain for traditional forms of teaching or the implicit suggestion that reform required the separation of the child from his or her social milieu. Notwithstanding these points of agreement regarding the deficiencies of Palestine's *ḥederim* and *katātīb*, it was in articulating the proper relationship between religious traditions and political activism in the modern era—and the role of education in navigating this terrain—that Palestine's different forces found themselves at odds. It is to these clashes we now turn.

5 THE BOUNDARIES OF RELIGIOUS KNOWLEDGE

Surely the church is a place where one day's truce ought to be allowed to the dissensions and animosities of mankind.

—Edmund Burke, *Reflections on the Revolution in France*

IN THE INTRODUCTION TO THIS STUDY, I offered a variation of Bruno Latour's "modern constitution" as a tool to understand the colonial attempt to delimit proper and improper approaches to education. At the center of this model sat the need to absolutely distinguish between "pure" pedagogic practices and their corrupted forms, associated with Zionist and Palestinian nationalist endeavors. Thus, British administrators would claim that the Arab Public System nurtured healthy national pride rather than national chauvinism; that it taught public service without veering into mass politics; that it embraced religious education as a moral rather than a political practice; and that all policies were guided by pedagogic best practices rather than the cynical use of education as a form of social engineering. The fact that all parties concerned constantly transgressed the boundary between proper and improper practices is obvious enough, although, I have argued, it was precisely through the *denial* of this categorical muddling that colonial power was most effectively asserted—not as force but as alleged neutrality. The following two chapters expand on this central theme by analyzing colonial approaches to religious education and civic engagement, on the one hand, and the "transgressive" alternatives put forth by Palestinian nationalists and Zionists, on the other.

Beginning this analysis brings us into direct confrontation with the fundamental assumptions on which British educational planning was based: education as a practice distinct from, and indeed outside, the realm of mass politics; and the classic liberal notion of religion as properly, or at least ideally, apolitical.

Thus, "politics" figures in the writings of British officials as a force that upsets the educational equilibrium rather than as an inevitable component of modern, national schooling under centralized state supervision. However, educators assigned a monumental task to religious education. This amounted to nothing less than instilling in children a universal moral system that was presumably shared by Palestine's three major monotheistic religions yet bore a striking resemblance to a particular form of English Christianity. I have suggested that this understanding of religion as a private and pious force seemed to shape the Palestine Education Ordinance, which exempted religious schools from most forms of government supervision. Thus, schools imparting only religious instruction were entirely freed from the legislation and became subject to inspection and other bureaucratic requirements only with the introduction of secular studies like history, geography, or mathematics. Moreover, it was through the cultivation of religious virtues that children could presumably be shielded from the destructive pull of mass politics. Thus, religious education represented a linchpin in the effort to maintain the "traditional" order in which rule through religious authorities was thought to offer an antidote to popular mobilization.

Building on this theoretical frame, this chapter argues that the Government of Palestine developed an approach to religious education in the Arab Public System that linked Islam to the cultivation of individual moral virtues. The innovation here lay not in the idea of religion as a site of moral fashioning but in the equation of religion primarily with individual ethics in a way that excluded material or public concerns. The result of this conceptual shuffling was to remove other realms of human experience—commerce, for example—and fields of knowledge, whether of the Arabic language or the history of the Arab peoples, from the legitimate purview of religious affairs.

I also demonstrate how contemporary Arab-Muslim educators responded to this educational schema. Here, too, we find that the curricula and textbooks they produced reflected a heightened concern with individual moral fashioning through ritual practice (*ʿibādāt*) and devoted less attention to elements of sharia that regulated social behavior (*muʿāmalāt*). In this respect, the educational content of Islam underwent an arc of secularization similar to that which occurred in Egypt, which has been cogently analyzed by Gregory Starrett with regard to modern schooling and Talal Asad in his study of sharia court reform.[1] However, based on a case study of al-Najāḥ National School in Nablus, I suggest that there were limits to this epistemic common ground and that the reorganization of life into religious/spiritual and secular/material spheres was not accepted hook, line, and sinker. Exploring articulations of Islam as a civilizational rather than juridical system, associating religion with individual moral conduct, could actually facilitate attempts to overcome Palestine's sectarian divisions by allowing leaders to imagine an Islam shared by all Arabs, including non-Muslims. Thus, while the legal jurisdiction of religion was increasingly restricted to the individual's conscience and personal status, this did not signal the acceptance of a worldview in which Islam was separated from mass politics. Rather, Islam and Arabism could work hand in hand as mutually reinforcing foundations of political engagement.

As one final introductory note, the notion—so common in colonial circles—that religious education was historically linked to either otherworldly concerns or to instilling a sense of respect for rulers requires some attention here. As I noted in Chapter 1, premodern Islamic education was more often than not associated with the conservation of the social order, functioning as "a pillar of *stability* rather than as a force for *change*."[2] This cannot, however, be conflated with the idea that Islamic schools were traditionally apolitical, and not merely because religious scholars and institutions assumed a wide variety of orientations toward the ruling classes over time. More crucially, asking whether premodern Islamic education was political in nature risks anachronism by eliding over the relatively recent formation of politics as a discrete sphere of human activity.

As Talal Asad has argued, "This separation of religion from power is a modern Western norm, the product of a unique post-Reformation history," and moreover, it has been only through "the theoretical search for an essence of religion" that we have been able to "separate it conceptually from the domain of power."[3] Our contemporary conception of the political is further bound to that of national "state space"—including not only the nation-state's ventures into mass education, public health, and management of the economy but also the emergence of the public sphere as the privileged site of mass politics.[4] With these considerations in mind, asking whether premodern forms of Islamic education were political in nature is akin to asking whether medieval theologians were hostile to socialized medicine. The reality is that modernity engendered new forms of political engagement whose relationship with education and religious knowledge had to be formulated, not merely rearticulated. The details of that relationship, and the manner in which it was contested between Palestinian and British educators, require our attention. We should not, therefore, imagine this as a battle between a traditional Islamic approach and a modern colonial one. Both positions forwarded views regarding religious education and its relationship to political action that were *necessarily* novel, connected as they were to the historically contingent forces of mass politics, state bureaucracies, and new forms of intellectual authority.

Understanding these discursive currents requires a close analysis of politically opposed educational spaces: the Arab Public System, managed directly by the Mandatory government, and the nationalist schools created by Palestinian leaders. The following comparison questions the extent to which we should view these schools as oppositional in terms of either curricula or social function. Both systems were intimately involved in politics of one kind or another, as the government's insistence on the political neutrality of education represented a very real form of colonial politics. Rather, it was the *nature* of this political activity—and whether it was recognized as political at all—that became subject to dispute.

BOUNDARY MAKING: ON SECULAR TIME AND SACRED VIRTUES

One fruitful path into the Government of Palestine's approach toward Islamic religious instruction is through the curricula it created for use in the Arab Public System. Curricula, like textbooks, are both important and imperfect historical sources. At the level of discursive analysis, they are indispensable resources for reconstructing the colonial point of view regarding modern education. But because they tell us nothing of how teachers communicated lessons or the impact they had on students, social historians are understandably wary of favoring the study of textbooks or syllabi over the reflections of students and teachers. In putting curricula at the forefront of this analysis, I am conscious of these limitations. It is my hope that this may serve as a basis for complementary endeavors by other scholars that further enhance our knowledge of the period.

As discussed at length in Chapter 3, the Government of Palestine introduced a new syllabus for both town and village schools in 1921. In the words of Director of Education Humphrey Bowman, "Before the war, education in such village schools as existed was confined to repetition of the Quran. The present syllabus, while including instruction in the faith of the pupils, is on a wider basis, and embraces reading, writing, and arithmetic as well as the elements of history, geography, and hygiene."[5] The Egyptian syllabus served as the immediate model, and the Department of Education chose to use the teachers' handbook (*Irshādāt al-ʿamaliya*) published by the Egyptian Ministry of Public

Education for Palestinian teachers as well.[6] That said, for colonial administrators intent on keeping Palestinian schools free of political agitation, Egypt's educational system also served as a cautionary model of what *not* to do, particularly with regard to Lord Cromer's extreme restriction of educational opportunities and the discontent that this fueled. Humphrey Bowman rather diplomatically alluded to Cromer's shortcomings in his memoir, noting that his "pious aspirations" to offer Egyptians greater educational opportunities "were not fulfilled," possibly because "of the Whig tradition in which he had been brought up from and from which he could never quite escape."[7] According to Elizabeth Brownson, Humphrey Bowman "was determined to avoid the blunders made there [in Egypt]—and to be sure, he made entirely different ones."[8]

The village syllabus was designed around an agricultural bias in the hopes of quelling the migration of peasants to Palestine's urban centers. New subjects geared toward increasing agricultural productivity were thus part and parcel of the government's attempt to render traditional life more livable. However, the introduction of new subjects into the curriculum was only one part of the story. Even more important for our purposes, the syllabus created divisions between existing types of knowledge and, in particular, fostered a sense of separation between Islam and "secular" subjects such as the Arabic language, the historical record, and the human body. One consequence of this contraction of religious topics was that it largely freed religious education from matters concerning material relations or the political sphere. Such instruction could therefore be reconstituted as the basis of a universal, and largely individual, code of ethical precepts. To understand this shift, and the tensions it generated, we must look not merely at the government curriculum for religious instruction but at what was newly *excluded* from the category of religion itself.

For instance, the curriculum treated the Arabic language, which had historically been a core subject of study within the *kuttāb* and madrasa (and indeed, many of the classic treatises on the Arabic language were published by Muslim theologians), as a distinct subject aimed at developing permanent literacy.[9] Further departing from the traditional order of the *kuttāb*, the 1925 version of the syllabus stated that Arabic-language instruction should foster an interest in classical and modern Arabic literature. Memorization was to be avoided, and "vulgarisms and provincialisms in pronunciation, grammar and vocabulary must be carefully eradicated."[10] Interestingly, memorization was still allowed within the context of religious education, but vulgarisms were discouraged: thus, "the Qur'an should be memorized perfectly and read with the intonation practiced by the early Moslems," a feat requiring that "the affected method of reading the Qur'an followed in the old maktabs [*katātīb*] should be discarded."[11] In this instance, modernization came to depend precisely on abandoning contemporary practices in favor of reconstructed—and supposedly more authentic—classical models. The revival of the Arab national spirit served as a familiar trope in British intellectual circles, and purging "correct" Arabic of its colloquial corruptions was a natural extension of this narrative.[12] This argument was not merely a colonial creation but formed a crucial component of the Arab *nahḍa*, in which intellectuals scorned Arabic dialects and demanded that the new Arabic literature be produced in *fuṣḥa* (standard Arabic).[13] In effect, the government syllabus seems to have echoed attempts by contemporary Arab intellectuals to construct a national-linguistic heritage that predated, and was distinct from, a specifically Islamic milieu. That this emphasis on Arabic as the carrier of national identity was not deemed incompatible with the effort to keep nationalist politics at bay points yet again to the attempt to demarcate appropriate educational goals (instilling a "healthy national feeling") from inappropriate ones ("hysterical racial pride").

Similarly, hygiene represents a subject that could have quite easily been subsumed under the category of religious education. Indeed, children did study "practical knowledge of the principles of ablutions" as part of the class dedicated to Islamic religious instruction.[14] In treating hygiene as a distinct field of knowledge, the curriculum indicated that these practices were not to be regarded as part of a particular religious ritual—even one that crossed the boundary between the spiritual and the material—but rather as universal norms grounded in scientific reason. However significant these innovations, it is by comparing syllabi for Islamic religious instruction and history that the approach to religion as a distinct type of personal experience becomes most apparent. In this sense, the curriculum offers a rich site for analyzing, in Talal Asad's words, "How, when, and by whom are the categories of religion and the secular defined?" and "What assumptions are presupposed in the acts that define them?"[15]

As numerous authors have noted, the teaching of history and geography constituted a continual source of tension between the Department of Education and the Palestinian Arab public.[16] Nationalists regarded the government curriculum as a classic colonial attempt to obviate the identity formation of the Arab child by turning his attention to foreign events while simultaneously neglecting the history of modern Palestine.[17] There is certainly much truth to this claim, though it does not fully capture the matrix within which these curricular decisions operated, how the boundaries between sacred and secular events were established, and what significance was attached to each.

The general structure of this curriculum narrated a teleological story at whose apex sat European modernity, its commercial triumphs, scientific advancements, and political conquests. Thus, the child may study figures from the Arab past in classes devoted to ancient or medieval history, but modernity as a historical period was reserved almost exclusively for European (and, to a lesser extent, North American) developments. The second class, for instance, included the following topics under the heading of "modern history": Christopher Columbus; Sir Francis Drake, his voyage around the world; Oliver Cromwell and the struggle between king and Parliament; James Watt and the invention of the steam engine; George Stephenson's railway line; William Wilberforce and the abolition of slavery in British domains; Horatio Lord Nelson and the Battle of the Nile; Charles Gordon and the suppression of the slave trade in the Sudan.[18] To the extent that lands outside the Euro-American context appeared, they were objects of colonial conquest or, as the Sudanese example suggests, improvement. Yet the curriculum was not totally bereft of Arab historical figures or events. For instance, teachers were given a list of "great men" whose biographies formed the basis of lessons, particularly in the lower grades. They included "the principal characters in Bible history," Socrates, Josephus, the rightly guided caliphs, 'Abd al-Malik ibn al-Marwan, Harun al-Rashid, Charlemagne, Mohammed al-Ghazali, Richard the Lionheart, Salah al-Din al-Ayyubi, Christopher Columbus, Napoleon Bonaparte, and Ibrahim Pasha, to give only a very small sampling.[19] There are two questions we must therefore address: First, if Arab history was not wholly excluded, what topics were fit for inclusion and why? Second, how did caliphs and jurists come to be included in secular history rather than within religious instruction, and what were the interpretive consequences of this shift?

On the one hand, the figures and events deemed worthy of inclusion functioned as milestones within an unbroken chain of Arab national heritage extending back to pre-Islamic times: the *Jahiliyya* poets Hatim al-Ta'ī and 'Amr ibn Madi Karib initiate a chronology that included the rightly guided caliphs, great military heroes (Khalid ibn al-Walid, Tariq ibn Ziyad, Jawhar al-Siqilli, Salah al-Din), and renowned artists and scholars (al-Shafi'i, al-Farabi, al-Ghazali, al-Mutanabbi) and culminated in nineteenth-century reformers (Muhammad 'Ali, Ibrahim Pasha, 'Abd al-Qadir al-Jaza'iri). This was by now a familiar narrative, a similar version of which appeared within history textbooks written by Palestinian nationalist educators, such as those by Muhammad ʻIzzat Darwaza.

Thus, it was not that Arab history was entirely ignored. On the contrary, central figures from the classical period and even the nineteenth century commanded a great deal of attention. What was neglected, however, was contemporary Arab history as seen from the perspective of national revival, foreign betrayal, and colonial conquest. For instance, while the government syllabus and ʻIzzat Darwaza's nationalist textbook both concluded with lessons on "the Great War and its results in the Arab land" (*al- ḥarb al-kubra wa atharuha fi al-bilād al-ʻArabiya* in Darwaza's text, suggesting a rather literal mirroring of the government curriculum), the content of those lessons was presumably quite different. Nonetheless, the topical similarities between these two, allegedly oppositional, history curricula gesture at a recurring point of tension within the government's educational planning: students were expected to gain the literary skills required to appreciate classical and modern Arabic literature, and to deduce moral lessons from the great military and political heroes of the Arab past, but were to avoid relating to this knowledge as a source of inspiration for their own political identities.

As indicated by the list of "great men," the child's first introduction to history was a mixed one in many ways. It included both Arab and foreign figures, taken from sacred and profane settings. Here biblical figures could inhabit the same historical space as al-Shafiʻi and King Alfred. Not only figures from the Judeo-Christian tradition found their way into the syllabus, as intermediate classes covered the family of Muhammad, "his mission and life in detail," the spread of Islam, and the decay of the caliphate.[20] This removal of characters and events from the annals of sacred history can be read as an attempt to naturalize the historical record, wherein the rapid spread of Islam, for example, is attributable to the "organisation of the Arab Empire" and its "fiscal system" rather than divine providence.[21] Similarly, lessons should stress "the effect of climate, physical conditions, means of communications, and environment on the development of the different races."[22] What is evident from this example is the fragmentation of Islamic history into discrete theological and political components, to be dealt with in the contexts of religious instruction and secular history, respectively. Thus, the history curriculum posited a new interpretive framework for explaining familiar episodes from the human past. What occurred within the old-fashioned *kuttāb* was not genuine history, perhaps less on account of *what* was studied than because of how the march of time was encountered and explained.

Within rural schools, "Mohammedan" (in the 1921 syllabus) or "Moslem Religious Instruction" (in the revised 1925 version) commanded a relatively large share of the weekly school hours, topped only by the extensive time spent on the Arabic language.[23] To assuage the Muslim population "that the importance they always attached to the moral and religious basis of education was not to be neglected," the curriculum for religious education was created by a "classical scholar of well-established reputation in the Arab world."[24] This scholar was likely Sheikh Hussam al-Din Jarallah, who tied in the election for grand mufti before the British appointed Hajj Amin al-Husseini to the post.[25] Jarallah held a number of official posts throughout the period, serving as the chief clerk for the sharia courts and a district inspector for the Department of Education. In 1926, he was seconded to Transjordan to assume a position as the minister of justice. He later returned to Palestine, where he continued to hold positions within the sharia courts and served as a member of the *awqaf* commission.[26] Following the Jordanian occupation in 1948, King Abdullah appointed Sheikh Jarallah as chief qadi and mufti of Jerusalem, supplanting his longtime rival.

Jarallah was a modernist scholar and former student of Muhammad ʿAbduh. While no writings of Jarallah's have been published, we can glean some information about his views from an interview with his daughter, Saʿida.[27] She remembers her father as a progressive figure among Palestine's ulema who believed strongly in the education of women. He sent Saʿida to Schmidt's College, even though it was a Catholic institution, and then to the Women's Training College. In 1938–39, he sent her—alone—to continue her studies in England, a decision that apparently generated no small share of controversy. Further stressing her father's progressive credentials, Saʿida recounted the following anecdote that occurred following the 1948 war:

> I remember one time there was a big feast and King Abdallah was attending. One of the people told the king that Shaykh Hussam teaches his daughters how to play the piano and sends his daughters to foreign schools. My father stood in front of the king and cited some of the Prophet's sayings about education and culture in front of everybody. He told him that the Prophet said "you should pursue your education even if it takes you to China"—and that education was a

> requirement for every Muslim man and woman. We were the first to go to Zion (shorthand for Dames de Sion, a girls' school) in a boarding school and the first to learn to play the piano. This was very difficult sixty or seventy years ago. Muslims were very strict in those days.[28]

Even if Sheikh Jarallah was not the "classical scholar" referred to in Tibawi's account, we can nonetheless detect clear traces of Islamic modernist thinking in the new curriculum, which stressed uniformity in religious studies, the linkage of ritual practice to symbolic meaning, and the primacy of the Qur'an as a source for religious guidance.

Given the popularity of "Protestant" approaches to Islam within reformist circles of the late nineteenth and early twentieth centuries, it should be no surprise that the Qur'an served as the center of religious education in government schools. "The Qur'an should be the source of authority in deducing doctrines, ritual, moral axioms, and civil transactions."[29] The Qur'an and Sunna functioned as the vessels for the transmission of these virtues, as it was through the moral exemplars contained therein that the child acquired "fear of his maker in all his religious and worldly [*dunyawiya*] acts."[30] Furthermore, the first goal of religious instruction (*al-diyāna* or *al-ta'līm al-dīnī*) was "the propagation of superior moral virtues by means of good example."[31] As this passage suggests, Mandatory officials endorsed a view of religious education as a means of character formation that was not dissimilar to contemporary British views of education at home. Taking into consideration Jonathan Sheehan's excellent study of approaches to the Bible in late nineteenth-century England, it is not altogether surprising that British administrators in early twentieth-century Palestine would regard religious education as a means of diffusing individual ethical and civic virtues rather than an integral component of either material or communal life.[32]

The syllabus further divided its contents into two segments: "Qur'an" and "Religious Instruction." The former consisted of an ordered timetable for reading the Qur'an in its entirety by the end of the final year of schooling, prescribing which sections should be read and which committed to memory. The creation of a large network of public schools in which each child learned the same portion of the Qur'an at the same time must itself be appreciated as a novelty, one that "encouraged growing numbers of believers to think of their faith as objective, systemic, and exclusive" and that looked to exclude "popular traditions of religious knowledge."[33] Thus, the incorporation of religious education into the school curriculum was not the mere continuation of the past but a significant attempt to create a uniform approach to the Qur'an's teaching and interpretation. In the same vein, the introduction of an official textbook for the upper grades reflected the urge to ensure that teachers followed a standardized curriculum. This necessarily stripped the teacher of some of the autonomy he possessed within private *katātīb*, and the development of detailed syllabi and textbooks should be understood as an attempt to mitigate the uneven influence of individual teachers. This was one area in which the colonial approach converged with previous attempts by reformers like Muhammad 'Abduh, who argued that only a unified approach to religious education, purged of its irrational elements, could combat the destructive creep of ignorance (*jahl*) among Ottoman Muslims.[34]

In the class titled "Religious Instruction," lower classes focused on the life and attributes of Muhammad, his family, migration to Medina, death, and burial. These were, significantly, all topics that appeared in the history syllabus as well, though here particular stress was paid to the Prophet as a moral guide: "his self-abnegation and humility," "his interest in the well-being of children," "his refraining from revenge when revenge lay in his power." Through the incorporation of "moral training"—"virtues whose practice is inferred from verses in the Qur'an"—the upper grades combined the earlier emphasis on Muhammad's biography with the reformist stress on the Qur'an as the authoritative source for deducing ethical principles. These included, for instance, "respect due to parents," "obedience due to rulers," and "the etiquette of visiting."[35]

The emulation of Muhammad's behavior was as old as Islamic education itself. What is interesting for our purposes is that this emphasis came at the expense of teaching the material, social, or political dimensions of Islam. The curriculum thus promoted a view of religion as largely limited to the biography of Muhammad, the text of the Qur'an, and the "universal moral values" that were thought to represent an ethical core shared by Christianity, and to a lesser extent, Judaism. In contrast, many Muslim religious thinkers and leaders appeared not within the syllabus for religious instruction but within that for Arab history. Thus, Abu Bakr and al-Ghazali took their place in the curriculum alongside other heroes of the classical Arabic tradition in much the same way that Socrates and Julius Caesar were used to symbolize the intellectual and political triumphs of the Greco-Roman period. Prominent Muslim figures *did* migrate from sacred to secular history as exemplars of the Arab nation, and it was this movement that facilitated the approach to Islam as a defined group of beliefs, ritual practices, and ethical norms.

Stripped of most of its political leaders and cultural heroes, Islamic religious instruction could thereby be reconstituted as part of a universal—or perhaps more to the point, universalizing—moral system that was largely removed from those affairs now claimed by the secular. In this instance, the modern concept of history was linked to the nation in a way that religion—imagined as a source of ethical values rooted in belief rather than material practices—could not support. Echoing the earlier transformation of the Bible into an ethical text of neohumanistic heritage, religion was imagined as a moral common ground that could rise above the political clamor. If any degree of particularism was allowed to creep into the classroom, it was through the historical study of the great men of the past, hence the heightened level of supervision over schools' history curricula and constant battles over history texts.[36]

That being said, we should not conflate the way the curriculum was designed with the way in which it was received. At least according to Tibawi's account, the attempt to separate Islamic religious education from its political context was partially undermined by the mediating role of Palestinian teachers. "Texts from the Quran or Hadith of the Prophet were expounded in such a way that the outcome might as well be presumed to come from a political treatise. Conversely, political events and current local affairs were so subtly represented in religious garb, with an irresistible appeal to the minds of the young, that gave the impression that the outcome was in accord with the wishes of the early caliphs or indeed of Muhammad himself."[37] While my focus has not been on the reception of the government curricula—a topic that, however difficult to assess, nonetheless is deserving of its own study—we should remain mindful of the gap that in all likelihood separated the Education Department's intentions from the experience of actual students.

In sum, emerging against the backdrop of the *kuttāb* in which reading, writing, and tales from the past were inseparable parts of learning the Qur'an, the Arab Public System claimed to offer a new and improved form of education. Its syllabi are significant as discursive objects that both reflected an emerging epistemic order and helped solidify its categorical divisions between the individual and communal, the theological and historical, and the sacred and profane. It is worth reiterating that this approach to religion as a depoliticized entity was directly at odds with the actual administrative structure of Palestine, whose governance through religious units obviated the emergence of a nonconfessional public space. More cynically, we might say that it was precisely *because* religion was conceived of in apolitical terms that the British chose to govern through it. Either way we are left with a bundle of contradictions that characterized colonial officials' approach to Arab and Islamic education: they desired secular education without secularism, national education without nationalism, religious education without sectarianism.[38]

INTERSECTIONS

It is telling that one of the first issues of the Arabic newspaper *Filisṭīn* featured an editorial on the state of education in Palestine. Reflecting the hopes of the second Ottoman Constitutional era, the piece drew attention to the need to transform public schools to train a new generation of citizens: "All that the era of despotism begat must pass with it, and as to the era of freedom, everything in it must be new." Metaphorically, the author exhorted readers to don new garments (*athwāb jadīda*) and to throw off the garb of despotism. Yet perhaps most important is that the success of this project was represented as hinging on the creation of new textbooks, without which "the nation will remain in its former state . . . of hypocrisy, and fraud." Indeed, it continued, "in our country we are in need of a general overhaul of [text]books to create new ones accompanied by principles of the constitutional era."[39]

The impulse toward creating standardized textbooks to transmit the values of an enlightened era to a new generation of citizens hints at the degree to which public education in Palestine, even in its nascent form, was understood as part and parcel of the new political order. The recognition of education's political importance only increased among Palestinian leaders following the Balfour Declaration and the British occupation, and again, textbooks proved a crucial (and contentious) factor in attempts to prepare the next generation for a new set of political challenges. This was all the more important in the face of attacks on Arab unity—either through the severance of Palestine from Greater Syria or sectarian attempts to sow dissension between Muslims and Christians—attacks that could be somewhat mitigated by the production of textbooks that would allow schoolchildren in Nablus to learn the same lessons as those in Jaffa.

The embrace of educational uniformity was not, then, something that came to Palestine only in the wake of the British occupation. Rather, the drive to standardize education, and religious instruction in particular, formed a key part of the late Ottoman agenda as the Sublime Porte looked to public schools as a means of fostering social utility and imperial loyalty in equal parts. Within this late Ottoman context, we should note the 1887 memorandum that Muhammad

ʿAbduh addressed to the sheikh al-Islam at the close of his Parisian exile.[40] As modern Islam's great textualist, to borrow a phrase from Paul Sedra, ʿAbduh is often associated with his turn away from judicial precedence (embodied in the practice of *taqlīd*), mysticism, and popular customs in favor of a textually orthodox "true" Islam that granted primacy to the Qur'an and Sunna. In his 1887 letter, we see ʿAbduh's attempt to envision a new form of Islamic schooling that would correspond to this intellectual position and that would halt the tide of "ignorance" sweeping the masses away from true Islam. The memorandum offers an instructive example of the attempt to transform historically diverse patterns of Islamic learning into an educational system that aimed at, even if it did not achieve, a certain level of bureaucratic standardization and curricular uniformity.

ʿAbduh's principal argument was that religious education in the Ottoman Empire had failed and that the consequences were not primarily, as it might have been in earlier times, the erosion of the general moral order or the weakening of communal piety; rather, and far more dire, deficiencies in religious education were gradually undermining the state itself. The timing was not insignificant, as he submitted his recommendations in 1887 following a slew of political and military defeats that stripped the empire of several key provinces: Serbia and Montenegro (gained independence in 1878), Bosnia-Herzegovina (occupied by Austria-Hungary in 1878), Cyprus (occupied by Britain in 1878), Tunisia (occupied by France in 1881), and Egypt (occupied by Britain in 1882). Most Ottoman Muslims, ʿAbduh argued, were floundering in a sea of ignorance (*jahl*) regarding the true nature of Islam, which had weakened the empire politically by opening the door to Christian missionary activity. Ignorance was first and foremost a disease of the masses and the religious leaders who catered to their needs, characterized here as "believers along the lines of the ignorant [ones] that preceded us."[41] His use of *jahl* and its derivatives is highly suggestive of the period of *Jahiliyya* (the "age of ignorance" prior to Islam) and corresponds with the overall sense that contemporary Muslims have deviated from the proper path:

> The passage of time has indeed injured the souls of Muslims, and the days have harmed the tenets of their belief as the bonds of their conviction have weakened, which has enveloped them in the darkness of ignorance [concerning] the foundations of their religion, and weakness has indeed followed the decay in morals, the regression of character, and degeneration in spirit, until most of the public has become similar to domestic animals.[42]

We find similar sentiments in contemporary Bengal, where the urban upper classes (*ashraf*) attributed the backwardness of Bengali Muslims to the idea that they were not authentically Muslim. As Parna Sengupta has shown, this view fueled a bifurcated form of advocacy in which the *ashraf* pushed for higher-level educational institutions for themselves (in addition to increased placement in the colonial bureaucracy) and the extension of "modern, state-supervised primary-level *religious* schooling" for the ignorant masses.[43]

Following ʿAbduh's thoroughly negative assessment of the moral state of Ottoman subjects, he outlined a detailed and hierarchical plan for Islamic education in the empire's public schools. He recommended three tracks of religious instruction tied generally to class: primary schools that "stop at the principles of writing, reading and something of arithmetic" for children who would work in trade, agriculture, or industry; a slightly more advanced track in the *sultaniyya* schools (professional and military academies) for those who would serve the state in some future capacity; and an expansive curriculum in madrasas for "the sons of Muslims that grasped what was presented" prior to this point and "revealed excellence in their understanding" of the Islamic sciences. What united these three different courses of religious education was ʿAbduh's emphasis on standardized curricula and centralized supervision of both the teaching staff and pupils. Indeed, ʿAbduh composed a list of the subjects that must be included (and avoided) within each stratum, adding, "It is necessary to establish [for them] religious textbooks in accordance with this perspective." For students in primary schools, their religious education should mention nothing of Islamic sectarian battles and focus on teaching a practical understanding of behaviors that were permissible (*ḥalāl*) and prohibited (*ḥarām*). He also recommended an abridged textbook for history centered on the biography of Muhammad and his companions and the moral virtues that facilitated the early Arab conquests. All this should be taught in a fashion that was succinct and easy to comprehend.[44]

His prescriptions for the upper two tiers introduced more advanced topics and methods, such as the principles of jurisprudence and the methods of disputation. Yet even at the highest level of madrasa study, ʿAbduh attempted to establish a standardized series of topics and texts that would have effectively overturned the prevailing style of learning, in which individual teachers possessed a wide degree of autonomy in selecting the subject matter on which they lectured.[45] In ʿAbduh's scheme, because these schools would produce future members of the ulema, they required the utmost supervision from the

Ottoman state and the sheikh al-Islam himself. If the dire state of contemporary political life stemmed from deficiencies in religious knowledge, he argued that enacting his recommendations would facilitate the overall rebirth of the nation through implanting in its subjects' hearts "a love of and respect for religion."[46]

In offering this short digression from the Palestinian context, my intent is to highlight the degree to which British and Arab reformers found points of overlap with regard to the design of modern schooling. Members of both groups identified the decentralized and uneven nature of education as a problem in need of solving by means of curricular standardization, state control of education, and the proper training of teachers. In this they merely reflected what were, by the close of the nineteenth century, common assumptions regarding the development of mass education. We can nonetheless detect a fundamental difference between 'Abduh's position regarding Islamic education and that of British colonial officials who would follow. Religious education served a functional role within both schemas, as all parties linked the cultivation of proper religious education to larger political goals. However, insofar as 'Abduh linked the reform of religious education to the regeneration and modernization of Ottoman subjects, it was never conceived of as a means to maintain a current order or to divert the masses from political engagement. On the contrary, traditional practices lay at the root of the problem, a fact that rendered new forms of Islamic education crucial to the empire's political struggle against European incursions. For all his invocations of "true" Islam, 'Abduh's educational ideas were in fact linked to progressive and even revolutionary currents within the Ottoman state that were distinct from more instrumental attempts to use Islamic education to prop up the flailing empire.[47] In more general terms, what was unique about 'Abduh's pedagogic program was his harnessing of Islamic education to a larger program of social change.

Taking stock of this background is necessary to understanding the broader intellectual context that Palestinian educators inhabited, as ideas pioneered by 'Abduh in the late nineteenth century would become standard operating procedure in Arab modernist circles, particularly among educators and select members of the ulema. In his diary from the First World War, for example, the Palestinian soldier Ihsan Turjman recounts discussing the works of Muhammad 'Abduh and Qasim Amin at the home of the Palestinian educator Khalil Sakakini with a group that included Is'af Nashashibi, Haj Amin al-Husseini, and Ishaq Darwish.[48] Moreover, 'Abduh's positions regarding Islam and education largely established the foundation for the development, during the interwar period, of new schools, curricula, and textbooks created by Arab educators in Egypt, Palestine, and Transjordan.

The remainder of this chapter follows the traces of this modernist legacy by examining educational materials that Arab-Muslim educators created in the first half of the twentieth century. At the center of this analysis sits a case study of al-Najāḥ National School in Nablus and, in particular, the relationship between Islam, secular history, and political activism promoted therein. I have suggested that there was some degree of overlap in the government curricula and textbooks created by Muhammad 'Izzat Darwaza, the first headmaster of al-Najāḥ. We explore these points of intersection in further detail and ask what, if anything, they tell us about the negotiation of religious and secular forms of knowledge. Exploring these points of convergence adds further nuance to our understanding of Arab modernists—who are too often either dismissed (or celebrated) as colonial mimics—as intellectual figures and political actors. While not an exhaustive review, this exercise is nonetheless suggestive of the diverse paths forged by Palestinian nationalists in their attempts to create new forms of schooling that were responsive to concerns regarding both cultural authenticity and social utility.

We begin by acknowledging that the leadership of al-Najāḥ largely shared the Department of Education's view of religious education as the site of individual moral fashioning. Whether we choose to regard this fact as an instance of cross-civilizational common ground or as the colonial penetration and reworking of an Islamic episteme (in the Foucauldian sense) is an important question, and there are arguably elements of truth in both approaches. The Islamic tradition is a rich and varied one with no shortage of material to draw on in creating a natural association between religious education and moral training. Yet the way in which these traditions were mobilized at this particular point in time cannot be regarded as a neutral fact that exists apart from the uneven power dynamics in which Muslim Arabs toiled during the "liberal age."[49] Acknowledging that the modernization of Islamic education occurred within the context of European colonialism should not be taken to imply that it thus became somehow less "authentic." There is no historical period devoid of its power imbalances. Yet, we cannot approach the transformation of educational—and indeed, religious—practices *as if* they were the mere products of internal disquiet. Rather, respect for historical nuance requires accounting for the multidimensional contexts in which these transformations occurred.

It is also noteworthy that al-Najāḥ's leadership did not believe that an emphasis on individual moral formation should separate Islam from either social life or political activism; rather, the student's ethical development facilitated his interventions on behalf of the national community at large. Moreover, and in fascinating ways, the notion of religiosity as a form of individual ethics could actually serve as the conceptual basis for an Arab national politics that transcended supposedly age-old communal divisions. In this sense, the colonial epistemic order was not without its practical advantages. Whereas government policy reflected a tendency to conceive of religiosity in terms of private faith and ethical conduct, and to perceive these values as antithetical to national politics, the leaders of al-Najāḥ seemed to have accepted the former conceptualization as a means of political mobilization rather than a force that restrained it. Points of commonality with government curricula did not, therefore, signal the acceptance of a form of Islam divorced from political action. Like his contemporary Taha Hussein—whose autobiography was required reading at al-Najāḥ by the late 1930s—'Izzat Darwaza embraced the idea of an Islamic civilization system that was intertwined with the fate of the Arab nation. Thus, while the contraction of Islam's legal jurisdiction to laws of personal status and a pronounced emphasis on individual ethical formation may suggest an attempt to relegate religion to the private space, we should not necessarily equate these shifts with the wholesale adoption of secularism as a movement to liberate public reason and therefore, the political sphere, from religious sensibilities.

THE *NAHḌA* IN NABLUS

In 1918, a group of educators and intellectuals in Nablus founded al-Najāḥ National School to cultivate a new generation of elites poised to become future leaders, "possessing refined intellects . . . nurtured by useful sciences [*al-'ulūm al-nāfi'a*], culture and nationalism."[50] The school's founders were associated with the Nablus branch of the Arab Club, and al-Najāḥ became known during the Mandate period as a center of nationalist agitation. In addition to Darwaza, the school employed a number of Palestine's leading political activists, including Jalal Zurayq, Akram Zu'aytir, and Muhammad 'Ali Darwaza.[51] In its curricular materials, the school stressed both the ethical content of its instruction—as "character [*khulq*] is the basis of success in life"—and its belief in the essential unity of the Arab nation, emphasizing that its doors were open to non-Muslims as well.[52] The latter were exempted from attending lessons pertaining to Islam, and exercises in "their religious rituals" were offered in the students' own places of worship.[53]

Though he is perhaps better known for his activism as a Palestinian nationalist, Muhammad 'Izzat Darwaza served as headmaster of al-Najāḥ School from 1921 to 1926.[54] A member of the 1920 Congress of Damascus that elected Emir Faisal king of Greater Syria, and later a cofounder of the Istiqlāl (Independence) Party in Palestine, Darwaza was unwavering in his opposition to Zionism and the extension of Mandates over Arab territories following the First World War. He also authored numerous textbooks for use in private Palestinian schools, particularly history texts. While these books were never used in government schools because of their nationalist overtones, they were used extensively in al-Najāḥ and other private schools in Palestine.[55] By the late 1930s al-Najāḥ employed a number of Darwaza's works, including *Lessons in Arab*

FIGURE 6. The staff and graduating class of al-Najāḥ, 1932, including several notable Palestinian figures. Seated in the front row, from right to left, are the activist and journalist Akram Zu'aiter, the poet Muhammad Adnani, the mathematician and writer Qudri Tuqan, and 'Abd al-Hamid al-Sa'ih, one of the authors of *Principles of the Islamic Religion*. Courtesy of the Library of the Institute for Palestine Studies, PC81/235.

History from Antiquity to the Present, *Lessons in Ancient History*, and *Lessons in Medieval and Modern History*.[56]

It is readily apparent from reviewing the textbooks that Darwaza adopted many of the assumptions prevalent within colonial circles about the backwardness of Arab peoples and the need to adopt the tools of Western progress. For instance, his work on medieval and modern history is almost exclusively confined to European and American developments, reflecting the notion that Arab lands had not yet passed through the gates of modernity. The text begins with the fall of the Western Roman Empire and ushers students through the rise of the Anglo-Saxons, the "age of discovery," the colonization of the Americas, the Napoleonic wars, and the Industrial Revolution. It concludes by addressing the student directly and highlighting the political implications of material progress:

> I think that after reading this lesson, you are very distressed about your country and your nation and say to yourself, "All the inventions are in Europe and America, and the wondrous industries are in Europe and America; everything we use in terms of clothing, pots, bedding, kerosene stoves, cars, iron railways, airplanes, lamps, pens and paper, and other things, all of it is produced in the factories of Europe and enormous America by means of modern machines powered by steam and electricity."[57]

Modernity here functions both as a characteristic that differentiates Euro-American nations from Arab lands and an advantage that facilitates colonial domination of the former over the latter. However, this need not be the case forever, and Darwaza charges his readers to use their despair as a source of inspiration in their struggle to transform the homeland through hard work and innovation. By adopting the tools of European progress, Darwaza promises that "then your country will advance and you will exchange your sadness for joy," adding that such transformations were deeply rooted in tradition itself. "Indeed, your ancient forefathers already fought hard [*ijtahada*] and were therefore successful."[58] It is noteworthy that the verb *ijtahada* means both "to struggle to overcome something" and, within the realm of Islamic jurisprudence, "to offer an independent legal ruling." The term acquired significant symbolic weight at the turn of the twentieth century because of its revival by Sunni modernists, who believed the practice of *ijtihād* could facilitate a broad range of social and political changes within Islamic societies. Darwaza was no doubt capitalizing on this dual meaning when he urged his young readers to embrace the tools of European progress and use them to restore the Arab nation to its former grandeur—an act for which, as he implies, there existed the most prestigious of precedents.

The curriculum for al-Najāḥ shared much common ground with that used in government schools, beginning with the privileged place given to the Arabic language. The first four classes devoted an overwhelming number of their total hours of instruction to the study of Arabic, as the table below demonstrates.

Elementary classes used two primary texts for Arabic-language instruction, both of which are significant in terms of tracing the disassociation of Arabic from an Islamic framework. The first was an Arabic primer, *al-Jadīd fi qirā'a al-'Arabiya* (The new [way] for reading Arabic), by Khalil al-Sakakini, a Palestinian Christian intellectual and educator. The second text, *Qusūs atfāl* (Children's stories), by Kamil Kilani, adapted popular stories like "Hayy Ibn Yaqzan" (The life of Ibn Yaqzan) and portions of *1001 Nights* into simple—though not colloquial—language. The choice of these texts gestures at an understanding of Arabic that was relatively novel: that is, its study existed independently from (and was given greater weight than) the study of the Qur'an. That a school that touted its Islamic credentials could so easily adopt an Arabic textbook by one of Palestine's foremost Christian intellectuals testifies not only to al-Sakakini's influence or al-Najāḥ's progressive tendencies but to a larger shift wherein the

Distribution of subjects for elementary classes

Subject	*First class*	*Second class*	*Third class*	*Fourth class*
Qur'an and Islamic religious instruction	4	6	6	6
Arabic	16	13	10	8
English	—	—	6	7
Arithmetic	5	5	5	5
History	—	2	2	2
Geography	—	2	1	2
General instruction*	4	—	—	—
Object lessons	—	2	2	2
Drawing	1	1	1	1
Physical education	3	2	1	1
Weekly total	33	33	34	34

Source: *Barnamaj al-Najāḥ al-wataniya Nablusi*, 8.

* *Al-mu'alūmāt al-'āma* was given only in the first class and consisted of leading the students in observation of plants and animals, general instruction about health and hygiene, and "geographical and historical stories."

study of Arabic had become disassociated from the study of Islam—a position that would have been untenable a few decades earlier. Similarly, the adoption of reading primers like those created by Kamil Kilani reflected an effort to identify an Arabic literary heritage that was not overtly Islamic in tone but could be regarded as shared national property.

The production of such primers constituted a key step in a transformation away from verbal expression (both in terms of telling stories from memory and hearing them recited) toward a social order that tried to cultivate "a habit for rapid silent reading."[59] The popularity of primers also testifies to the spread of modern pedagogic ideas about the distinctiveness of childhood and the need to create curricular materials that catered to the child's immature sensibilities. On both counts, the *kuttāb* was woefully inadequate. Similar trends also swept through Zionist schools of the period, suggesting a point of pedagogic overlap in what were otherwise separate school systems. In a similar vein, much of al-Najāḥ's curriculum for Islamic religious education mirrored that used within the government's Arab Public System, with religious instruction divided into two components (at least in elementary classes): a schedule for reading and memorizing the Qur'an and instruction in matters of ritual and moral guidance. This is yet another example of how distinct educational networks were linked by certain administrative and pedagogic practices, even while their leaders accused one another of various educational and political misdeeds.

Al-Najāḥ School also adopted standardized textbooks for Islamic religious instruction, the appearance of which represented a significant development in the history of modern Islamic education. If we recall Muhammad 'Abduh's letter to the sheikh al-Islam, we can appreciate the importance of such texts in a modernist program geared toward a rationalized, univocal form of Islam. Educators published a number of such texts in the first half of the twentieth century, not only in Palestine but also in Iraq, Egypt, and Transjordan. Many were written by scholars associated with al-Azhar, some of whom were also employees of education ministries in surrounding Arab countries. For instance, al-Najāḥ relied on a series of books, *Ṣafwat durūs al-dīn wa al-akhlāq* (Primary lessons in religion and morals), prepared by Mustafa 'Inani and 'Aṭiyah al-Ashqar for use in Egyptian elementary schools.[60] As the preface states, in 1932 the Ministry of Public Education "saw fit to enlighten the teaching of religion in its schools," and thus the Egyptian government launched a textbook competition to solicit new publications. 'Inani and al-Ashqar's book emerged victorious and became the official text for elementary religious education in Egypt.

'Aṭiyah al-Ashqar was a former public education inspector, while 'Inani was a senior inspector for the Arabic sciences at al-Azhar. The latter figure also authored a textbook for use in secondary schools, *Kitāb al-dīn al-Islāmī* (Book of the Islamic religion), along with Hassan Mansur and 'Abd al-Wahab Khayr al-Din, both of whom were affiliated with Dar al-'Ulūm in Cairo (today Kuliya Dar al-'Ulum). The college was established in 1872 to teach both Islamic and modern sciences, chiefly to al-Azhar graduates. After the British occupation of Egypt, the college became the de facto center for training public school teachers. Its future graduates would include the activists Hassan al-Banna and Sayyid Qutb, both of whom began their careers as educators. A similar series of texts, *Mabāda fi al-dīn al-Islāmī* (Principles of the Islamic religion), was published in Palestine in 1947, written by 'Abd al-Hamid al-Sā'ih, Ibrahim Mahmud Sanwir, Ahmed al-Khalifa, and 'Ali Hasn 'Auda. All four men were active participants in interwar political and educational programs, boasting affiliations with al-Azhar (al-Sā'ih and 'Auda), the SMC (al-Sā'ih), Dar al-'Ulum and the Government Arab College in Jerusalem ('Auda), and the Jordanian government, in which Sanwir held a number of official posts following 1948.

Principles of the Islamic Religion is a six-part series created for use in primary and lower secondary classes. The first volume notes prominently on its cover that it was designed "in accordance with the Department of Education's latest curriculum," while the second part proudly announces that "the Department of Education in Palestine and the Ministry of Education in the Hashemite Kingdom of Jordan have decided to teach this book." Such pronouncements mirror that which appeared on the cover of *Ṣafwat durūs al-dīn wa al-akhlāq*: "The Ministry of Public Education (Egypt) has chosen to use this book in its schools." Given the British colonial presence that existed in all three countries, it is not surprising to find a great deal of commonality in the structure and content of the textbooks, which may point to further curricular overlap between the Arab Public System in Palestine and national schools like al-Najāḥ, which often adopted textbooks published in Egypt. At the very least, it suggests that the nature of education in these two school systems was not necessarily as different as their leaders liked to imagine. Perhaps most important, these textbooks shared certain common features stemming from the legacy of Islamic modernist thought. These included a concern for authentic scriptural meaning, an emphasis on individual moral development, the privileging of ritualistic elements of Islam (*'ibādāt*) over socioethical ones (*mu'āmalāt*), and an accentuation of the social utility of religious practices.[61]

It is useful to recall here the widespread disdain for teaching the Qur'an by rote memorization, a method that supposedly prevented the true meaning of the text from being effectively imparted. As Gregory Starrett has argued regarding approaches to religious education in nineteenth-century England, the text of scripture was of secondary importance to the moral lessons it was supposed to impart, "and in any case the text had to be understood in order to be useful."[62] Whereas premodern modes of learning the Qur'an can be understood as a form of embodiment in which "students embody, or possess the words of God within their very beings,"[63] modernists stressed the need to convey the authentic meaning of passages to children so that they would understand their ethical content. As discussed previously, the Arab Public System in Palestine maintained the practice of memorizing the Qur'an, though it did so in a reformed fashion that stressed comprehension by instructing teachers to clarify the meaning of difficult terms.[64] Looking at *Ṣafwat durūs al-dīn wa al-akhlāq*, we see this heightened concern with "proper" comprehension reflected in the very structure of the book. Each section begins with a vocabulary table of uncommon terms, followed by a passage from the Qur'an within which the new words appear, and concludes with an explanation of the verses' meaning and significance. The authors use the same structure for introducing the student to hadith, resulting in a form of authorial didacticism in which the student (and the teacher) is guided down the narrow path of true meaning. A similar attempt to impart uniformity is evident in those portions of the texts related to ritual practices (*'ibādāt*). Precise instructions regarding the ablutions to make before prayer are followed by directions regarding the proper times for prayer and the postures to assume.

Designed to combat what reformers viewed as the corruption of Islam in their midst, religious textbooks of this type necessarily shied away from a multiplicity of interpretations in favor of a singular narrative that, as in the case of these examples, received the sanction of the state. This is not to claim that students in *katātīb* were not traditionally subject to a singular version of Islam—they were, that offered by the teacher. Yet this was offset by the varied customs of families, villages, and communities, expressions of Islam that existed in everyday life rather than in codified texts. At the very least, the lack of administrative or curricular uniformity prior to the absorption of *katātīb* into a system of state-funded schools made it more difficult to dictate which opinions and practices were genuinely Islamic.

As those elements of Islam concerned with ritual practice, *'ibādāt* occupy a central role in many of these texts, one that often overshadows attention given to *muʿāmalāt*. Teachings regarding the latter are conspicuously absent from *Principles of the Islamic Religion*, whose volumes devote substantial attention to laws related to prayer, fasting, pilgrimage, and charity alongside lessons on hadith, the divine attributes (*tawḥīd*), etiquette (*tahdhīb*), and the biography of Muhammad. Read as an attempt to articulate the modern contents of "the Islamic religion," the text does so in a way that is remarkably restrictive from a classical perspective. In juridical terms, *muʿāmalāt* may regulate everything from how a commercial transaction is carried out to what goods one produces for sale. As these instances suggest, the defining characteristic of *muʿāmalāt* is their social nature—indeed, the term is a derivation of the verb "to treat (someone)." It is telling that, in lieu of a legalistic treatment of commerce or social relations, the textbook raises commercial issues in a moralistic manner. Thus, the student is told to imitate Muhammad, cast here as a budding capitalist: "The Prophet would guard his profits [literally, booty] and trade, for he was active and a lover of work."[65]

A final significant feature of these texts was their tendency to proffer explanations of Islamic religious obligations that highlighted their social utility. This could range from the pragmatic—ablutions were essential because "the clean pupil is loved by God and the people"—to the ethical.[66] For instance, according to *Principles of the Islamic Religion*, the fast of Ramadan is undertaken to teach children the pangs of hunger so they will understand the imperative of giving to the needy.[67] While this humanitarian rationale may strike us as a modern interpretation, it is also found within a number of classical sources, particularly from Shia scholars.[68] What is unique is not the explanation itself but the privileging of it over others that might stress, for instance, the fragility of human life before God the creator. Similarly, the Hajj is described as an opportunity to meet Muslims from other countries and establish communal ties with them, stressing the practical benefits that stem from completing one's obligation over those that regard it as commemorating the resanctification of Mecca.[69]

Taken as a whole, these texts offer us an opportunity to see reformist Islam positioning itself not merely as an intellectual stance but as a form of pedagogy well suited to deployment by the modern state. Although some of the features analyzed here may seem merely shifts in method—such as the impulse to standardize the teaching of the Qur'an—efforts to articulate a version of "authentic" Islam and propagate it through state channels generated consequences whose impact reached far beyond the schoolhouse. When we consider that the project of mass public education is political at its core, that the link between individual behavior and civic duty is presupposed in the formation of modern school systems, the leap from pedagogy to politics appears little more than a small hop. Moreover, the political implications of this development are clearly visible in the later emergence of groups that attempt to regulate "un-Islamic" behavior and states like Saudi Arabia that propagate their own version of true Islam in regard to public education and international missionary work.[70] Though a complete analysis of the link between these texts and more recent forms of Islamic education is beyond the present scope, there is much to suggest the relevance of these early efforts to render Islam both knowable and useful to efforts by contemporary states to propagate their own official brands of Islam.

A FORK IN THE STRAIGHT PATH: DIVERGENT VIEWS OF ISLAM AND POLITICAL ACTION

From the emphasis on moral fashioning to the association of Islam with ritual action rather than *muʿāmalāt*, much of what has been described thus far is harmonious with ideas about religious education that were popular in British colonial circles. A closer look at al-Najāḥ's program of study points toward the limits of this concord and helps explain why Palestinian nationalists derided the same government school system that they also imitated in key ways. In what follows, I suggest that the crucial element of dissonance stemmed not from divergent definitions of Islam but from differing conceptions of its role in the life of the Arab nation as a political body. Here we also see that the "Protestant" view of Islam as a defined set of beliefs and rituals could actually facilitate the national project rather than restrain it.

There is perhaps no better example of this than ʿIzzat Darwaza himself, who was both an author of interpretive works on Islam and the cofounder of a political party that consciously tried to transcend the sectarian lines that threatened to divide Palestinian society. Together with leaders like Hamdi al-Husayni, Darwaza was the leading force in a movement that "tied communal-religious organization to imperialism, but nationalism to true independence."[71] Moreover, there is no sense that he found his commitment to the revitalization of Islam at odds with his belief in cross-communal Arab unity. Rather, his writings reflect a unique conceptualization of the relationship between Arab identity and Islam that accepted key tenets of secular modernity while rejecting the notion of religion confined to the private space.

At the center of Darwaza's thought was an assertion that the Arab nation and Islam existed in a mutually reinforcing relationship wherein the fortunes of one directly impacted the position of the other; neither could flourish in the modern period alone. "Arabness grew stronger through the strength of Islam, and Islam grew stronger through the strength of Arabness." As he states in his memoirs, it was his belief in an essential Arab-Islamic symbiosis that won the support of al-Najāḥ's school committee, which was initially divided regarding his appointment: "I synthesized social, historical, national and Islamic discussions for the students, and this was most likely what caused them to decide to include me in the body of founders and offer me the task of directing the school."[72] Darwaza's textbooks represented an attempt to translate this intellectual posture into terms accessible to students learning about the Arab and Islamic past. Consider the following passage from Darwaza's text, *Studies in Arab History from Ancient Times until the Present*, which was used in the upper elementary classes at al-Najāḥ:

> The *hijrah* ranks among the greatest events in the history of the Prophet and Islam. It shows us that the Prophet and his companions abandoned their nation, relatives, and possessions, and risked their lives in pursuit of the call of Islam. This was the beginning of the greatness of Islam and the Arabs. Afterward, Islam grew stronger to a large extent, and because of that the Arabs acquired great strength and glory. Therefore, among the obligations of Muslims and Arabs is to respect the history of the *hijrah*, to celebrate the first year of the *hijrah*, and to follow the example of the Prophet and his noble companions in their sacrifice and resolve.[73]

As is evident in this passage, which is taken from the text's biography of Muhammad, Darwaza did not believe that the essential connection between Arabness and Islam created an exclusionary framework. On the contrary, commemorating the Prophet's *hijrah* to Medina is recast here as an obligation on Arabs as a national body. Because the greatness of the Arab nation is organically linked to the advance of Islam, customs that were religious in nature could be transformed into national obligations with little conceptual difficulty. Reinforcing the point, Darwaza concluded his biography of Muhammad with the following hadith: "If the Arabs are degraded, Islam is degraded" (*idha dhalat al-'Arab dhal al-Islām*).[74]

Perhaps most remarkably, this essential connection between Islam and the Arab nation is actually what facilitates communal action across sectarian lines:

because, Darwaza suggests, Islam guarantees freedom of religion and does not command individuals to abandon their own customs, it can act as both a pillar of Arab national heritage and a preserver of religious difference. This is implied in a number of passages dealing with the spread of Islam. For instance, when Muhammad and his followers arrived in Medina, he concluded a pact with the Jews living there to respect their freedom of religion, "because the Islamic religion does not command by force that one should leave his religion." This approach was said to offer a stark contrast with the Byzantine rulers of Greater Syria who oppressed the people "regardless of their sect" by imposing high taxes and "interfering in their religious freedom [*huriyatuhum al-dīniya*]." It was for this reason that Arab armies were welcomed into Jerusalem as liberators, bearing a letter that guaranteed the inhabitants of Palestine both religious freedom and the protection of property.[75] With this historical understanding as a backdrop, it becomes clearer how al-Najāḥ could boast of being an Islamic institution that opened its doors to non-Muslim students. Indeed, its curricular materials and mission statement speak to this outlook, professing that the school was located "in an Arab, Islamic country and that the eye of the pupil shall not encounter [in the school] anything other than what strengthens his Arab and Islamic affinities." At the same time, "the school opens its doors also to non-Muslim students" who "have lived with their Muslim brothers a life of affection and complete serenity in what promises to thwart the sectarian tendency implanted by [past] generations."[76]

Finally, we consider one additional textbook, *Kitāb al-dīn al-islāmī* (A textbook for the Islamic religion), which al-Najāḥ School used for religious instruction in its secondary classes.[77] The book was coauthored by Mustafa 'Inani along with 'Abd al-Wahab Khayr al-Din and Hassan Mansur, both of Dar al-'Ulum. In contrast to earlier grades—which mimicked the government's division of Islam into the Qur'an and ritual practice—al-Najāḥ's secondary classes did away with this bifurcated approach and focused exclusively on "The Islamic Religion" (*al-diyāna al-Islāmiya*), with subject matter increasingly geared toward the social and political dimensions of Islam. Thus, students in upper secondary classes were to study the "wisdom of instituting *'ibādāt* and *mu'ālamāt*" and attend lectures on Islamic social theory as well as "religious and social topics that have a direct relationship to the contemporary life of Muslims."[78] In lieu of moral exhortations or detailed descriptions of proper ritual practice, the text delves into realms that secular modernity would deem outside the scope of religious matters altogether: governance, intellectual freedom, the natural sciences, and commercial activity.

Let us look, for example, at the chapters dealing with the scientific achievements pioneered during the "golden age" of Islam. This material occurs within the context of Islamic religious instruction, which is fitting given the text's emphasis on the singularity of Islam's support for scientific inquiry. Indeed, the rational sciences appear as part of a continuum that includes jurisprudence and other religious studies, suggesting something similar to the classical view of *'ilm* as an all-encompassing category. The reason is, the student is told, that "the Islamic religion came to break the shackles of the mind."[79] Channeling the legacy of Jamal al-Din al-Afghani, the text quotes Herbert Spencer's famous statement about the incompatibility of knowledge and religion only to argue for Islam's exceptional nature.[80] The text then transitions to discuss "the service of Muslims to science," surveying a predictable assortment of scholars, the great libraries of the 'Abbasid Empire, and the madrasas founded by Nizam al-Mulk.

This was not meant as a mere historical lesson but—sprinkled with a carefully curated assemblage of Qur'anic verses and hadiths—as an attempt to establish scientific inquiry and the pursuit of material progress as one of the Muslim's essential duties to God. Thus, the text relates to students that the sciences serve as both a way to know God and "to overcome the hardships of this world," adding that "the Islamic religion prescribes learning the sciences regardless of their type or end goal."[81] Not surprisingly, the first verses students encountered were taken from Sura al-A'rāf:

> O, Children of Abraham
> Wear your beautiful apparel
> At every time and place of prayer
> Eat and drink, but waste not by excess,
> For Allah loves not those who waste
> Say: Who has forbidden the gifts of Allah,
> Which He has produced for his servants,
> And the things, clean and pure,
> (Which He has provided) for sustenance?
> Say: They are in the life of this world for those who believe
> And (purely) for them on the Day of Judgment.[82]

Lest the point be lost, the text includes yet another set of verses (Sura al-Baqara, 21–22), with an explanation that God calls believers to two types of works: *'ibādāt*, such as prayer and fasting; and "worldly works, to be useful in their worldly lives—which are a means to their final lives—such as the useful sciences, commerce and industry, and others."[83] Material goods and the scientific knowledge required to produce them are not simply acceptable within this framework but part and parcel of the duties imposed by God himself.

Just as science and industry lie within the realm of religious concerns, so too do matters dealing with governance. Here we find the clearest challenge to the colonial epistemic order and the equation of religious values with inner faith. Following a discussion about modes of juridical reasoning and different Islamic legal schools, the text turns to the topic of *shura* (consultation). "Allah made *shura* the basis of governance in Islam and commanded his Prophet (the blessing of God be upon him), saying, 'And consult them in the matter.' And he clarified what Muslims must do in their government, saying, 'And command them to consult among themselves.' "[84] However, as the text claims, the corruption of later rulers led to the decline and eventual disappearance of *shura* as a religious duty, so much so that people began to think that Islam demanded a form of authority that was individual and despotic. Enticing students to look at this past not merely as history but as sacred duty, the section concludes with the following directive: "Look at the most advanced states in the current era and [see] their strength is found in their laws being based on consultation [*shura*], and that the will of their people is respected. This is the secret of their greatness, happiness, and progress."[85]

The political implications are not difficult to deduce, particularly in the context of British rule; nor is the intertwining of religious obligations with worldly concerns hard to discern. Rather, this review of curricular materials points toward the flexibility of Islamic symbols and discourses to assume a functional role in modern political thought. On the one hand, we could view this emphasis on social and political utility as an instance of secularization or even civil religion, whereby religious terms and customs morph into the basis of practices geared toward communal solidarity and welfare. On the other hand, the latter concerns were historically included within the umbrella of Islam itself, and indeed, these lessons appear within texts devoted to religious instruction. In this sense, rather than represent a transition away from religion and toward the secular, the text asserts that Islam seamlessly encompasses elements of both domains. Examples like this suggest what Jonathan Sheehan has called "a different vision of secularization," one that "focuses less on the disappearance of religion than on its transformation and reconstruction."[86]

However partial in nature, the comparison offered in this chapter between the Arab Public System and al-Najāḥ National School has revealed that there was a great deal of conceptual overlap between the two, particularly at the primary level. However, as I have suggested, this similarity yielded to points of difference when articulating the broader role of Islam within an Arab national project. In particular, I have suggested that the encouragement of religious instruction within Palestine's public schools must be conceptualized within a broader imperial paradigm that linked religion to the preservation of traditional native society. Chiefly concerned with matters of ritual and individual moral conduct, this mode of religiosity was presumed to offer an effective counterweight to nationalist passions. It is worth reiterating that the key issue is not whether Islamic education was historically disconnected from political life. Rather, we are elucidating a historically contingent relationship between religion, education, and mass politics that became possible only within the context of modernity.

Yet, as I have argued, at the precise moment when British officials were encouraging religious education as a stabilizing practice, Arab educators were reimagining the relationship between Islam and modern nationalism in a way that rendered religious education a key component of political activism. Despite points of overlap with colonial views of Islam as conceptually bounded and chiefly concerned with individual moral development, al-Najāḥ and its leaders contested the notion that religious education was therefore unconcerned with—or far less, corrupted by—political activism. Certainly 'Izzat Darwaza would have agreed with Jerome Farrell about the existence of a common Christian-Muslim morality but not with his view of true religion as distinct from mass politics. Rather, as administrators at al-Najāḥ emphasized, this commonality was what enabled Arab brothers from across confessions to transcend the sectarian past while striving for a new national future. In fact, the juridical and conceptual restriction of "the Islamic religion" created a discursive space for imagining a cross-communal Arab identity and mutually constitutive Arab-Islamic social order. It is here that we see British officials and Arab educators like ships passing in the night: one claiming religious education as the key to maintaining the traditional order; the other claiming it as an essential part of a revolutionary future.

6 BORDER CLASHES

The continuity of tradition does not mean preserving the past in the same form to this day. That type of continuity spells stagnation. True continuity is selective.

—Mordechai Segal, *Oraḥot ha-ḥinuch*

IN THE LATE SPRING OF 1928, the Committee to Clarify the Question of Religious Education met to discuss which steps, if any, could be taken to strengthen "the religious feeling" (*ha-regesh ha-dati*) in Zionist schools. Composed of some of the *yishuv*'s leading educational figures, the committee revealed through its deliberations just how difficult such a task would be, not least because members brought with them divergent notions of all the key concepts involved: religion, Judaism, tradition, ethics, secularism, community, commandments, ritual, and so on. For instance, the chief rabbi of Jaffa–Tel Aviv, Shelomo Aronsohn, linked the fact that Labor and General Zionist schools did not compel children to perform active or "practical" commandments (*mitzvot ma'asiot*) to a dangerous decline of religion in general.[1] Yet others argued that the decline of traditional observance neither lessened the religious spirit of the *yishuv* nor signaled the victory of secularism, for, in the words of Yitzhak Alterman, "as long as we don't relinquish the sacred writings [*kitvei ha-kodesh*] in schools, we are unable to speak about the [Zionist] secular school in the European sense of the word [secular]."[2]

I begin with this anecdote to highlight the extent to which the content and function of religion, or *dat* in modern Hebrew, was a subject of active contestation among Zionist educators rather than a question of minimal concern that mysteriously returned later in the century. Surveying the widely disputed terrain of Zionist historiography—in which nearly every foundational claim about the movement has been subject to debate, revision, or outright dismissal—the association of Zionism with secularism remains largely intact, as does the related claim that Zionist schools were clearly divided into "religious" and "secular" camps.[3] We find it pop up as self-evident in the reports of journalists and government committees, the writings of scholars, and popular depictions of *kibbutzniks* abandoning ritual observance for the tilling of fields. To be clear, I am not ignoring the large body of scholarly work on religious Zionism but questioning whether "secular" is a useful label for a movement constituted by men and women who were often deeply engaged with the sources of Jewish tradition. As Gideon Shimoni has argued,

> In respect to their Jewish identity profile, they [members of the Second Aliyah] were a remarkably homogeneous group. Most had emerged out of a traditionalist religious background but had abandoned it in their youth. For them and thereafter for successive generations of pioneering youth movement and the He-halutz organization, the adoption of the pioneering ethos of Zionism meant transformation of one's life through the act of ascent to Eretz Israel and dedication to a life of pioneering labor. It also meant the creation of a new social order and a new type of Jew, usually designated by the term *ivri* (Hebrew). In many respects this ethos served as a functional equivalent for traditional religion.[4]

Though there was much that distinguished the new kibbutz school, for instance, from the *ḥeder* of old, I suggest that the idea of a binary between religious and secular orientations obscures more than it reveals. As a term whose common usage variously suggests the separation of life into private-spiritual and public-material realms, a rejection of the truths of revealed religion, or the reorganization of human life on the basis of reason alone, "secular" is neither an accurate nor helpful adjective with which to describe Zionist educational practices. Despite their substantial points of internal discord, Zionist schools of different ideological persuasions were largely united by their conviction that sacred texts could be repurposed and related to as the wellsprings of Jewish national identity, even as thinkers posited radically different views about what this entailed. What was established as foundational was not to believe but to engage—to read the holy texts, to struggle with their major figures, and to argue with a God who may or may not exist.

In short, Zionism did not merely replicate the structure of secularism as it developed within Christian contexts. Rather, Zionist thinkers and educators expended a great deal of creative energy on articulating a new and synthetic form of Jewish identity that would bridge the material and the spiritual, the communal and the political, the religious and the secular. Looking at Zionist educational practices, we find that the engagement with and selective appropriation of *kitvei ha-kodesh* served as a privileged tool for imagining the national self—not the splitting of religion from politics but the reworking of the former for the sake of the latter. In examining this history, I hope to contribute to the growing body of scholarship that revisits the relationship between Judaism and Zionism and considers how secularism has historically unfolded beyond the European context.[5]

However, these Zionist attempts to articulate a synthetic Jewish identity were at direct odds with the British colonial impulse to separate religion from the messy business of nationalist politics. As I have shown, the Department of Education attempted to maintain and even expand the role of religious education in both Jewish and Arab schools, propelled largely by the belief in religious instruction—if done properly—as a tool for inculcating universal moral ideals that would mitigate nationalist fervor. On the whole, British officials did not consider that religious education could serve more radical purposes—and not because they were especially dense or oblivious to what now seems obvious. As I have suggested, our task is to excavate the conceptual frames in which the association of religion with tradition and "universal" values appeared natural.

Within this epistemic context, any revolutionary use of religious education violated the boundary meant to distinguish true religion from its corrupted forms. As in instances of Muslim "fanaticism," if Judaism meddled in the work of mass politics, it did so at the expense of its religious nature; indeed, it became something else entirely. There was arguably no greater offender of this educational model than the one being developed under Zionist auspices. In the view of Jerome Farrell, who served as the director of education for the second half of the Mandate period, the religious education given within the Mizraḥi system was "formal and dead, a matter of ritual and obsolete tabus." The General schools hardly fared any better in his estimation, as "the majority [of teachers] seem to have replaced religion by racialism." But worst of all was the situation within Labor schools, which were "in general secularizing and many are actively *anti-religious*."[6]

With these conceptual battles in mind, this chapter details how competing visions of religious education (and Judaism itself) served as a dynamic source of tension throughout the Mandate period. The Zionist view of education, religion, and politics as deeply intertwined practices produced increasing animosity between Jewish educators and the Government of Palestine as the years passed, though the government had little recourse to impose its will on Zionist schools because of, ironically, the nature of its own sectarian politics. Thus, the Zionist example offers a stark contrast both to the government's administrative control of the Arab Public System and to the "Protestant" approach to Islamic religious education it tried to develop therein. Here, too, we find the Mandatory government woefully at odds with its subjects regarding what a religious education was meant to do.

THE COMMITTEE AND ITS WORK

We begin this analysis by examining the deliberations of the Committee to Clarify the Question of Religious Education. The Zionist Board of Education formed the committee in March 1928 at the request of Rabbi Shelomo Aronsohn. In a presentation to the board about the need for such a committee, he argued that the new nationalist education, unmoored from its religious foundation, risked creating a generation of Jews unrecognizable to the greater body of Israel. Aronsohn claimed that education in the diaspora could never hope to be holistic, due to the "foreign homeland [and] the different languages that are unsuitable for a complete national education," yet the return to Zion had not capitalized on its potential to unite the different parts of the Jewish body and soul. The result was that in the homeland, ironically, "we lack in education what was always with us," the religious commandments and customs that had sustained Jews for hundreds of years. Not only were schools failing to acclimate children to perform ritual commandments, but the creep of biblical criticism threatened to definitively divide Zionists from the Jewish masses. "An education like this is against nature, against history." This was not merely a matter of ideology, however, as Rabbi Aronsohn argued that it was precisely this gap between diasporic Judaism and the new Hebrew education that left the former unwilling to support the latter, and this at a time when the *yishuv* remained overwhelmingly dependent on funding from abroad. If the present situation were remedied, his logic followed, "the whole nation will come to the aid of education, to its reform, and to its protection."[7]

Indeed, the association of Zionism with secularism was actually something of a liability during the Mandate period as the *yishuv* faced off with Jewish leaders abroad who were dissatisfied with the supposedly antireligious character of Zionist schools. It was one thing for the ideologues of the Second Aliyah to articulate radical positions and call for the "negation" of the diaspora, Judaism included; it was quite another to absorb and educate tens of thousands of children from families of varied background and religious persuasions. Composed in larger part of families and, after 1933, Jews fleeing Nazi persecution, the immigrants who came to Palestine during the Mandate period often expected that their children would receive some semblance of a traditional religious education. Most in fact preferred the schools maintained by the centrist General Zionists, which accounted for half of the total enrollment of the Hebrew Public System. The other 50 percent of students were divided between Religious Zionist and Labor schools.

Until 1932, Zionist Schools were technically under the supervision of the Jewish Agency, which itself was composed of Jews living in both the diaspora and Palestine, many of whom were dismayed by the drift of Zionist schools away from *halachic* observance. For instance, in 1929, a member of the British Board of Deputies introduced a resolution stating, "That in the opinion of this Board, representatives of the Anglo-Jewish Community on the Jewish Agency should support the upkeep of such educational institutions only as are conducted in a manner which is not contrary to the teachings and practices of traditional Judaism."[8] Commenting on the resolution and the accusation of religious animus that stood behind it, Dr. Isaac Berkson, who would later head the Department of Education of the Va'ad Leumi, argued that this perception was far from accurate. His statement, which directly touches on the conceptual confusion surrounding terms like "religion" and "tradition," is worth quoting at length:

> So many different things are meant by religion and tradition. I have no hesitancy in saying that certainly as far as the General Schools are concerned they are in harmony with the Jewish tradition. Question may be raised with reference to the schools of the Labour Federation. . . . Even in these schools the teaching is "not directed against traditional Judaism," but the life in the communities where these schools are situated, the Kvutzoth and the Workers' Settlements, is often not in harmony with Jewish tradition. As is well known the rules of "kashruth" are not observed. Naturally enough the life of the children both in and outside of the school partakes of the same character as the rest of the life of the community. In these schools caps are not worn when the Bible is taught, but undoubtedly there is a deep respect toward the Bible. If the social idealism of these groups is to be taken into consideration, much may be said for the idea that their teaching is in harmony with the Torah, but they emphasize the moral rather than the theological or ceremonial aspects of Judaism, naturally as they conceive the moral aims of Judaism, in the light of modern social movement.[9]

It was within this context of general contestation over the nature of the Jewish tradition that the committee was convened. Along with Rabbi Aronsohn, its members included Hadassah founder Henrietta Szold; Eliezer Meir Lipshitz, the founder and head of the Mizraḥi Teachers' Seminary; Shoshana Parsitz, an activist and educator who held various official positions within the Zionist administration; Yosef Mohliver, a prominent educator and principal of the Hebrew Gymnasium in Jerusalem; and Aharon Michal Barchihu, a well-regarded teacher, principal of the Betzalel School, and representative to the Zionist Congress, in addition to high-ranking members of the education inspectorate. Several areas of discussion arose during the course of the committee's three meetings, touching on issues as minute as whether teachers should cover their heads while teaching the Hebrew Bible to those as grandiose as the distinction between religiosity and piety (*datiut* and *adikut*). The committee's meetings were productive in the sense that its members agreed on certain recommendations regarding the approach to religious texts and the general cultivation of "religious feeling"—none of which were, however, ultimately accepted by the Board of Education. But for our purposes the committee's deliberations have importance beyond whether or not their decisions were implemented on an official level. On the one hand, they illustrate just how porous and contested remained the boundaries among a whole set of foundational concepts: nation, religion, religiosity, God fearing, tradition, ethics, secular, and so on. On the other hand, what emerged from these deliberations was a realization that a return to traditional education was insufficient to capitalize on the revolutionary potential of religious texts and practices; rather, the future vitality of the national project—understood by almost all as organically linked to religion, however defined—hinged on cultivating a new and dynamic religious sensibility among the next generation. Here too, it was the new that would make the old meaningful once more.

One of the central questions that framed these deliberations was whether the Zionist school could serve as a vehicle for creating a new form of Jewish subject or, conversely, would inevitably reflect its surrounding environment. Holding the latter opinion, one member of the Board of Education, Joseph Azaryahu (a prominent educator who also served as the head inspector for General Zionist schools), cast doubt on the usefulness of convening such a committee in the first place. Responding to Rabbi Aronsohn's account of the neglect of religious education, Azaryahu qualified that

> the question is how to repair the thing [the deficiency of religious education] and whether it is in our hands to do so. To our regret, I must say that it is not in

> our power to rectify it, to turn the wheels of history backward. A single generation ago our lives were different than they are now, this is a fact whether we want to admit it or not. In order to educate children with a religious spirit, the teachers must be religious in their spirits and souls. Teachers like this are indeed few in number. And if the non-religious teacher comes to teach religion, the prayer will be bland and meaningless [*tiflah*]. The home, the parents' house, is for the most part free-thinking [*ḥofshim*—sometimes rendered as "secular," meaning unrestrained by the dictates of *halacha*], and could it be that the school will greatly influence a child from a free-thinking home?[10]

On one side then, we have the assertion that the march of time has largely obviated traditional forms of Jewish observance and that the "wheel of history"—fashioned here out of purely linear materials—will inevitably spell the future decline of religion. What I find fascinating is not only that such predictions never materialized—and that modernity is fully capable of generating new forms of religious practice rather than undermining them is readily apparent—but that there were others within the *yishuv* who viewed the power of schools quite differently.

Responding to Azaryahu, Rabbi Aronsohn retorted, "Mr. Azaryahu asks whether it is possible to fight against [the conditions of] life. The people of Israel have witnessed much greater feats of strength. The essence of Zionism is overcoming reality, an aspiration that is against nature, what with the resurrection of the language and so on." Was not the entire Zionist project an attempt to turn the wheel of history in another direction? To force through human effort that which was not possible through the meanderings of natural processes alone? We should note that these declarations about human agency and the course of history do not come to us from the usual camps; rather, it is the representative of Orthodox Judaism who makes this challenge to his secular colleague. Further complicating the mix, Rabbi Aronsohn found support for his position in Yitzhak Alterman (father of the famous Hebrew poet Natan Alterman), an education inspector for the General trend who would later manage the Department of Education for the municipality of Tel Aviv. "I do not agree with Mr. Azaryahu's opinion that it is impossible to fight against life," he said. "It is possible to turn the wheel of history backwards and we are compelled to do so." For Alterman, Rabbi Aronsohn's highly pragmatic recommendations—to increase the number of hours devoted to the study of Mishna, for example—were in fact quite inadequate and represented only a superficial solution to the problem at hand, which was no less pressing than the regeneration of spiritual life in the *yishuv* as a whole. "Here I will be more religious than Rabbi Aronsohn," Alterman stated, in describing his desire to think about the question of religion "in the fullness of its scope."[11]

A few months later, Alterman was able to expand on these concerns in a special presentation before the committee's members: "It's possible we stand at the beginning of a period that will formulate a new relationship to this question [of religious education]." The challenge before them was thus both vexing—undoubtedly divisive and bearing the traces of past theological and political splits—and exciting, as the material reality of Jewish life in Palestine rendered new forms of physical, national, and spiritual union possible. How educators chose to respond to this challenge would "change the face of the generation" to come, reflecting the extraordinary power that Alterman assigned to education as a *formative* process. The presentation itself consisted of a series of propositions, beginning with the assumption that there was no environment, even in the most secular milieu, in which the child would not have to confront the question of religion. Because it was unavoidable in this sense, it was incumbent on educators to develop the means for cultivating a positive and innovative approach to it. One of the chief means of doing so was through the study of *kitvei ha-kodesh*, meaning the Hebrew Bible, Mishna, Talmud, and various rabbinic commentaries:

> I think that even those who oppose a religious foundation for the school do not agree that we should relinquish the sacred writings in their capacity as the foundation for our national culture. The self-justification from the free-thinkers [i.e., secular Jews], that sacred writings are parts of literature and no more, this self-justification is a testament to their naivety. The child learns a verse in its form: In the beginning God created, and God said "let there be light" and there was light. Everything is the creation of our God! And if we don't give up on the sacred writings in schools, then this strengthens the prior proposition, that even if we assume it were possible to for an environment to be completely cleansed of religious symbols, here the child arrives at an aspect of it [religion]—the part of *kitvei ha-kodesh*—and in the end he will encounter this question and determine a stance toward this force—The same God that created the heavens and the earth, the light—what is he in the end? Is he dead or does he live and sustain? It is incumbent upon the educator to give an answer. More than this, he must establish an attitude.[12]

It was on this basis that Alterman argued that as long as schools concerned themselves with teaching *kitvei ha-kodesh*, it was impossible to speak of any

Zionist schools as secular in the European sense. On the contrary, "in our quarters schools are not devoid of a religious foundation. The difference among them is the way in which they relate to the question [of religion] and the attitude of educators toward it." One school may celebrate the centrality of divinity, and another may shirk from it, "but our schools are not secular [*ḥiloniyyim*]."[13]

While the centrality of the Hebrew Bible and other sacred writings was common across the different streams of Zionist education, including within the Labor movement, the issue of religious education became thornier when educators tried to deal with the teaching of ritual commandments (*mitzvot*) in schools. The question was particularly pressing with regard to General Zionist schools, which by the late 1920s educated more children than the Labor and Mizraḥi trends combined.[14] Unlike the Labor schools, which enjoyed the greatest autonomy and developed the most unconventional curriculum, the differences between the General and Mizraḥi schools were subtler. In the words of Dr. Joseph Luria, director of the Zionist Department of Education, these differences boiled down to the study of Talmud and the issue of compulsion:

> The difference between *ḥaredi* [meaning here Mizraḥi] elementary schools and General ones is that in the first, much time is given to the study of the Talmud, which they begin in the fourth year and to which they dedicate ten hours weekly in each class. On account of this they are compelled to minimize general studies, especially nature subjects, singing, drawing, and physical exercise. There is yet another distinction, and it is—the relationship to the practical obligations of religion. Indeed, in General schools students also learn prayer, in several they also study the *Shulḥan Arech*, *Orach Ḥaim*, and in several settlements it is customary to find communal prayer in the schools, but the education of children in carrying out practical commandments [*mitzvot ma'asiot*] is not part of the General schools, and they relate to this as to something that is transmitted to the heart of each [student] from his parents.[15]

The question of whether schools ought to do more to train students in the performance of *mitzvot* was not a mere pedagogic one but related in fundamental ways to the broader ideological struggle over the function of Judaism as religion in the context of a *national* home. As Gideon Shimoni has argued, it was the members of the Second Aliyah—many of whom would later rank among the *yishuv*'s most important political and cultural figures—who first incorporated a derisive view toward Jewish ritual observance into the new worship of labor. The ideological rhetoric of the Second Aliyah's labor Zionist core, he writes, "was antirabbinical, contemptuous of halakhic minutiae, and disdainful of the *galut* [diaspora], past and contemporary. . . . The main ideological thrust was toward the divorce of the new Hebrew identity from all religious authority and influence and the 'normalization' of Jewish national culture on a secular basis."[16] Setting the nature of this "national culture on a secular basis" aside for a moment, it is certainly true that the young men and women who formed the Zionist vanguard envisioned the creation of a new Hebrew identity through the "negation of diaspora," and the turning away from traditional *mitzvot* was central to this process. This new Hebrew man was to be the antithesis of his diasporic (and truly, eastern European) counterpart, whose stereotypical image was the yeshiva scholar: physically diminutive from a life hunched over books, timid before his gentile neighbors, and cut off from the material world due to his overriding obsession with legal minutiae and ritual observance.

Yet this ideological, and indeed idealistic, negation of the diaspora became more problematic when the *yishuv* faced the realities of financing the national home project and its very real dependence on funding from Jewish communities abroad. If, for the pioneers of the Second Aliyah, the gap between their daily life and that of their counterparts back home was a source of pride, by the mid-1920s this rift had become a fiscal liability. This is reflected throughout Rabbi Aronsohn's presentation to the Board of Education and in the later discussions of the Committee to Clarify the Question of Religious Education. In Rabbi Aronsohn's terms, the financial health of Zionist education was largely dependent on strengthening the religious content therein. "The same portion of the people that supports schools in *Eretz Israel* desires the observance of religion in general. It demands that children will be educated in the spirit of religion and Torah. Much damage is attributed to not [carrying out] this desire. There was indeed an idea that religion was created for the diaspora, but is not necessary in *Eretz Israel*. . . . This is incorrect. Religion is the strongest foundation of nationalism." About this latter sentiment the committee was largely in agreement, and this was true even of a liberal figure like Henrietta Szold, who expressed her belief that "in education there is no distinction between nationalism and religiosity."[17]

It was over what this meant in practice that members of the committee and the Board of Education found themselves divided. Rabbi Aronsohn argued that all Zionist schools should instruct their students in the performance of practical *mitzvot*, claiming that "with this issue there is no distinction of political party"; that is, religious heritage constituted the very fabric of nationalism in a way that transcended petty factional squabbles. What is most fascinating about his position was that he viewed religious instruction as a tool for forging a new reality. It was true that the present moment was different from that of the past, wherein, as Yosef Mohliver stated, the *ḥeder* was a continuation of the home environment. Joseph Azaryahu put it in even stronger terms, arguing that "in the past, the *ḥeder* did not create a religious atmosphere, rather the opposite, it was an organic part of life."[18] As mentioned previously, Azaryahu thought it impossible to instill in children values that were not reflected in the broader environment of which they were a part. In this, he questioned the transformative potential of modern education itself, which, from the state's earliest forays into mass schooling, had been associated with reshaping the social order. On the contrary, Rabbi Aronsohn argued that *mitzvot ma'asiot* served as exercises in social training that not only created self-disciplining subjects (in the Foucauldian sense) but also ensured the long-term viability of the national project. Within this context, ritual acts were not taught because they were an organic part of everyday life but because they served as a means of transforming it.

Rabbi Aronsohn gave voice to this idea in his repeated calls for training or acclimating children to the performance of commandments, beginning with the recitation of simple blessings in kindergarten. Supporting this position against that of Azaryahu, Yitzhak Alterman argued that the mere fact that children in the *yishuv* were not already religiously observant was beside the point. Many schoolchildren were also unlikely to speak Hebrew in their homes, yet the spread of the Hebrew language ranked among Zionism's clearest accomplishments. What were the schools but a vehicle for disrupting the home environment? Or in Alterman's terms, "We build a lot on training."[19] Moreover, there was no reason to believe that the relationship between individual religious feeling and religious acts was causal rather than cyclical, meaning that the latter was not necessarily a result of the former but could in fact be the cause: "The religious experience does not always cause the religious act and conversely a religious act always has the power to awaken a religious experience. In the same way an artistic act can cause an aesthetic experience. It is not always that the experience gives rise to the act."[20] Within such a paradigm, it was wrong to deduce that the decline of religious observance was irreversible, as in fact it was the very training of children in "the religious act" that could subsequently produce a new religious sentiment. Even more important for our purposes was the notion of what this religion entailed. This was no return to the habits of the forefathers but a radical attempt to rethink the basis of religiosity from the perspective of modern political and social needs.

It was for this reason that Alterman found Rabbi Aronsohn's rather familiar recommendations—such as acclimating children to performing ritual commandments in schools or increasing the number of hours devoted to sacred texts—wholly inadequate. What was required was nothing less than a complete overhaul, beginning with the "very low" state of Jewish ritual, which Alterman claimed contained none of the awe-inducing splendor of "the religious rites of Notre Dame." The revival of the religious spirit within the next generation demanded that educators "enrich the form of ritual" and "create unforgettable religious impressions." Simply devoting more hours to the study of Talmud could not carry out such an important task, and Alterman recommended an assortment of practices that went beyond the usual texts and commandments: religious celebrations for the child's entrance into school or for completing the study of a particular book, parties for Shabbat and holidays for schoolchildren, special Shabbat and holiday services for children, theatrical performances, and the performance of old customs, like *tashlich*, in a new and "celebratory manner."[21] Alterman recognized that creating this new religious sensibility was a unique but necessary challenge:

> Today we need more than most, because the underlying environment leads us toward estrangement. Religious education of the usual type is worthless, and we require more means of education than our forefathers did. Our possibilities are limited, but just as with the Hebrew language we were extremists and proclaimed [the need for] mass knowledge [of it] precisely at the moment of decline, so too in our religious lives we must strengthen the religious consciousness of the masses precisely when we are most vulnerable to attack by our accusers [literally, when Satan prosecutes us]. Just as we overcame it [with regard to Hebrew] for the sake of the national truth, we will also be victorious here for the sake of the eternal human truth that the people of Israel brought to the world.[22]

The idea that tools from the past were insufficient to shape the religious sensibilities of future generations emerged as the common theme of Alterman's lengthy and somewhat rambling presentation, and on this point the committee was mostly in agreement. Such an approach was also obvious enough to Rabbi Ya'akov Berman, the lead inspector for Mizraḥi schools. At the most basic level, he acknowledged that Jewish religious education must necessarily assume multiple forms in the modern period and that the new religious education would differ in key ways from that of the old. Here he drew on the example of modern Orthodoxy in contemporary Germany: "In Germany when Orthodoxy came to create religious education it was compelled to bring forth with it changes. They understood that modern education must also give religion new and modern garb." For Rabbi Berman, there was no question what this "modern garb" might look like in the context of the *yishuv*: "If we want to give a religious education to our children—that may occur only if we assume that the foundation of nationalism is religion."[23] Far from being a religious Zionist position alone, the members of the committee were largely in agreement that, in Szold's terms, "Hebrew nationalism," as an "original creation of the Hebrew nation," was a creation within which "religion and nationalism advance in a single line" and were inseparable.[24] The difficulty came in balancing this commitment to religious texts and traditions as the unifying sources of Jewish identity with a liberal concern for individual freedom. Even if educators hoped to unite the various schools around this "essence" of religiosity (Szold's term), there would still necessarily be multiple models for doing so. "Even if the goal is singular and unified across all streams [i.e., Labor, General, and Mizraḥi schools], it cannot be imagined possible to move toward that goal along a single path."[25]

In formulating their final recommendations to the Board of Education, the committee attempted to reconcile these competing impulses to arrive at a sort of centrist position. Children should be acclimated from a young age to perform acts like ritual hand washing and blessings after meals but not obligated to do so. All parties agreed that modern biblical criticism, which undermined the divine provenance of the Torah, had no place within schools and that sacred texts should be "taught with covered heads." But above all there was a concerted effort to create holistic religious experiences through the use of modern pedagogic strategies geared specifically toward children's sensibilities. Mirroring the contemporary attempt to create a unique body of children's religious literature, the committee recommended schools organize special children's congregations for Shabbat and holiday services. What united such gestures was the realization that simply acclimating the child into the adult world of Jewish practice—with its customary attention to textual study and the strictures of *halacha*—was no longer enough.[26]

The fact that the Zionist Board of Education rejected these recommendations is noteworthy, but from the perspective of social history, it is of equal importance that committee members—a diverse group of school inspectors, headmasters, and policy makers—agreed on them to begin with. Both by fact of its existence and due to the nature of its deliberations, the Committee to Clarify the Question of Religious Education gestures toward the theoretical difficulties involved in approaching Zionist education through preformed notions of the "religious" and "secular." Moreover, turning away from this paradigm allows us to see a very different dynamic at work in Zionist attempts to fashion a new type of Jewish identity. Here, rather than move from the old to the new, the traditional to the modern, or the religious to the secular, we can discern a concerted effort to think through these binaries in dialectical terms. Viewed accordingly, secularism does not come to replace religion but to offer it new life.

RELIGION AT LARGE

I have suggested thus far that in its commonplace meaning, "secular" is a misleading label for Zionist schools, which on the whole did not seek the negation of Judaism or the invention ab initio of a new identity but the appropriation, selective privileging, and reworking of traditional Jewish texts, concepts, and behaviors. More than anything else, it was the assertion—which found varied expression across school trends—that the Jewish religious tradition could be mined in service of a new political reality that brought Zionist leaders into confrontation with the Mandatory government. Even leaving aside Mizraḥi schools and their explicit religious Zionism, the notion, common among Labor educators, that one could cherish the Bible even without its God was both confusing and deeply unsettling to British officials. Indeed, the materiality of Judaism seemed to be well suited to advancing a form of Jewish identity that was at odds with normative constructions of religion as private, faith based, voluntary, and decidedly nonjudicial. As Mordechai Segal, one of the Labor movement's preeminent educators, articulated it, "Yes, indeed, there is tradition without religion, the tradition stemming from the life and creativity of a nation's innumerable generations. We should present it, clarify it and shed light upon it, endear it to [students], bring it closer and adopt it, and frequently emphasize its value to humanity beyond faith and ritual."[27] Nothing could be further from British officials' moralizing liberalism than an attempt to preserve a religious tradition for the sake of nationalist ends, all the while dispensing with its God.

While my purpose is not to offer a comprehensive overview of Zionist educational practices, which varied greatly and have been the subject of extensive scholarly inquiry, we can nevertheless begin to discern some general patterns as we examine the points of friction between the government's approach to religious education and that pioneered by educators in the *yishuv*. At the most basic level, so-called religious subjects occupied a central place in the curriculum of every "stream" of the Hebrew Public System, particularly the Hebrew Bible.[28] The Va'ad Leumi stressed that each school shared certain common features and that it would be erroneous to characterize any of them as truly antireligious:

> A bare description of the three types of schools may convey several erroneous impressions: that the "General" and Labor schools are anti-religious; that only the Labor schools give instruction in practical activities; that the system is tripartite with only an external, administrative unity. All three assumptions are unwarranted. The Mizraḥi, indeed, "consistently hold the religious viewpoint in education; religious education is not a matter of instruction in this or that subject, but implies an all-pervading outlook on life.'" But the "General" schools are by no manner of means anti-religious. They put the study of the Bible in a foremost place and do not omit the study of the Rabbinical literature, and they observe the traditional customs. . . . Likewise the Labor schools insist upon a good knowledge of the Bible. At most it may be said that their spirit is non-religious.[29]

The Department of Education of the Zionist Organization consistently stressed the centrality of the Hebrew Bible as the carrier of both the Hebrew language and "Hebrew spirit" and viewed it as a unifying force within schools often rent by ideological divides.[30] As Yairah Amit has argued, "The various educational curricula developed in the Land of Israel and inspired by the Zionist movement regarded the Bible as the ideological basis and historical evidence of a productive Jewish society living on its land."[31] Likewise, Anita Shapira has characterized the Hebrew Bible as "the primary text for shaping identity in the Jewish society that was then coming into being."[32]

Scholars who have studied Zionism during this formative period have often understood the place of privilege allotted to the Hebrew Bible within the context of naturalizing the sacred, wherein Jews borrowed terms, concepts, and imagery from the biblical context and rearticulated them within a nationalist-political idiom.[33] Such accounts tend to stress that with the secular turn, subjects like the Hebrew Bible were disassociated from Jewish theology and instead constituted a source text for the development of nationalism. Labor Zionism in particular adopted "numerous symbols and practices from traditionalist Jewish religion but transformed and complemented them with universalist, largely Socialist, values."[34] Though this shift is sometimes portrayed as one from religion to nationalism, parochialism to universal values, and theology to secularism, there are reasons to question this narrative. For instance, how could the Jews rid themselves of theology while still speaking in terms of national destiny? What exactly should we make of this "Hebrew spirit" that lay in waiting for its final expression? Why the overwhelming sense of sanctity attached not to the mere act of labor but to the very specific working, improving, and redeeming of *Eretz Yisrael*? I suggest that, at least as far as Zionist education was concerned, this shift did not signal the abandonment of Judaism but its careful renegotiation into a politically useful form.

In the words of Joseph Azaryahu, who also chaired the committee charged with creating the General school curriculum in the early 1920s, conditions in Palestine presented a unique opportunity to teach traditional Jewish texts in a new way and with new goals. Referring to the role of the Hebrew Bible in school curricula, he wrote:

> The principal, "dominant," goal of teaching the Bible in our schools is therefore its pedagogical impact on the pupils. This goal justifies placing it in the leading position in our school curriculum, because it transforms the Bible from being merely an object of knowledge, ordinary study material that the school provides, to the level of spiritual formation and transformation, an educational factor, designed to form the students' mental being, implant in them the morality of Judaism, the aspiration for social justice, the love of the people and the admiration for its ideals and heroes, awaken in them religious exultation and yearning for the highest, for the good and the ultimate holiness, feelings which the tumultuous workaday life in our time extinguishes in the souls of our contemporaries and leaves them dry of dust. That is the power of "the book of Books," and its potential benefit for the education of our youth.[35]

While there was obviously something different about Zionist education that distinguished it from the Jewish religious schooling of past times, accounts that suggest a clear transition from the religious to the national or secular do not fully convey the complexity of the Zionist educational program, even within the left-leaning Labor movement. In this regard we should note that while the leftist educator Mordechai Segal, the founder of the Kibbutz Teachers College, endeavored to publish *The Bible without God*, his effort to do so failed. On the contrary, "most [Labor educators] taught the Bible 'with God,' however humanistically they interpreted the idea."[36]

Similarly, as we saw in the deliberations of the Committee to Clarify the Question of Religious Education, there was a great deal of concern during the first decade of the Mandate that modern biblical criticism might find its way into classrooms, as it had done previously in the Herzliya Gymnasium.[37] Beyond representing a politically expedient choice given the dependence on funding from less "free-thinking" communities abroad, attempts to exclude modern biblical criticism from schools must be understood within the context of Zionist attempts to present children with a synthetic account of Jewish history that was as attentive to claims made by the Bible as it was to those of Josephus. Furthermore, the fact that biblical criticism was roundly repudiated and explicitly rejected by Zionist educators well into the 1970s suggests that the secularization of the sacred text was an uneasy and ultimately incomplete project.[38]

Turning to the curricula in question, we find that the Zionist approach to the Hebrew Bible offers a clear contrast to the approach toward religious texts the Government of Palestine advanced within the Arab Public System. If the effort in the latter case was, as I have argued, to separate religion from secular history and thereby constitute Islam in religious terms as a source of individual ethics rather than communal politics, Zionist schools sought to create a synthetic form of Jewish identity that rendered such differentiation all but impossible. A few concrete examples will help make the point clearer.

Looking at school curricula across the three Zionist trends, we confront clear articulations of what might be termed "composite or synthetic history," as biblical events migrate into general history lessons, and vice versa. Indeed, sacred and secular historical narratives were not meant to exist as independent realms of study but served as complementary, mutually enforcing bodies of knowledge. We can see this not only in the expected fashion of biblical history becoming incorporated in a modern nationalist narrative as a sort of primordial title deed to Palestine but also in more surprising ways. For instance, the Hebrew Bible curriculum for fifth-year students in General Zionist schools had two components: prophets (Samuel II, Kings I and II, Jonah, and Amos) and topics drawn "from the history of ancient nations." The latter included subjects such as "the Egyptians: the land and its borders, the Nile and its influence on the landscape; the residents, their occupations, and ways of life; their beliefs . . . the rule of the king." Similar topics are assigned for Tyre and Assyria, often with directives back to particular sections of the Hebrew Bible or to related lessons in the geography curriculum.[39] It is also significant that the curriculum for General schools only included a discrete history component (*divrei ha-yamim*) once students reached the sixth year of study. During the early years of their education, students across trends principally learned about the past through the many hours (between four and six each week) devoted to the Hebrew Bible and, for the youngest children, *moledet* (literally, homeland or homeland studies).[40] The view of the Bible as the chief historical source for the Jewish people extended into the period of Israel's independence, so much so that memoranda written by the Ministry of Education in 1957 explained that fifth-graders would not be required to study history because historical material was learned through Bible lessons![41]

Schools maintained by the General Federation of Jewish Labor (the Histadrut) shared this commitment to a synthetic view of Jewish peoplehood, in which the Bible, the Land of Israel, and the Hebrew language were all essential parts. Educators affiliated with the Labor movement approached the teaching of the Hebrew Bible in diverse ways, as enumerated first by Jacobus Schoneveld and more recently by Yuval Dror.[42] As the latter concludes, Schoneveld's classification of Labor pedagogy "spoke of religious and secular elements" but did not perceive that "all the approaches to teaching the Bible in the schools of the Labor Movement and the Kibbutzim stressed critical, nationalistic, universal humanist, and moralistic and personal elements. One stretches the issue to speak of clear-cut classifications."[43] What we have instead is an attempt to formulate a synthetic approach to both Jewish identity and history in which the Bible remained the cornerstone, even if its all-powerful figure became more of a footnote. It was indeed a peculiar posture (though in some sense a deeply Jewish one) to assert that there was a religious tradition in which God was a rather unimportant detail. All the same, describing such reconfigurations of the Jewish tradition as "secular" neither captures their internal dynamism nor conveys the larger impulse to forge a modern Jewish identity that would obviate the need for "secular" and "religious" aspects of the self. Whereas diaspora existence was associated with being a man in the street and a Jew at home, Zionism seemed to offer a path toward unification.

The curriculum for Labor schools, published in 1937 as "Guidelines A," stipulated that early grades should begin with stories of key individuals and episodes from the Hebrew Bible, either conveyed orally or taken from a series of textbooks called *Sipurei ha-Mikrah* (Bible stories).[44] Topics of study included Adam and Eve, Noah, the three patriarchs (Abraham, Yitzhak, Ya'akov), Joseph, Moses and the Exodus from Egypt, in addition to later books such as Yonah, Ruth, and Esther. First published in 1919, *Sipurei ha-Mikrah* was a collaborative series of school readers composed and edited by Yehoshua Ravnitski, Chaim Nahman Bialik, and Simhah Alter Guttmann (who went by the pen name S. Ben-Zion). Serving in various capacities as writers, educators, and publicists, the three men ranked among the upper echelons of the *yishuv*'s Ashkenazi cultural elite, and their textbooks are therefore of particular interest to the question of religious education in Labor Zionist schools. The first book in the series is devoted to the Book of Genesis, beginning with the opening lines of the Torah ("In the beginning God created the heavens and the earth") and continuing in abridged form through the death of Abraham. Among the book's noteworthy features is a word bank, which appears before each section of the text and introduces vocabulary terms, and the questions (presumably composed by the editors) that follow each portion of text. These range from "Who created the heavens and the earth?" and "How did God create the light?" following the creation story, to "What did Abraham say to his servant with regard to Yitzhak?"[45] As these questions suggest, even though the authors clearly abridged the Torah in many sections, God managed to survive the editorial process mostly intact. Thus, the choice to use *Sipurei ha-Mikrah* can hardly be attributed to wanting to excise the divine presence from the national epic of the Jewish people. However, the text did come with many pedagogic advantages when compared with the actual Torah—such as bite-sized portions of text and leading questions focused on reading comprehension—that supported a more robust interpretive scaffolding than appeared in the stories' original form. In this respect, the texts share certain features with the textbooks for Islamic education analyzed in Chapter 5 and display a heightened concern for guiding children (and their teachers) down a more narrowly defined hermeneutical path.

Another volume in the series, referred to by the authors only as "the fifth book," is also of note when considering the approach toward sacred and secular time. Geared toward older children, the text includes selections from the Books of Kings interwoven with other selections taken from the Books of Jeremiah, Ezra, and Nehemiah. There are no annotations that demarcate which portions of the text come from which source, as the attempt is to present a unified narrative that recounts the history of ancient Israel. The story begins with the fracture of the unified Kingdom of Israel into two states and the ascent of Reḥav'am to the kingship in the Kingdom of Judah. Selections from Jeremiah foretelling the destruction of Israel because of the people's sinfulness are interspersed, which in turn lead to recounting the actual Babylonian exile. The latter portion of the text includes passages from the Books of Ezra and Nehemiah, which narrate the return to Zion at the behest of Cyrus, the rebuilding of the Temple and the walls of Jerusalem, and perhaps most significant from a Zionist perspective, the purging of "foreign" elements from among the population. The book ends with an abridged passage adapted from the final verses of Nehemiah:

> Also at that time I saw that Jews had married Ashdodite, Ammonite, and Moabite women; half of their children spoke the language of Ashdod and the language of various other nations and did not know how to speak Judean. I censured them, cursed them, flogged them, tore out their hair, and adjured them by God, saying, "You shall not give your daughters and sons in marriage to their sons or yourselves." One of the sons of Yoyada the son of the high priest Eliyashiv was a son-in-law of Sanballat the Horonite and I drove him away from me. I purged [the priests and Levites] of every foreign element, and arranged for the priests and Levites to each work at his task by shifts. Oh my God, remember it to my credit![46]

Given the Zionist preoccupation with the threat of assimilation—symbolized here by foreign wives and languages—these verses from Nehemiah could hardly be a better end to a narrative arc composed of sin, exile, return, and redemption. Beyond the obvious points of resonance for those engaged in a new return (*shivat Zion*), the history recounted here is impossible to classify as either "religious" or "secular" but points instead to a different hermeneutic universe in which that division is quite simply nonsensical.

Beginning in the sixth grade, students stopped using *Sipurei ha-Mikrah* and began studying the Bible in its original Hebrew form. Already by grade three, the curriculum was heavily biased toward the latter portions of the Bible (the *-nakh* portion of Tanakh, including prophets and "Writings" such as the Books of Esther and Ruth) rather than the Torah (first five books of Moses), and this trend accelerated in the years that followed. Thus, rather than study Genesis or Exodus, students devoted themselves to reading the prophetic writings of Joshua, Judges, Samuel I and II, Kings I and II, Jeremiah, Ezekiel, Isaiah, Amos, Jonah, and Zechariah, in addition to the Books of Job, Ruth, Esther, Nehemiah, and Daniel, among other selections. While many scholars have noted the place of privilege that Zionist schools afforded to the prophetic writings—a relative novelty as far as Jewish education was concerned—this was arguably not merely because of the ethical exhortations for which the prophets are known. Returning to the issue of sacred versus secular history, these later biblical books were equally important as archival sources relating to Jewish national existence in the Land of Israel. In this capacity, they not only overshadowed the place of the Torah in Zionist curricula but also served as an authoritative source that detailed Jewish national existence in the land.[47] Similarly, and much as we would expect, the history curriculum used in Labor schools included numerous references to biblical writings and exhortations to teachers to construct a unified narrative of the Jewish past that had little regard for the religious or secular nature of the sources in question. The formal history curriculum in fact began with the Babylonian exile and the first return to Zion, which was to be studied alongside passages from Jeremiah, Hagai, and Ezra.[48] In short, rather than exist in distinct ontological spheres separated either by time (ancient/modern) or content (ethical-universal/historical-national), we find that Zionist schools did not approach secular and sacred history as distinct interpretive practices but as mutually constitutive narratives that served to animate and legitimize each other.

Another significant feature of the history and geography curricula—one that was shared across all three trends—was the great extent to which the inclusion of events and personalities hinged on their relation to the Jewish people and the Land of Israel. As Shmuel Feiner has argued, this nationalist approach to the writing of history represented a change in direction from that pioneered by European *maskilim*, for whom the importance of history as a pedagogic tool was linked to its capacity to recount major events from and historical shifts occurring within the non-Jewish world.[49] In contrast, the Department of Education of the Zionist Organization articulated a perspective in which other lands, peoples, and events become relevant only through their contact with the Jewish people, cast here as the epicenter around which historical time revolves:

> In the study of geography, the homeland [*moledet*] stands at the center. Special attention must be paid to adjacent lands and to those that are most important to inhabitants of Eretz Yisrael. In [the study of] history, the syllabus privileges knowledge of Jewish history and the teacher is restricted to only those events in general history that are related to the history of our people.[50]

Drawing an example from the General school trend, the geography curriculum began by surveying the Land of Israel before moving outward to Mount Sinai, "the road of the exodus from Egypt," and Babylonia, the first land of exile. In each instance, the place studied appears not precisely as an entity of independent interest but of historical importance to the Jewish people.[51] Thus, when surveying Syria, the teacher is to stress "the economic and cultural relationship between it and Eretz Yisrael" and to discuss the Jewish communities of Damascus, Beirut, and Aleppo.[52] The Mizraḥi syllabus added that the survey of lands surrounding Eretz Yisrael should be done "in connection to what is taught about them in the Torah and the early prophets," a directive that was largely harmonious with the approach in Labor schools detailed previously.[53] In the final year, students were to review "the value of Eretz Yisrael in our national and religious life; the new and old settlements, the races [in the land], the history of Eretz Yisrael from the Middle Ages until the days of the New Yishuv, and the commandments that are dependent on the land."[54]

This narrative structure differed significantly from that of the curriculum developed for use in the Arab Public System, in which substantial attention was paid to European and American history while Palestine itself was presented in international terms as an object of perpetual conquest. While the Zionist curriculum in this regard may offer an example of what Jerome Farrell termed "national chauvinism," it is perhaps more complicated than that—and ultimately in my view, points to a sort of theological residue in the practice of history as a national project.[55] In truth, this structure of narration echoes not only contemporary nationalist histories but also that within the Hebrew Bible itself in which great empires, rulers, and peoples exist on the periphery of a story whose central object is the genealogy of the Israelites. The student of Tanakh would encounter, for instance, the ancient Egyptian or Persian kingdoms and might glean something of their military or intellectual power. However, such empires do not stand as independent entities within the narrative structure of the text but are significant only as agents who affect the formation and destiny of the people of Israel. Within this context, the outside world serves as little more than the setting for the unfolding of Jewish history rather than as an object of inquiry bearing its own intrinsic worth. The contrast with the approach to Palestinian history in the Arab Public System could not be more striking.

Indeed, the very reason given to justify the study of history within Zionist schools communicated a sense of divine destiny or special purpose for the people of Israel. It was precisely this sense of national purpose that Benjamin Elazari-Volcani had earlier dismissed as "national theology," that "trend of thought that subsumed Jewish nationalist ideas within theological categories of thought born of misguided metaphysics and nostalgia."[56] However, not only was Volcani's voice countered by others within the *yishuv* during the Second Aliyah, but the shifting demographic realities of Mandatory Palestine helped swing Zionist education even further away from his radically materialist position. According to the General school curricula, history served as a tool "to awaken in the hearts of students an internal [sense of] participation in the fate of our nation and in the fate of the great members of the generations who have worked and suffered."[57] Articulating the same sentiment in more overtly theological terms, the Mizraḥi syllabus stated:

> Teaching our history in relation to the general history of nations brings the child to realize that divine supervision uncovers historical paths for us in a special manner. The continued existence of our small and poor people in the midst of a great multitude of enormous nations, strong and steadfast nations, that despite their political and cultural strength have passed and gone, fosters an understanding of the strength of Israel's Torah and the divine supervision [*hashgacha pratit*] that protects us. This realization is what creates a firm connection between the student and the nation of Israel to Eretz Yisrael, the land of our people's birth and the soil of the law, the prophets, and the sages.[58]

For our purposes, we should interrogate the difference between the "the fate of our nation" and its divinely directed destiny, keeping in mind that together, these two school trends accounted for approximately 75 percent of the students enrolled in Zionist schools. In both instances we find ourselves equally estranged from truly secularized explanations—whether cultural, materialist, or structural—and instead encounter continual appeals to fate, destiny, and national spirit as the driving forces of Jewish history. The situation in schools managed by the Labor movement, with their oft-noted commitment to materialist readings of Jewish historical sources (including the Hebrew Bible), was obviously more complicated. Yet here, too, we find, as evident in *Sipurei ha-Mikrah*, a redemptive narrative that continued to resemble the traditional pattern of sin, exile, and return: from the exile in Babylonia and the hopes for redemption (*geulah*), to the return to Zion and the building of the Second Temple, the expulsion of Jews from their land and their bitter existence in the diaspora, and finally to the rise of the Zionist movement and its triumphs, like the "redemption [*geulah*] of the Jezreel Valley" at the hands of the able pioneer.[59]

This sanctification of settlement and agricultural labor was a particularly pronounced part of early Zionist education and often accompanied attempts to appropriate Jewish customs and holidays and reinvent them in ways that stressed their relationship to the material life of *Eretz Yisrael*.[60] Tracing its roots to the ideological currents of the Second Aliyah, this key theme found its purest expression in the figure of A. D. Gordon, for whom "labor was not only a rational value for the individual's expansion of self and his social relations" but also "the key to a cosmic religious experience that bonds man to nature." In was due to such ideological convictions that, at the age of forty-eight, Gordon immigrated to Palestine "to participate in the process that would restore the Jewish nation to its natural homeland environment, that is, to its cosmic source."[61] Though usually associated with the Labor movement, this trend was prevalent in General and Mizraḥi schools as well and offers a fascinating example of the ideological maneuvers that educators undertook *within* the corpus of traditional Jewish texts.[62]

During the 1920s, a new generation of Hebrew poets such as Avraham Shlonsky continued to emphasize the essential dignity of labor as a force of spiritual renewal, often by appropriating biblical language and ritual imagery only to overturn their classical meanings.[63] For instance, in one of his most famous works, "Amal" (Toil), newly built homes and roads are likened to phylacteries as the narrator is led to his morning labor in lieu of—or perhaps, as a form of—prayer. At times, the glorification of land and labor played dissonantly off the existing corpus of Jewish ritual texts. In his poem "Metropolis," Shlonsky concludes by blessing "he who weighs his yoke upon us" (*baruch machbid olo aleinu*), offering a stark contrast with the customary supplication, "May the compassionate one break the yoke from our necks."[64] Several of these discursive elements found their way into the Zionist mainstream, even if their revolutionary nature was not fully appreciated, through their incorporation into the educational programs of each party. In fact, in the face of so much ideological controversy, the sanctification of land and labor represented a sort of common denominator: malleable enough that each trend could offer its own interpretive flavor, stable enough that the symbolic fabric was not torn asunder. We could point to numerous examples of this tendency; for the purpose of this discussion, I highlight only a few.

The first involves a shift in discursive privilege within the study of *kitvei ha-kodesh*. For instance, the upper two classes of General elementary schools studied Mishnah, the redaction of the oral law. In the seventh class, students studied five of the sixty-three sections of the Mishnah. The first was *Pirkei Avot* (Ethics of the fathers), a compilation of ethical teachings and sayings that includes almost no legal rulings. The other four tractates—*Bikkurim*, *Pe'ah*, *Shevi'it*, and *Brachot*—were all selected from Mishnah *Zera'im* (Seeds).[65] Specifically, *Bikkurim* concerns bringing the "first fruits" of the land as an offering at the Temple; *Pe'ah* discusses the laws of charity related to the harvest; *Shevi'it* addresses the laws related to the sabbatical year in which the land is allowed to rest; and *Brachot* offers guidelines surrounding major ritual prayers and blessings.

Taken as a group, these selections reflect many of the ideological shifts discussed thus far. For instance, the emphasis on *Pirkei Avot* fit well within the modern attempt to locate the ethical core of Judaism as an abstract and singular entity and to further identify a Jewish ethics that could be disentangled from the legal minutiae of *halacha*. Though the study of the text was not novel in and of itself, its study in isolation represented a departure from the customary order in which law, literature, ethics, and practice constituted an organic whole. Similarly, General schools included prayers in the Hebrew-language curriculum "in order that the student will know them and understand their ethical value."[66] Exposure to major prayers and blessings was also meant to acclimate children to Jewish ritual practice and was no doubt designed to ameliorate concern about a rift between the *yishuv* and diasporic Jewry. This had been a practical concern ever since Baron de Rothschild reportedly visited his agricultural colonies early in the twentieth century and found, much to his dismay, that schoolchildren could not recite the *shema*, the most fundamental of Jewish prayers.[67] Yet it was the three tractates taken from the agricultural portions of the Mishnah—which stressed the historic rootedness of the Jewish nation in the Land of Israel—that commanded the most attention. Suffice it to say, these tractates, while continually studied by Jewish communities, did not attain such a prominent position outside the *yishuv*. For the sake of comparison, Mizraḥi schools, whose curriculum adhered more closely to the customary selections of Mishnah studied among Ashkenazim, did not teach any of these agricultural tractates.[68]

Privileging these texts also meant leaving many others out, such as the central texts related to the laws of the Sabbath, the holidays (with the exception of Rosh Hashanah), family and ritual purity, civil damages, the courts, marriage, divorce, idolatry, sacrifices, and the Temple service. Certainly this shift in discursive focus is noteworthy, yet the privileging of certain parts of the Jewish textual tradition over others need not be read as a shift from religious to secular Judaism. We are not dealing with the invention of traditions as much as the parsing and selection of some over others. The practice of making these choices is important and ultimately testifies to the flexibility of the Jewish hermeneutic tradition; it need not, however, be conflated with secularism. On the contrary, Zionist education was deeply invested in stressing certain forms of religiosity or, perhaps more accurately, of cultivating a modern form of Jewish identity that need not split the self into its religious and secular parts.

THE POLITICS OF DENIAL AT WORK

Having looked in some detail at the educational practices associated with the Zionist movement, we must finally account for the ways in which the British colonial government related to these developments. There is a common trend in historical (and polemical) writing about Mandate Palestine to regard Zionism and British colonialism as marching harmoniously in stride. Certainly from the perspective of Palestine's Arab population, any distinctions between the two forces were mostly insignificant in light of the cooperative attempt to transform Palestine into a Jewish state and the eventual dispossession of Palestinians that this process entailed. However, Zionist historiography has tended to overemphasize the acrimony between the Mandatory government and the Zionist leadership in an attempt to highlight the movement's self-reliance and to disassociate the Jewish state from Western imperialism. Moreover, it is true that many Zionist figures regarded British officials negatively and dismissed them as colonial agents intent on curtailing Jewish autonomy and, in the educational context, controlling the Hebrew Public System.[69] Moshe Aharon Beijel, a prominent Labor educator, was among those who chafed at attempts by the Government of Palestine to supervise Jewish education. He believed that the director of education wished "to fit our varied lives into a framework that is foreign in its preparation—based on his experience in other countries." He further wondered

> how any foreign man, even an educator from the government Department of Education, can dictate to us about the structure of our schools? As if we were born yesterday? We know that the European pedagogy is sophisticated, but we also have a pedagogy; we have methods of education and instruction of our own. We have experience in our education, we have been engaged in the education of our sons for thousands of years, and Europe, when did it begin doing that?[70]

In reality, the nature of the British-Zionist relationship was far more complicated than either side would like to admit. I have already shown that Palestine's legal structure afforded significant advantages to the Zionist community, including a level of educational autonomy that was totally unavailable to the Arab population. However, relations began to sour in the 1930s and became increasingly hostile after Jerome Farrell succeeded Humphrey Bowman as director of education in 1937.

The Department of Education complained that separate management structures for each of the three streams of Zionist education—Labor, General, and Mizraḥi—led to administrative redundancies and financial inefficiencies that rendered the Hebrew Public System "uneconomical and ineffective."[71] But beyond these administrative faults, the greatest source of contention between the Zionist school system and the Government of Palestine concerned the politicization of Jewish schools. While concerns of this nature existed throughout the

Mandate period, Humphrey Bowman had managed to find a modus operandi with Zionist leaders that Farrell was incapable of replicating. Farrell's distaste for Jews and Arabs alike no doubt contributed to these tensions, but they were also reflective of changes in an overall political context that—by the time he assumed the post of education director in 1937—had deteriorated markedly. It was in this year that the Peel Commission published its report recommending the partition of Palestine into Jewish and Arab states, and concerns were often voiced about the role of nationalist education in eroding relations between the two communities. It was within this context of increased tension between the Zionist Organization and the Mandatory government that the Department of Education for the first time acted on its long-standing threat to withhold a portion of the block grant from the Va'ad Leumi if certain reforms were not enacted.[72] As discussed previously, Farrell was also the driving force behind the department's decision to extend direct aid to a number of Orthodox religious schools unaffiliated with the Va'ad Leumi. Both acts were no doubt designed to challenge Zionist dominance of Jewish education in Palestine or to at least moderate its approach. We therefore explore the source of offense in greater detail.

At the most basic level, the fact that nearly every Zionist school was administered by one of the three major political parties represented a direct challenge to the British ideal of education devoid of political influence. This created a situation full of pedagogic misdeeds in addition to the aforementioned administrative inefficiencies. In a related vein, the government lamented that members of the Zionist Teachers Association viewed themselves not so much as "public officers" but as "leaders in an industrial dispute whose primary and ultimate object is political power."[73] These complaints were part of a larger problem in the eyes of the Mandatory government: harnessing Judaism to a political cause that viewed education as one of its primary "weapons" upset not merely the proper educational order but the political-theological one as well.[74] Looking at this case in detail offers an exemplary demonstration of the politics of denial at work, as the explicit politicization of Zionist schools was denounced as morally unsound by the same government that viewed religious education as a tool to keep the masses out of politics.

It seems from the archival records that one of Jerome Farrell's favorite activities during his tenure as director of education was to author reports in which he criticized the politicization of the Hebrew Public System.[75] In this he was not alone, as both the McNair and Anglo-American Commissions expressed alarm regarding the subordination of Jewish education to Zionist political ends. The

McNair Commission was appointed by the secretary of state of the colonies with the express purpose of investigating Jewish education in Palestine and published its findings in 1946. Members of that commission went as far as to direct a confidential letter to the secretary of state for the colonies "to stress one matter to which we attach importance but which, if we expressed our views fully in our Report, might, in the present state of affairs in Palestine, cause embarrassment or frustrate some of our recommendations." That matter, "one of the most disturbing aspects of education and home life in Palestine," was none other than "the extent to which young children are preoccupied with political and other ideological matters." The letter continued to lament the presence in Zionist schools of youth movements affiliated with each of the major political parties: "The fact is that most, if not all, of the political parties and ideological groups are making a deliberate attempt, by means of a technique which the totalitarian States have made familiar, to organise children under the respective banners at a very early age without regard to the interests of the children's education."[76] Using much milder language, the published version of the report touched on the inefficiencies and pedagogic damage done by the trend system, in which "Jewish political parties have played a very prominent part in the provision of schools and teachers."[77]

The McNair Commission also criticized the behavior of teachers, who not only went on frequent strikes when their salaries were in arrears but refused to curtail their political activism in a manner befitting public servants. While the Government of Palestine had forbidden teachers in the Arab Public System from joining any political group or association since 1925 (other than the "neutral" YMCA), in 1946 the McNair Commission could merely plead that Jewish teachers "must realize their position, as public servants entrusted with the care of children, makes it necessary for them to place some degree of restriction upon their participation in public controversy, whether religious or political."[78] Echoing arguments repeatedly forwarded within British administrative circles, the commission took for granted the existence of a neutral educational field governed merely by pedagogic requirements on which political concerns exercised an unnatural influence. Not only was this understanding undermined by the material dependence of systems of public education—both in Britain and in the empire—on political decision making; it similarly masked the fact that attempts to shield schools from political influence represented a very real form of colonial politics.

Given these observations, the McNair Commission's ultimate recommendation that the Jewish community be given more autonomy in educational matters seems somewhat contradictory. As "one of the chief instruments in the building of the Jewish national home in Palestine," the report noted, "education means to the Zionist Jew something more than it does in England or in most other countries." Because "the strain of national idealism which pervades Jewish education is often puzzling to those trained in one of the British educational systems," the commission argued that "the responsibility for the management of the Jewish schools should be in the hands of the Jewish community."[79] Published the same year, though broader in scope, the Anglo-American Committee of Inquiry reflected a similar contradiction. While criticizing Jewish schools for inculcating "a spirit of aggressive Hebrew nationalism," the report nevertheless recommended that the Jewish community should serve as a model for delegating control of Palestinian education to the Arab community: "A large share of responsibility for Arab education might well be assumed by an Arab community, similar to the Jewish community already established in Palestine."[80]

These inconsistencies were not lost on Jerome Farrell, who detailed his observations on both reports in an extraordinary memorandum to the Colonial Office in November 1946. Authored in the final years of Mandatory rule in which Britain, bankrupt and reeling from the material and human costs of the Second World War, was in the process of imperial disengagement, Farrell's lengthy report represents the ultimate distillation of British frustrations regarding Zionist education in Palestine. Were Palestine to remain an imperial possession, his immediate concern was that the Colonial Office might entertain these recommendations regarding increased educational autonomy for Jewish and Arab communities in Palestine. Commenting on the reports, Farrell warned, "If unselfishness, peace and goodwill are principal aims of education it will be difficult to reconcile the two relevant recommendations which each Report in effect makes and which, bluntly stated, are (a) that a 'fiery nationalism' shall be eradicated from the schools, (b) that control of education shall be vested in fiery nationalist politicians."[81]

Farrell took further issue with the McNair Commission's conclusion that Zionist leaders' sense of "national idealism" mandated their autonomous control over Jewish education. "The phrase 'national idealism' is misleading," Farrell wrote:

> I should prefer "racial" or even "tribal" to "national" and "chauvinism" or "indoctrination" to "idealism," a word which to English minds inevitably suggests high and unpractical moral standards. There are no doubt many individual Jews who are idealists but the Zionist Organization's official policy and power direct

> the tribalism of the Jews to strictly selfish, practical and material ends. The aim is of course attained, as in Nazi Germany, by the unscrupulous manipulation of childish and adolescent emotion.[82]

This was only one of several instances in which Farrell compared Zionist educational practices to the political indoctrination of totalitarian regimes, particularly in Nazi Germany. In another context he likewise expressed concern that channeling government funds through the Va'ad Leumi rather than the LEAs was a dangerous step toward "the excessive centralization of the continent and of Nazism."[83] Comparisons with totalitarian states are telling, as the latter openly embraced the form of social engineering that Farrell claimed was contrary to liberal values. If we recall the modern educational constitution proposed earlier, such practices were situated directly across the absolute (yet continually transgressed) boundary from pedagogic responsibility—the purported base of British policy.

Significantly, Farrell's memo charged Zionism with severing Jews from the two great "civilising influences" available to them: first, the gentile cultures of Western European countries and, more important for our purposes, religious Judaism. Zionists were thus depicted as having forfeited their membership in the civilized world:

> The immoral or hypocritical attitude of the Zionist leaders is not that of most Western Jews but few of these migrate to Palestine and those who remain in the Diaspora do not fully understand the differences between their own ethical outlook and that of the Poles, Russians and other Easterners who constitute the larger part of Palestinian Jewry and direct its internal policy. These have not been long, widely and intimately subjected to civilising influences either at home or in Palestine and, having abandoned religious practices, are without any basis for the development of moral principle.[84]

Indeed, Farrell emphasized, "there is no common moral and theological ground upon which politically organised Jewry and a Christian civilization can stand together in harmony."[85] As he emphasized later in the memo, there was simply no way that Jewish identity could form the basis for political action without violating the principles of "common humanism," principles that, we might add, were seemingly uncompromised by the political acts of "Christian civilization." Farrell assumed a quasi-confessional mode in stating:

> I must admit that for many years, and despite many indications, I myself failed fully to understand why in the national home, Palestine, it should be neces-

> sary to reinforce the natural separatism which dispersed Jewry had exhibited through millennia by exaggerated attention to Hebrew language and other, more unprofitable, Hebrew studies. Ultimately, however, though late, the reason became clear, that the aim was not a passive, cultural and religious Judaism but the nurture of an active, selfish and aggressively secular, and imperialistic spirit liable to direct itself to domination over neighbouring peoples.[86]

There is no conceptual space in Farrell's framework for a religious Judaism that is something other than cultural or passive. Beyond pedagogic irresponsibility, Zionism was thus guilty of promoting a political-theological hybrid that simultaneously overturned the Jew's "natural" passivity and violated the sublime principles of religion itself. Traces of this attitude existed among many British officers in Palestine, including Farrell's predecessor, Humphrey Bowman, who spoke charitably of Orthodox Jews, particularly those who had been in Palestine prior to the First World War. These were the *watani* Jews who granted coherence to the idea of the Holy Land, "the most unoffending and inoffensive Jews in the world: holy men and their families, and religious students."[87]

Of course, Zionists were not the only group guilty of using education as an instrument of political indoctrination, only the most successful. In the same memorandum, the director of education stated, "The attitude of Palestine Zionists to education is essentially identical not only with that of the Nazis and the Russian Communists but also with that of Jamal Hussaini and other Arab politicians who wish to use the Arab schools to inculcate fanatical anti-Zionism." However, he noted with satisfaction, "the Arab politicians have been less successful and their influence touches in any considerable degree only Moslem private schools [e.g., al-Najāḥ School and its counterparts in other cities]. . . . Thus a large majority of the Moslem and Christian population is still educated in the common principles of conduct which inform Christianity and Islam."[88] Farrell's colleagues in the Colonial Office praised his assessment as an "extremely careful and fair minded analysis."[89]

Despite Farrell's protestations, the reality was that the Government of Palestine had largely tied its own hands in dealing with Zionist education. Sectarian legislation such as the Religious Communities Organization Ordinance allowed Zionist political organs to represent the official "Jewish community of Palestine," a status that came with a great deal of administrative autonomy. The Education Ordinance further contributed to the sectarian division of education in Palestine wherein the religious community, singularly defined, became the only political unit capable of making a claim for educational autonomy. While government inspectors attended meetings convened by Zionist education administrators, their recommendations were taken as suggestions rather than demands. A memorandum prepared by the Jewish Agency reflected this attitude: "While the Jewish authorities are prepared to entertain recommendations and proposals on such points from the Government Department of Education, we cannot look upon such recommendations as being mandatory."[90]

Indeed, officials in both Palestine and the Colonial Office expressed dismay that the Government of Palestine had been unable to exert more influence over the direction of Zionist education, and there was often a sense of puzzlement over why precisely this was the case. Expressing his views on another of Farrell's lengthy reports, this one addressing the Va'ad Leumi's financial mismanagement of Zionist education, H. S. Scott from the Colonial Office admitted that "the whole administrative work of the Va'ad Leumi is indited [*sic*] in paragraph 40 [of Farrell's report]" but still found it "difficult to understand how it was that the Government continued to deal so gently with the inefficiency of that body."[91] The Hebrew Public System's larger measure of financial self-sufficiency clearly made it more difficult for the Government of Palestine to enforce its will as it did in its dealings with Arab education. Yet government financial assistance to Zionist schools was not altogether insignificant, accounting for between 10 and 15 percent of the Zionist education budget throughout the period.[92] Moreover, the government had for many years failed to impose even the limited sanctions that were within its authority.

In reality, this astonishment with regard to the Government of Palestine's ineptitude was in many respects misplaced. Officials in London had continually constrained the administrators in Palestine in their dealings with Zionist political bodies, as we saw in the Colonial Office's response to the Education Ordinance, which originally gave the Palestine government wide powers of supervision. This was not merely the case with education but represented a larger source of strain between colonial administrators on the ground who were quickly able to deduce the difficulties inherent in the national home project and those in London who continued to push for its implementation. Officials in the Colonial Office could point the finger ever elsewhere, such as in arguing that the Va'ad Leumi refused to enact meaningful education reforms because "it is so much easier to engineer a grievance, to fire in telegrams from all quarters of the globe and to batter at the doors of No. 10 [the Prime Minister's residence], than to sit down quietly to the job of constructive work."[93]

Perhaps worst of all was the late realization that the autonomy granted to Zionist schools, based in part on the Religious Communities Organization Ordinance, was itself completely unjustified:

> This independence would be claimed with better reason if the Va'ad Leumi were in fact as well as in name the council of a religious community, but it is rather a racial and national assembly with a "party" (i.e., Zionist) bias and a secular, not a religious, ideology. Non-Zionist Jews are excluded from the "party" by their own religious scruples or from an effective share in it by the suspicions of the "party" managers.[94]

As was the case in his later memo, Farrell's frustrations reflected not merely his own antipathy toward Palestine's various "Semites," the existence of which should not be overlooked, but also the unresolvable contradictions embedded within British support for the Zionist cause. On the one hand, he clearly saw Jews as a nation and Judaism as a religion, and on the other, he viewed the mixing of religion and nationalism as a violation of both the rules of liberalism and the ethics of "common humanity." Not surprisingly, the fact that he viewed these two sets of ethical parameters as essentially the same went unstated. The irony was that the act of granting Jews political rights as a religious community allowed Zionism to capitalize on this autonomy for nationalist ends. In the end, we are led back to the fundamental contradictions inherent in British policy making in Palestine—Jewishness should constitute the basis of national rights, but, as a religion, Judaism should rise above the nationalist tumult. These reflections should invite us to think further about the relationship between the sectarian and the secular, on the one hand, and the multifaceted relationship between Zionism and colonialism, on the other.

This chapter has attempted to unravel the different threads that ran through Zionist and colonial views of religious education within the *yishuv*. These two groups found themselves at odds over the nature and purpose of this education and even over the definition of "religion" itself. The Department of Education repeatedly expressed concern over the political nature and antireligious spirit of Zionist schools—and the consequent alienation of Jews from common humanity—an anxiety that helps explain the government's support for Orthodox schools. Yet administrators found nothing particularly savory about these older forms of communal schooling other than their perceived indifference to mass politics. The mistake was in equating traditional forms of religious education that developed largely prior to and outside the world of mass politics with the dubious assumption that religion was therefore a conservative force in and of itself. In fact, in the face of strong government opposition to the inclusion of politics in the classroom, there seems to have been no serious attention paid to the ease with which Jewish religious studies could be politicized. On the contrary, the director of education repeatedly asserted that the Zionist schools had fallen into a sort of "racial self-worship" because they were not adequately religious.[95]

A review of Zionist educational programs suggests that contrary to Farrell's admonition, a dynamic—albeit contested—engagement with the Jewish religious tradition was present within all three trends. This survey of the Hebrew Public System reveals that Zionist education was deeply invested in articulating a new relationship between Jewishness and mass politics, for which secular is a poor characterization. This analysis has highlighted how easily theological meanings could coexist with, and even generate, historical narratives regarding the eternal connection between the Jewish people and the land—with the corresponding political implications. But in an even larger sense, the attempt to construct a synthetic identity that bridged the spiritual and material, and the public and private, can be read as a rejection of secular liberalism as a political and social model. To *not* have to leave one's Jewishness at home: Was this not both the core of the Zionist promise and simultaneously a condemnation of the modern European manner of coping with difference?

This is not to claim that there was nothing different about Zionist education that distinguished it from the past forms—only to question why that difference has been so readily equated with the secular. In this regard, I suggest that taking Zionism's secularity for granted does the political work of disassociating the movement's early days from its complicated present, in which Orthodox education has been linked to the rightward tilt of Israeli politics. Have we not noticed that assertions of Zionism's secular roots are often heard from those same quarters that lament the "return" of religion in contemporary Israel and that ascribe responsibility for the country's prolonged conflicts to either religious settlers or the growth of ultra-Orthodoxy?[96] These tend to be the same narratives that look nostalgically to the pre-1967 years as Israel's golden age, before the secular dream was upended by messianic imperialism. I have suggested that a critical examination of Zionist education complicates this reading and suggests points of continuity between that past and Israel's present.[97]

To reiterate, this is not an argument that past and present forms of education are essentially the same but that they draw on a common reservoir of narratives, terms, and symbols whose interpretive flexibility is almost endless. Much as we would expect if we treat religions as materially embedded practices rather than essential objects, the Jewish textual tradition can in fact give rise to different and often contradictory arguments regarding Zionism, *Eretz Yisrael*, the position of non-Jews, governance, violence, and peace. Rather than regard one form of engagement with this tradition as secular (rational, ethical, tolerant) and the other as religious (xenophobic, fanatic, insular), I have approached educational practices along a spectrum that asserted, in varied ways, that an authentically Jewish life was grounded in Torah. Determining what that meant and who decided was of course no simple matter; rather, the Zionist educational project offered an opportunity for ever-expanding groups of individuals to theorize anew about the relationship between Jewish theological principles, communal practices, and political life—opening new hermeneutic vistas as they asserted their own right to interpret and to educate. The plurality of "Jewish values" we now encounter—including some that are diametrically opposed—was already a feature of Zionist education during this formative period.

In conclusion, and to shift registers slightly, these reflections seem to substantiate Gershom Scholem's anxieties about the secularization of the Hebrew language, famously voiced in a letter to Franz Rosenzweig: "That sacred language on which we nurture our children, is it not an abyss that must open up one day?"[98] What remains useful about Scholem's question is its implicit suggestion that the Hebrew language, and arguably the entire sacred complex embedded within it, is not a force that Zionism's cultural and political elite might actually be able to control. In fact, though initially initiated by the quasi state for particular political ends, the instrumental utilization of religious texts, customs, and idioms has increasingly escaped the state of Israel's best attempts to direct them.[99] The corollary to harnessing the Jewish religious tradition to mass politics has been the ongoing contest, in Israel and the diaspora, over whose policies represent the most "authentically" Jewish position. Little wonder then that in our contemporary age, ongoing attempts to fuse the material and spiritual, the political and the communal, and the secular and the religious represent either the source of Israel's salvation or the fuel for its eventual destruction. It all depends on whom you ask.

CONCLUSION

The Invisible Cross

> Like that unmarked race, which, in the related discourse of racism, became invisible or white, Christianity invented the distinction between the religious and the secular and thus *made* religion. It made religion the problem—rather than itself. And it made it into an object of criticism that needed to be no less than *transcended*.
>
> —Gil Andijar, "Secularism"

> There was no way to teach a man to read the Bible . . . which did not also enable him to read the radical press.
>
> —Raymond Williams, *The Sociology of Culture*

HAD THE OPINIONS ABOUT RELIGIOUS EDUCATION that prevailed during the early twentieth century materialized, a study like this would have been firmly rooted in a past that was quickly fading from view. The eventual obsolescence of religious observance was likely part of David Ben-Gurion's political calculus when he made broad concessions to Agudat Israel to guarantee its support for the Zionist project.[1] Similarly, intellectuals like 'Izzat Darwaza and Taha Hussein saw the advance of Islamic civilization as being accompanied by the retreat of sharia as an all-encompassing legal code for regulating human behavior. In more recent decades, modernization theory posited that societies would naturally secularize en route to modernity. To these miscalculations we may add the colonial one examined as part of this study, that religious education constituted a conservative force that would restrain social change rather than propel it.

With the benefit of hindsight, we can place the British approach to religious education on a continuum that, for most of the twentieth century, viewed religiosity as an antidote to unsavory forms of mass politics. In this context, it is worth recalling that Anwar Sadat's assassination by members of Egyptian Islamic Jihad came on the heels of his support for Islamic groups in universities as a counterweight to leftist organizations. In a related vein, Israel regarded Muslim Brotherhood–affiliated social service and charity organizations as a lesser threat than those linked to the Palestine Liberation Organization and allowed the former to operate in Gaza during the mid-1980s even as it cracked down on the latter. I have argued that the era of nationalism and mass schooling gave rise to new social conditions wherein the relationship between religious traditions and political identity had to be formulated anew. That this could be done in support of revolutionary change rather than in the name of mere continuity has become, at the beginning of the twenty-first century, almost axiomatic.

This was clearly not the case in Mandate Palestine, which has served as the immediate context for charting the intersection of actors who sought to formulate new ideas about the role of religious education in the age of mass politics. In contextualizing this analysis in an imperial frame, I have tried to be attentive to the fact that designating what is "religious" is itself an expression of power, not merely an objective determination based on certain attitudes toward the transcendent. It is this larger context of discursive authority that we must bear in mind when we analyze concrete instances in which the religious or secular nature of schools, communities, and cultures was actively debated. With regard to the Mandatory government, I have argued that a particular understanding of religion as a politically disinterested code of individual ethics lay at the heart of sectarian policies that linked educational autonomy to the religious community. It was, moreover, the Zionist movement that was able to best capitalize on this administrative structure, through the official designation of the Jewish community alone as both a religious and national entity. Moving beyond Palestine's legal order, I have argued that the Mandatory state promoted a new and improved type of religious education within both Muslim and Jewish communities as the paradoxical guarantor of the traditional order. Finally, I have shown that while certain Jewish and Muslim educators also found communal schools like the *ḥeder* and *kuttāb* woefully inadequate, they did not acquiesce to the government's view in toto but offered competing educational models in which religious texts and practices formed the cornerstone of nationalist politics. These schools differed in substantive ways from their communal forebears, yet approaching this educational history as signifying a transformation from the religious to the secular is not particularly useful. Rather than move in some sort of linear time from the former to the latter, I have suggested a more dialectical reading in which Jewish and Islamic texts, practices, and themes were mobilized in furtherance of secular nationalist goals.

This study has also tried to attend to the fact that educational trends in Palestine were rooted in a much broader geography that takes us to places like Cairo, Berlin, Warsaw, and Aligarh, where traditional patterns of communal education had come under fire by Jewish and Muslim reformers over the course of the last century and a half. Within European Jewish and Arab-Islamic contexts, the reformist agenda shared certain common features: a heightened emphasis on a pure language (Arabic or Hebrew) as a vessel of national heritage; a tendency to minimize exegetical traditions in favor of an unmediated approach to the sacred text; a desire to diversify the curricula studied within communal schools to include European languages and modern sciences; and an insistence on schools' hygienic and pedagogic improvement. Despite their notable differences, both movements singled out education as the key driver of social transformation and tied the attainment of a vast array of goals to the adoption of modern forms of schooling being pioneered in European contexts. Understanding the later history of religious education in Palestine requires taking stock of this modernist legacy and, crucially, the power disparities under which Jewish and Muslim intellectuals toiled.

With this background in mind, we can better make sense of the numerous points of overlap that joined British, Zionist, and Arab-Muslim educators in Mandate Palestine. It was, after all, during these decades that Jewish and Islamic education underwent a wholesale transformation wherein the modernist innovations of the prior century became common practices. As heirs to these reformist traditions, Jewish and Muslim educators were particularly conscientious of education's revolutionary potential and explicitly viewed schooling as a tool for preparing the next generation for their respective national struggles. This entailed not merely support for the expansion of communal school curricula to include practical subjects but also the mobilization of Jewish and Islamic textual traditions to highlight the sacred character of political activism. In this sense, we might offer a variation on the quote from Raymond Williams cited at the beginning of the chapter: there was no way to teach a man to read the Bible (or in this case, the Qur'an) that did not also enable him to read it *as* a radical text.

Despite certain points of overlap between British, Jewish, and Arab educators—ranging from opinions regarding school hygiene to pedagogic approaches to sacred texts—education in Palestine remained an endlessly contentious issue, particularly in regard to defining the role of religious subjects. I have linked these difficulties to the sense of ambiguity over what, precisely, the content of religion included. Was religion about faith or action? A personal matter or communal affair? Was its purpose to unite different "faiths" (a common phrase that betrays its own particularism) or to stress the historic mission of a single group? And how, perhaps most important, should religious traditions function in regard to the mass political movements that were rapidly transforming the nature of Jewish and Muslim life? I have tried to examine the negotiation of these conceptual boundaries—between the religious and secular, the universal and particular, the pedagogic and the political—against the background of Palestine's hardening sectarian boundaries. I have done so both to gesture toward the material processes by which certain types of division assumed a place of prominence and to highlight the historicity of those allegedly primordial religious tensions about which contemporary observers of Israel/Palestine hear so much.

Finally, I have attempted to reinscribe this history into that of the broader tendency by colonial powers—no less evident today—to act as disinterested mediators in an intractable conflict between Jews and Arabs (and with increasing specificity, Muslims). Within the context of education in Mandate Palestine, the politics of denial began with a refusal to recognize mass, state-sponsored education as an inherently political practice. I have argued that efforts to deny this fact hinged on what were rather fuzzy boundaries between pedagogic need and social engineering, public service and mass politics, national pride and national chauvinism, religious values and politicized religion. Only by appreciating this web of tenuous distinctions can we understand how British officials found nothing contradictory about, for instance, stressing civic engagement while forbidding politics in the classroom. Broadly speaking, the denial of this porousness was a defining feature of British rule in Palestine and continues to anchor broader liberal claims about the objective good. It represents nothing less than the power to render power invisible and to express this power through policies that insist they have nothing to do with politics. This complex array of administrative directives, statements, and decisions derived its power from the same spring of liberalism that has, in more recent times, rendered Western secularism a universal model of good behavior. Conversely, it was "native" movements across the boundary that separated colonial practices from their corrupted forms that represented the ultimate site of transgression.

In concluding this study, we should note one final example wherein the politics of denial was particularly evident: the treatment of Christian schools as disinterested, neutral meeting grounds where Jews and Arabs could escape the surrounding political turmoil that was attributed less to the realities of colonialism than to the innate fanaticism of feuding Semitic cousins. In the *Palestine Royal Commission Report*, for instance, the authors heaped praise on "mixed" (i.e., Christian) schools in Palestine that educated both Jewish and Palestinian Arab (Christian and Muslim) children. As J. S. Bennet from the Colonial Office summarized the situation, "The Commission had received evidence that in such schools as St. George's, Jerusalem, or the Jerusalem Girls College, it had been proved that Arabs and Jews could be successfully taught together, and not only work and play together but also make lasting friendships."[2] We should note his sense of surprise in observing that students from these different communities, whose historical relations have not been characterized by continual animus, were in fact capable of learning together. Nevertheless, public coeducation was never deemed a practical goal based on its level of difficulty—which was indeed substantial. As the PRC *Report* wrote of the situation:

> The worst feature is the nationalist character of the education provided, and for this we see no effective remedy at all. Ideally, as we have suggested . . . the system should be a single bi-national system for both races; but under the conditions imposed by the Mandate it seems virtually impossible to realize that ideal. It would involve a radical alteration in the present administrative organization.[3]

Writing seven years later in response to a memorandum by Jerome Farrell summarizing the "tragic history" of education during the Mandate, H. S. Scott of the Colonial Office wrote, "It is no doubt easy to be wise after the event," but "if the purpose of the Mandatory was to establish a composite state one would have thought that unity of treatment in education should have been adopted from the beginning." The danger of allowing separate systems of education to flourish, he continued, was that "the cultural rift between Jews and Arabs, which it was a mandatory obligation to close, would actually be widened and I fear that is exactly what has happened."[4] Scott's comments encapsulate the general lament that swept through much of the Colonial Office during the Mandate's final years. Generally speaking, officials spent the first part of the period arguing that a unified school system was undesirable and the final years lamenting the fact that it was no longer feasible.

Much of the confusion stemmed from the vagueness of the Mandate itself and the differing interpretations of what political and social reality it entailed. It is telling that in 1944, the Colonial Office could not exactly clarify what the Mandatory's policy had been or should have been. Was the goal, as Scott articulated it, to form a "composite state" with a binational character? Or was Palestine to be a Jewish state with the Arab majority rendered a minority through massive immigration? Was it to have an Arab majority with a large, autonomous Jewish population? The fact that an unambiguous answer to these questions was never forthcoming—or that the answer changed with every white paper—left education administrators without a clear sense of what role schools were to play in shaping the political future. Moreover, the mere suggestion that policy should be dictated by political, rather than educational, concerns violated the epistemic order on which colonial educators depended to distinguish social engineering from pedagogic necessity. This refusal to acknowledge the inherently political nature of mass schooling—to say nothing of the impossibility of insulating schools against the surrounding political drama—also foreclosed any potential to craft an education policy that might serve a positive political role. In this, the British diverged from their Ottoman predecessors, who envisaged the school as a crucial site of acculturation between the various religious and ethnic groups that constituted the empire.[5] It is true that the reality of the Ottoman system fell far short of this lofty goal. However, it is significant that the British did not set such a goal to begin with. The irony, of course, was that the Palestinian social reality was being radically transformed all around the schoolhouse regardless of attempts to preserve the vestiges of tradition.

Finally, the PRC's praise for "mixed" Christian schools offers confirmation of Ylana Miller's astute observation that the British tended to view Christianity as the only framework within which to articulate common civic interests in Palestine.[6] In its final report, the PRC included the following description of these schools:

> In most, if not all of them, a high standard of educational efficiency is maintained. Their curriculum is broader than that of the Jewish or Arab schools; their educational ideals and methods are western; and, in most of them, a specifically Christian type of character is aimed at. No encouragement is given to either Jewish or Arab nationalism, not so much by suppression of these aspirations as by diversion of interest into other channels. . . . They provide a fine example of what could have been achieved in happier circumstances.[7]

Within this passage, we can detect several key concepts that were continually mobilized to facilitate the politics of denial: the particularism of Jewish and Arab education versus the supposedly broader horizons of Western schools; the diversion of interest away from Jewish and Arab nationalism in favor of more productive channels; the benefits gained from students' exposure to a (presumably apolitical) "Christian type of character."

Alas, happier circumstances were not to be had, though in another sleight of hand, the passages just quoted function to elide the role of British policy making in exacerbating the very divisions that mixed schools hoped to overcome. As I have argued, the tendency to project a vision of Jewish and Arab separatism onto the past as a stable feature of Palestinian life does not account for the fact that not all forms of division are qualitatively the same. While they did not create communal divisions, British administrators pursued educational policies that accelerated Jewish and Arab separatism and gave statutory recognition to such separatism so that education *could not* proceed on any other basis. Rather than represent the mere continuation of the Ottoman social and political order, the educational policies adopted by the Mandatory government contributed to the eradication of any semblance of nonsectarian public space. Whether cloaked in the language of pedagogic best practices or administrative necessity, policies related to education finance and management linked autonomy to private religious initiatives (no matter how difficult such designations proved to be), foreshadowing the erasure of a common civic sphere as Palestine became not just administratively—but socially and politically—divided into competing "publics." Meanwhile, as the Mandate grew ever more burdensome, the tendency within colonial circles was to speak of Palestine in tragic terms as a place whose conflicts were almost supernaturally driven by a force beyond anyone's control: "Under a different form of Mandate a unitary Palestine state might have been built up with children of both races educated together in common schools."[8] Though it may sound like the words of an outside observer, this statement is from an official within the British Colonial Office, in other words, from the administrative organ that was charged with deciding what type of political form the Mandatory state would assume.

Questions regarding the relationship between religion—and religious education in particular—and political radicalism have only become more timely since the turn of the twenty-first century. In the days that followed the attacks of September 11, 2001, the term "madrasa" entered the American vocabulary alongside "jihad," and indeed, many commentators argued that the two were intrinsically linked. Likewise, one need not have spent much time researching the Israeli-Palestinian conflict to have heard that radical *yeshivot* (singular, *yeshiva*) encourage settler violence. Such claims have become commonplace over the last decade as writers associated with the so-called New Atheists—including figures like the late Christopher Hitchens, Richard Dawkins, and Sam Harris—have popularized the notion that religions are particularly prone to fanaticism and violence in a way that secular movements are not. There is obviously much to say in response to such claims, and they, too, are part of what I have termed the "politics of denial." But as the question of religion and violence is beyond the immediate subject, I here simply draw attention to the ahistoricity of religion that such arguments assume. Rather than approach religions as stable essences that are textually based and consistent across time and place, I have tried to highlight the ways in which religious traditions are plural, contested, and dynamic, almost always changing—even (especially) when their adherents deny it. The reality is that there is nothing inherent about what constitutes a religious education, and the association of religion with political radicalism is itself a rather recent development. To appreciate religions in their tremendous diversity also means to recognize that religious education can be mobilized in furtherance of a full spectrum of political and ethical goals. At a time of growing suspicion in Western countries toward religious "outsiders" and a tendency to view the traditions of others in one-dimensional terms, this is a fact we would be well served to remember.

NOTES

INTRODUCTION

1. At the outset of the war, more than half of the Arab children who attended school were in private communal institutions: approximately 8,705 in Muslim schools (predominantly *katātīb*) and thousands more in Christian (largely missionary) schools, and 8,248 in the Ottoman public schools. Tibawi, *Arab Education in Mandatory Palestine*, 20. Within the Jewish community, precise statistics of school enrollment by administrative body are unavailable, but it is unlikely that the number of students in schools managed by the *va'ad ha-ḥinuch* approached the number in private *ḥederim* and *talmudei-torah* (Orthodox communal schools) given the difference in population between the Old Yishuv (66,000) and the New Yishuv (13,900) at the outbreak of the war. Elboim-Dror, *ha-Ḥinuch ha-Ivri be-Eretz-Yisrael*, 2:21.

2. Casanova, *Public Religions in the Modern World.*

3. Asad, *Formations of the Secular*; Habermas, "Notes on Post-secular Society"; Habermas, *An Awareness of What Is Missing*; Taylor, *A Secular Age*; Fitzgerald, *Ideology of Religious Studies*; Fitzgerald, *Religion and the Secular*; Fitzgerald, *Religion and Politics in International Relations*; Masuzawa, *Invention of World Religions*; Anidjar, "Secularism;" Nongbri, *Before Religion*; Calhoun, Juergensmeyer, and VanAntwerpen, *Rethinking Secularism*; Calhoun, Mendieta, and VanAntwerpen, *Habermas and Religion*; Mahmood, *Religious Difference in a Secular Age.*

4. Gribetz, *Defining Neighbors*, 13.

5. As most influentially argued in Gellner, *Nations and Nationalism.*

6. In his authoritative study of British educational policies in Palestine, Abdul Latif Tibawi offers a general overview of "religion, nationalism and education policy" but ultimately demurs. "Here it is not possible without disturbing the balance of emphasis in this study, to cover the whole field of the interaction of religion and education. This field is so wide and crowded with events as to merit a special study." See Tibawi, *Arab Education in Mandatory Palestine*, chap. 7.

7. Shemesh, *Beit ha-midrash le-morim "Mizraḥi."* The late Motti Bar-Lev authored numerous works about religious (particularly religious Zionist) education in the state of Israel. Readers interested in a general overview should consult Bar-Lev, *ha-Ḥinuch ha-dati ba-ḥevra ha-Yisraelit.* More recently, Jewish religious education is taken up by the contributors in Dror and Gross, *Dor le dor.*

8. Greenberg, *Preparing the Mothers of Tomorrow*. For a general overview of the Supreme Muslim Council's educational endeavors, see Kupferschmidt, *The Supreme Muslim Council*, 139–44.

9. See Weissman, "Ḥinuch banot datiyot bi-Yerushalayim bi-tekufat ha-shilton ha-Briti." For the late Ottoman period, particularly details about the Old Yishuv's relations with the educational bodies of the Zionist Organization, see Elboim-Dror, *ha-Ḥinuch ha-Ivri be-Eretz-Yisrael*,vol. 2. A broader treatment of ultra-Orthodox life during the Mandate period appears in Friedman, *Ḥevra ve-dat*.

10. Horowitz and Lissak, *Origins of the Israeli Polity*.

11. It is noteworthy, for example, that in the leading study of Jewish education during the Mandate Period, only thirteen pages are devoted to describing the relationship between Zionist education and the Government of Palestine. See Dror and Reshef, *ha-Ḥinuch ha-Ivri bi-yamei ha-bayit ha-leumi*.

12. See, for example, Doumani, *Rediscovering Palestine*.

13. Khalidi, *The Iron Cage*, chap. 1.

14. Shafir, *Land, Labor, and the Origins of the Israeli-Palestinian Conflict*.

15. Lockman, *Comrades and Enemies*, 8.

16. See, for example, Abigail Jacobson's study of late Ottoman Jerusalem, *From Empire to Empire*. Also of note in this regard is Gribetz's *Defining Neighbors*. With regard to Arab and Jewish education, Yoni Furas has recently examined the "uncanny resemblance" that linked the nationalist practices of history across school systems, even as such practices contributed to driving these communities further apart. Furas, "In Need of a New Story."

17. Latour, *We Have Never Been Modern*, 38.

18. Ibid., 33.

19. Ibid., 39.

20. Ibid., 43.

21. Segev, *One Palestine, Complete*, 33.

22. As Segev argues, Chaim Weizmann was well aware that British officials viewed him as a sort of "king of the Jews" who represented a unified "world Jewry" and used this conspiratorial anti-Semitism to his advantage. See ibid., chap. 2.

23. Sir Henry McMahon to Sherif Hussein, October 24, 1915. Reprinted in Antonius, *The Arab Awakening*, appendix A.

24. For a more detailed discussion of the Paris Peace Conference and related summits, such as that at San Remo, which definitively decided the fate of former Ottoman territories, see Fromkin, *A Peace to End All Peace*, pt. 9.

25. Susan Pederson has masterfully chronicled the institutional history of the League of Nations Mandate system through her analysis of the Permanent Mandates Commission, including numerous episodes of interest to the historian of Palestine. See Pederson, *The Guardians*.

26. League of Nations, "The Covenant of the League of Nations," Avalon Project, Yale Law School, April 28, 1919, http://avalon.law.yale.edu/20th_century/leagcov.asp.

27. The exceptions, by and large, consisted of British Jews like Herbert Samuel, Pal-

estine's first high commissioner, and Norman Bentwich, who served as attorney general. Despite their obvious support for Zionism, their appointments were theoretically based on their status as British citizens.

28. As an education officer in the colonial service, Bowman was treading a well-worn path. It is estimated that from the years 1918 to 1938, some 20–30 percent of Oxford and Cambridge graduates served in the colonial education administration. See Symonds, *Oxford and Empire*, 307.

29. S. Boyle, *Betrayal of Palestine*.

30. Humphrey Bowman, diary entry, June 1, 1925, MEC, Humphrey Bowman Collection, Box 3B.

31. Ibid., September 26, 1929.

32. See "Hassam al-Din Jarallah," in Muhammad 'Amr Hamada, *A'lām Filasṭīn min al-qurn al-awal hata al-khāmis 'ashar*, 133–34. On the elections for grand mufti, see Al-Hout, *al-Qiyādāt wa al-mu'assassāt al-siyāsiya fi Filasṭīn 1917–1948*, 203–5; and Roberts, *Rethinking the Status Quo*, chap. 4.

33. The Council of the League of Nations, "The Palestine Mandate," Avalon Project, Yale Law School, July 24, 1922, http://avalon.law.yale.edu/20th_century/palmanda.asp.

34. Horowitz and Lissak, *Origins of the Israeli Polity*, 24.

35. For more on these intra-Zionist struggles, see ibid., chap. 3.

36. Roberts, "Rethinking the Status Quo," 196.

CHAPTER 1

1. For more on the South Asian context, see Khan, "Sir Sayyid Ahmad Khan on Islam and Science."

2. The more comprehensive overview of these trends within the Arab context is Albert Hourani's work, *Arabic Thought in the Liberal Age*. Other accounts, such as those by Ibrahim Abu-Lughod and George Antonius, remain informative even if their theoretical frameworks are no longer as compelling. See Abu-Lughod, *Arab Rediscovery of Europe*; Antonius, *The Arab Awakening*. Scholarship devoted to the *Haskalah* and Zionism is too numerous to enumerate. Among the more useful texts regarding each movement's education programs, see Feiner and Sorkin, *New Perspectives on the "Haskalah"*; Assaf and Etkes, *ha-Ḥeder*; Feiner, "Programot ḥinuchiot ve-idialim ḥevratiyim"; Elboim-Dror, *ha-Ḥinuch ha-Ivri be-Eretz-Yisrael*.

3. The similarities between these two efforts at communal modernization in regard to the "idea of Europe" have been noted by Lital Levy in her work on the literary production associated with the *Haskalah* (enlightenment) and *nahḍa* (renaissance) in the nineteenth-century Ottoman Empire. See Levy, "The Nahḍa and the Haskala."

4. Bentwich, *Education in Israel*.

5. Tibawi, *Islamic Education*.

6. Berkey, "Madrasas Medieval and Modern," 46 (emphasis in original).

7. Turniansky, "Heder Learning in the Early Modern Period."

8. Bentwich, *Education in Israel*, 6–7.

9. Mitchell, *Colonizing Egypt*, 85–89.

10. Hefner and Zaman, *Schooling Islam*, 5. Numerous works exist on Islamic education in the classical period, some of which are valuable not merely as secondary sources but as examples of the way in which Arab reformers of the last century approached this heritage. See, for example, Totah, "The Contribution of the Arabs to Education." For a more recent and comprehensive account, see Tibawi, *Islamic Education*. A contemporary treatment of the subject, which assumes greater critical distance from the modernist paradigm, appears in Billeh and Kadi, *Islam and Education*.

11. According to one historian of Ottoman education reform, "It did not belong to the ultimate educational goal of the traditional Islamic school system to transmit utilitarian-practical knowledge." We might question the extent to which religious knowledge was not "utilitarian-practical" to the societies in which it served, but the point here is that the knowledge required for one's trade or vocation was not part of the traditional school. Somel, *Modernization of Public Education*, 19.

12. Babylonian Talmud, Shabbat, 127a.

13. Ridder-Symoens, *A History of the University in Europe*.

14. Foucault, "Governmentality." Foucault makes this point through an etymological survey of the term "governing," which in its earlier usage indicated the (father's) running of a household rather than an act of the state.

15. Ramirez and Boli, "The Political Construction of Mass Schooling."

16. Gellner, *Nations and Nationalism*; Weber, *Peasants into Frenchmen*.

17. "Increasingly, the economic organization of Europe invested individuals with both the authority to conduct their own productive activities and the responsibility to support the state financially. Given the competitiveness of an economically integrating Europe, the productivity and loyalty of individuals became a central concern of state authorities." Ramirez and Boli, "The Political Construction of Mass Schooling," 13.

18. Rawls, *Political Liberalism*, 199.

19. Ibid., 217–19.

20. Mitchell, *Colonizing Egypt*; Scott, "Colonial Governmentality." Examples of historical works that have adopted a Foucauldian approach to understanding colonial history include Duncan, *In the Shadows of the Tropics*; Li, *The Will to Improve*. For an example that applies this theoretical apparatus to the history of education in the Middle East, see Sedra, *From Mission to Modernity*.

21. For a recent example of the ways in which individuals continued to exercise agency even in the face of oppressive power structures, see Lee, *Pétain's Jewish Children*.

22. Ramirez and Boli, "The Political Construction of Mass Schooling," 3.

23. Starrett, *Putting Islam to Work*, 58.

24. Bentham, *A Fragment on Government*. I borrow the language of "political rationality" from David Scott's article, "Colonial Governmentality."

25. Bowman, *Middle-East Window*.

26. Gordon and White, *Philosophers as Education Reformers*. For an extended treatment of the educational practices associated with British liberalism, see McLaughlin, *Liberalism, Education and Schooling*.

27. One of the more famous articulations of this complementarity came from the

political philosopher T. H. Green, who developed the idea of "Christian citizenship" to describe the ideal of civic behavior. See Boucher and Vincent, *British Idealism and Political Theory*, chap. 1.

28. Ramirez and Boli, "The Political Construction of Mass Schooling," 8.

29. Sengupta, *Pedagogy for Religion*, chap. 6.

30. Ibid., 7.

31. Nongbri, *Before Religion.*

32. Masuzawa, *Invention of World Religions.*

33. Boyarin, "Was There Judaism in Pre-modernity?"

34. Smith, "Religion, Religions, Religious."

35. Batnitzky, *How Judaism Became a Religion*, 6.

36. Ibid., 13–28.

37. Feiner, "Programot ḥinuchiot ve-idialim ḥevratiyim."

38. "Edict of Toleration for the Jews of Lower Austria" (January 2, 1782), GHDI, http://germanhistorydocs.ghi-dc.org/sub_document.cfm?document_id=3648.

39. Citations throughout taken from Wessely, "Words of Peace and Truth."

40. Ibid., 70–71.

41. For a sampling of the literature that makes this argument, see Chidester, *Savage Systems*; Figueira, *Aryans, Jews, Brahmins*; King, *Orientalism and Religion*; Lopez, *Curators of the Buddha.*

42. Fitzgerald, *Ideology of Religious Studies*, 6.

43. Locke, "An Essay concerning Toleration," 197.

44. In this regard, Jonathan Hess's study of German Jews as both the objects of "improvement" in regard to their Christian interlocutors and the proponents of "distinctly Jewish visions of universalism and modernity" is of the utmost importance. In Hess's terms, "Typically cast as a clannish and coercive form of legalism irreconcilable with the Enlightenment's insistence on individual autonomy, freedom of conscience and the very power of reason itself, Judaism seemed to provide the perfect point of contrast for intellectuals wishing to imagine a secular political order grounded in the principles of rationalism and universalism." Hess, *Germans, Jews and the Claims of Modernity*, 6.

45. Mufti, *Enlightenment in the Colony*, 2.

46. Hefner, "Introduction," 12.

47. Sengupta, *Pedagogy for Religion*, 63.

48. For an alternative interpretation of the functional role of memorizing the Qur'an, see H. Boyle, "Memorization and Learning in Islamic Schools."

49. Starrett, *Putting Islam to Work*, 38.

50. Government of Palestine, Department of Education, "Syllabus for State Elementary Schools," 32.

51. Messick, *Calligraphic State.*

52. As Nongbri has recently illustrated, the term used for religion in Modern Standard Arabic, *dīn*, carried quite different connotations prior to modernity, among them "judgment," "custom," and "retribution." Accordingly, an intellectual attempt to locate "religion" in the realms of non-European peoples often preceded material efforts by

colonial powers to reform Islam into a religion on modern lines. Nongbri, *Before Religion*, chap. 2.

53. This point is well made by Talal Asad in his treatment of Muhammad ʻAbduh, wherein he disputes the tendency to regard ʻAbduh as something of an anomaly and thus places his thought outside the boundaries of what is authentically Islamic. See Asad, *Formations of the Secular*, chap. 7.

54. Fortna, *Imperial Classroom.*

55. Sengupta, *Pedagogy for Religion*, 21.

56. Hourani first presented this idea at a 1966 conference held at the University of Chicago, and it was subsequently published as "Ottoman Reform and the Politics of Notables."

57. For a survey of the responses to Hourani's theory, see Gelvin, "The 'Politics of Notables' Forty Years After."

58. Ayalon, *Reading Palestine*; Campos, *Ottoman Brothers.* See also Khalidi, *Palestinian Identity.*

59. Ayalon, *Reading Palestine*, 60.

60. Ibid., 138–45.

61. Matthews, *Confronting an Empire.*

62. "Following a Bad Example," *The Times*, March 20, 1925.

63. Hunter, *The Indian Musalmans.*

64. Ibid., 189.

65. Ibid., 102, 200. The rebel preacher to whom Hunter refers is Sayyid Ahmad Barelvi (1786–1831), who called for a jihad both against the Sikh kingdoms of northwest India and the British presence in India more generally.

66. Ibid., 205.

67. Sedra, *From Mission to Modernity*, 168.

68. Ibid., 169.

CHAPTER 2

1. Abu-Lughod, *Arab Rediscovery of Europe*, 45–47.

2. Tibawi, *Islamic Education*, 53.

3. Somel, *Modernization of Public Education*, 51–53.

4. Benjamin Fortna has written a nuanced and highly readable survey of Ottoman education in the empire's last years, *Imperial Classroom*. For more detail about the distinct pieces of legislation and bureaucratic divisions that facilitated education reform, see Somel, *Modernization of Public Education.*

5. Somel, *Modernization of Public Education*, 44.

6. Ibid., 86–90, 108–11.

7. Tibawi, *Arab Education in Mandatory Palestine*, 181.

8. Advocates of Islamic revival often argued that the return of the caliphate to Arab hands was crucial to the movement's success, a view that was most famously pressed on European audiences in Blunt, *The Future of Islam*. See Hourani, *Arabic Thought in the Liberal Age*, chap. 11 (esp. 268–70).

9. Somel, *Modernization of Public Education*, appendix 4.

10. Ibid., appendix 5.

11. In practice this does not seem to have been the case. Memoirs of the late nineteenth and early twentieth centuries often depicted "that the schoolmasters of the public *ibtidai* [primary] schools and most of the instructors were wearing white turbans, i.e., were probably members of the ‘ulema." See Somel, *Modernization of Public Education*, 260.

12. Ibid., 180; Fortna, *Imperial Classroom*.

13. Because Hebrew still existed primarily as a liturgical language, transforming it into a spoken language required concerted effort on behalf of early Zionists. It was not until the first decade of the twentieth century that a network of educators began using Hebrew as the language of instruction in Palestine's schools. For a detailed discussion, see Saposnik, *Becoming Hebrew*, chap. 4.

14. In addition to the Alliance Israélite, a small sampling of private organizations that maintained schools in Palestine include the Latin, Orthodox, and Syrian patriarchs; the Anglican bishop; the Custode de Terra Santa; the Order of the Friars, the Church Missionary Society, the Jerusalem and East Mission; the Church Mission to the Jews; the Scots Mission; the Missionsgesellschaft fur das Heilige Land; the American Friends Mission; the Swedish Mission; and numerous Roman Catholic bodies. Tibawi, *Arab Education in Mandatory Palestine*, 21–23.

15. There is still much research to be done on the schools created by missionaries in nineteenth-century Palestine. A few recent works gesture at the contentious—and competitive—relations between missionaries and local communities, for example, van der Leest, "Conversion and Conflict in Palestine." Arieh Saposnik identifies the battle against missionaries as a pivotal struggle for Zionists in Ottoman Palestine. See Saposnik, *Becoming Hebrew*. See also Halperin, "Battle over Jewish Students." A broader geographic treatment appears in Dogan and Sharkey, *American Missionaries and the Middle East*; Khalaf, *Protestant Missionaries in the Levant*.

16. For more on al-Sakakini's educational initiatives, see Robson, *Colonialism and Christianity in Mandate Palestine*, 29–32.

17. For an extended discussion, see Almog, *The Sabra*.

18. Saposnik, *Becoming Hebrew*, 4.

19. Ben-Yosef, *Milḥemet ha-safot*.

20. Government of Palestine, Department of Education, "Note on Education in Palestine 1920–1929." The exact number of schools under Zionist control during this time is subject to some debate. For alternative figures, see Bentwich, *Education in Israel*, 14–15. For greater detail on the early administrative structure of the Zionist schools, see Elboim-Dror, *ha-Ḥinuch ha-Ivri be-Eretz-Yisrael*, vol. 2, sec. 1–2.

21. A detailed analysis of *why* the Ottomans chose to enter the war at all appears in Aksakal, *Ottoman Road to War*.

22. Schilcher, "The Famine of 1915–1918 in Greater Syria." Salim Tamari provides a more personal look at the war's impact in Palestine with the translation of and commentary on the diary of a Palestinian soldier from Jerusalem. See Tamari, *The Year of the Locust*.

23. Tibawi, *Arab Education in Mandatory Palestine*, 156–57.

24. Ibid., 155.

25. The 1923 *Annual Report* states that there were 312 government elementary and secondary schools and 367 maintained by private groups. By 1945–46, the last year for which there are complete data, the government maintained just over 500 schools; there were nearly 1,300 under Zionist or private auspices. See Government of Palestine, Department of Education, *Annual Report 1923* and *Annual Report 1945–46*.

26. Dror and Reshef, *ha-Ḥinuch ha-Ivri bi-yamei ha-bayit ha-leumi*, 153.

27. Self-financed should not be taken to mean supported in its totality by Palestinian Jewry. Particularly during the 1920s, most of the financing for the Zionist school system came from the Zionist Organization in London and donations from abroad. For the 1920–21 school year, the Zionist Organization contributed LE (Egyptian pounds) 97,387 toward the education budget, with only LE 12,081 coming from the *yishuv*. By the 1925–26 school year, the contribution of the *yishuv* had grown to LE 47,770, but LE 63,000 still came from the Zionist Organization. In 1931–32, on the eve of the transfer of educational responsibility from the Jewish Agency to Knesset Israel, the former still contributed LP 75,720 toward a total budget of LP 130,816, or approximately 59 percent of the total education budget for the Hebrew Public System. See Dror and Reshef, *ha-Ḥinuch ha-Ivri bi-yamei ha-bayit ha-leumi*, 11–14.

28. Jerome Farrell, "Note on the Draft Estimates of the Education Department for the Financial Year 1937–1938, with Special Reference to the Expansion of Urban Education," April 10, 1937, TNA, CO 733/329/13.

29. Palestine Royal Commission, "Testimony of Mr. H. E. Bowman," 48.

30. Government of Palestine, Department of Education, *Annual Report 1945–46*, 4.

31. Tibawi, *Arab Education in Mandatory Palestine*, 273.

32. For the 1921–22 fiscal year, the Government of Palestine spent LP 210,398 on police and prisons out of a total annual expenditure of LP 1,259,587, accounting for 16.7 percent of annual expenditures, and directed LP 50,079 (4 percent) toward education. In 1926–27, police and prisons dropped slightly to account for 14.7 percent of annual expenditures, still outpacing education (5.5 percent). See *Annual Report for Palestine and Transjordan for the Year 1928*.

33. Tibawi, *Arab Education in Mandatory Palestine*, 156.

34. Second Advisory Council Meeting minutes, November 9, 1920, TNA, CO 814/6-0002.

35. Palestine Royal Commission, "Testimony of Mr. H. E. Bowman," 47.

36. Jerusalem Municipal Council, untitled memorandum, August 16, 1928, TNA, CO 733/146/8.

37. Thompson, *Colonial Citizens*, 62–66, 73–90, 63.

38. As discussed in the Introduction, the Zionist Executive's Department of Education served as the chief administrative body for Zionist schools until 1932, when control over the *yishuv*'s education was transferred to the Va'ad Leumi.

39. Wasserstein, *The British in Palestine*, 243.

40. Elboim-Dror, *ha-Ḥinuch ha-Ivri be-Eretz-Yisrael*, 134.

41. T. I. K. Lloyd, untitled memo, May 7, 1927, TNA, CO 733/139/5.

42. Lord Plumer to Secretary of State for the Colonies Amery, April 14, 1927, TNA, CO 733/139/5.

43. Ibid.

44. E. J. Harding minute, May 13, 1927, TNA, CO 733/139/5.

45. Government of Palestine, Department of Education, *Annual Report 1927–28*, appendix A.

46. Agudat Israel protested this arrangement repeatedly, as its schools (and girls' schools only, because they featured a broader curriculum) were eligible only for the standard per capita grants given to private schools because the block grant to support Jewish education went to the Jewish Agency/Va'ad Leumi schools. See, for example, "Extract from Note of Interview with Rabbi Blau and Mr. Goodman of Agudath Israel," March 16, 1938, TNA, CO 733/362/8.

47. Jerome Farrell, "Report of the Royal Commission on Palestine: Recommendations with regard to 'Mixed Schools' and Language Instruction," November 20, 1937, TNA, CO 733/362/2.

48. "Testimony of Mr. H. E. Bowman, C.M.G., C.B.E., Director of Education. November 27, 1936," 50.

49. Halperin, *Babel in Zion.*

50. Ibid., 326–29.

51. The Decentralization Party (al-muntada al-'arabi) first emerged after the restoration of the Ottoman constitution in 1908 and promoted greater autonomy of the empire's Arab provinces. In 1913, the First Arab Congress promoted a platform of decentralization within an Ottoman framework, including the use of Arabic as an educational and administrative language. Hourani, *Arabic Thought in the Liberal Age*, 286–89.

52. An expanded discussion of the political and social impact of monolingual education appears in Schneider, "Monolingualism and Education in Mandate Palestine."

53. T. I. K. Lloyd, untitled memorandum, July 1927, TNA, CO 733/139/5.

54. Ibid.

55. Ibid.

56. L. S. Amery minute, June 1, 1927, TNA, CO 733/139/5.

57. "CO Attachment to Letter to Treasury," January 30, 1933, TNA, CO 733/224/11.

58. Haim Arlosoroff to High Commissioner Wauchope, February 2, 1932, TNA, CO 733/224/11.

59. For the 1927–28 school year, estimates were that there were 28,844 Jewish children enrolled in schools (Zionist and non-Zionist) and 39,739 Arab children. Government of Palestine, Department of Education, *Annual Report 1927–28*, table 24.

60. Colonial Office, untitled memorandum, December 12, 1932, TNA, CO 733/224/11.

61. "Meeting Minutes with Brodetsky," 1932, TNA, CO 733/222/1.

62. The Education Ordinance allowed for the creation of local education subcommittees, in lieu of a unified authority, in areas with a mixed population and stipulated that "school fees collected by any Sub-Committee . . . shall be expended only upon the

schools controlled by that Sub-Committee." Government of Palestine, "Education Ordinance, 1933," sec. 14, no. 60.

63. For an account of education in Mandate Syria, see Khoury, *Syria and the French Mandate*; and Dueck, *Claims of Culture at Empire's End*, 51–90. For accounts of British educational policy in Mandate Iraq, see Sluglett, *Britain in Iraq*, 273–91; and Bashkin, "'When Mu'awiya Entered the Curriculum'"; Pursley, *Familiar Futures*; and Falb, "The Formation of State and Subject."

64. For a discussion of why an Arab Agency was never created—and never could be within the terms of the Mandate—see Khalidi, *The Iron Cage*, 44–45.

65. Tibawi, *Arab Education in Mandatory Palestine*, 131–33.

66. Palestine Royal Commission, "Testimony of Mr. H. E. Bowman," 48.

67. Whether or not these schools actually succeeded in rationalizing peasant agriculture is a matter of dispute. Importantly for our purposes, education administrators viewed the acquisition of literacy as a necessary prerequisite to implementing any type of agricultural reform. Tibawi, *Arab Education in Mandatory Palestine*, 42–43.

68. Quoted in Bowman, *Middle-East Window*, 49.

69. Government of Palestine, Department of Education, *Annual Report 1929–30* and *Annual Report 1945–46*.

70. "Protocols of the Joint Meeting of the Local Arab and Jewish School Committee of Haifa," July 26, 1943, ISA RG8 1056/35-mem (in Hebrew).

71. Government of Palestine, Department of Education, *Annual Report 1929–30*, 26, 34.

72. Nardi, *Education in Palestine*, 82.

73. C. W. M. Cox, January 27, 1942, MEC, Humphrey Bowman Collection, Box 2, File 2.

74. Palestine Royal Commission, "Testimony of Mr. H. E. Bowman," 48.

75. Government of Palestine, Department of Education, *Annual Report 1945–46*, 7.

76. Humphrey Bowman, "The Education of Girls in Palestine," *Palestine Bulletin* (February 6, 1927), quoted in Fleischmann, *The Nation and Its "New" Women*, 39. While there were certain points of overlap, the goals and curricula of Jewish and Muslim private schools for girls tended to be more expansive. For an in-depth study of the Evelina de Rothschild School, see Schor, *The Best School in Jerusalem*. Similarly, Ela Greenberg has profiled the girls' schools maintained by the SMC. See Greenberg, *Preparing the Mothers of Tomorrow*.

77. Fleishmann, *The Nation and Its "New" Women*, 36–48.

78. Ibid., 38.

79. Palestine Royal Commission, "Testimony of Mr. H. E. Bowman," 48.

80. Quoted in Fleischmann, *The Nation and Its "New" Women*, 53.

81. For an extended case study of British colonialism and the preservation/invention of tradition, see Nicholas Dirk's seminal work on caste and governance in colonial India, *Castes of Mind*, chap. 8. However, as Ellen Fleischmann has argued, the preservation of tradition could be a double-edged sword. Palestinian women effectively exploited British sensitivities to upsetting traditional norms in an attempt to shame the Mandatory government and influence its policies. See Fleischmann, *The Nation and Its "New" Women*, chap. 6.

82. Fleischmann, *The Nation and Its "New" Women*, 38.

83. See (Miss) H. Ridler, "Special Problems in the Training of Women Teachers in the Near East," in Government of Palestine, Department of Education, *Annual Report 1926–27*, 28–30.

84. "Table Showing the Number of Applications for Entrance into the Government Women's Training College, Jerusalem," January 3, 1937, TNA, CO 733/346/17.

85. There are numerous sources that testify to the demand for female education among the Arab population. For example, petitions from villages requesting the government open a girls' school became a common occurrence. See Greenberg, *Preparing the Mothers of Tomorrow*; Miller, *Government and Society in Rural Palestine*, chap. 6.

86. Humphrey Bowman, diary entry, April 7, 1929, MEC, Humphrey Bowman Collection, Box 3B.

87. Miller, *Government and Society in Rural Palestine*, 97.

88. For an extended discussion of the school strikes, see Tibawi, *Arab Education in Mandatory Palestine*, chap. 7. For an analysis of the 1925 strike within the Government Arab College, see Davis, "Commemorating Education."

89. "Undertaking to Be Signed by Teachers," May 1925, TNA, CO 814/3.

90. Tibawi, *Arab Education in Mandatory Palestine*, 184.

91. Tibawi is quite unequivocal in arguing that, despite all regulations to the contrary, schools in the Arab Public System inevitably became sites for inculcating a sense of Palestinian identity and Arab nationalism. See ibid., 195–203. Similarly, the PRC lamented that schools in the Arab Public System had become "hothouses for nationalism." See Palestine Royal Commission, *Summary of Report*, 339–40.

92. Susan Lawrence to Arthur Wauchope, undated [May/June 1935)], TNA, CO 733/273/5.

93. A. G. Wauchope to Susan Lawrence, undated [May/June 1935], TNA, CO 733/273/5. An extended study of history teaching and textbooks, among both Jewish and Arab communities, can be found in Furas, "In Need of a New Story."

94. Bowman, *Middle-East Window*, 310.

95. Ibid., 311.

96. Jerome Farrell, "Notes on Jewish Education and the McNair Report," November 30, 1946, TNA, CO/733/476/2, sec. 21.

97. Ibid., sec. 5.

98. Ibid., sec. 22. As Jonathan Gribetz has shown, Farrell's view of Christian and Muslim communities united in religious and cultural terms against the Jewish outsider was shared by Palestinian religious and political leaders during the early years of the Mandate and was already present in nascent form in the late Ottoman period. Gribetz, *Defining Neighbors*, 235–36.

CHAPTER 3

1. A sampling of this important scholarship includes Makdisi, *The Culture of Sectarianism*; Weiss, *In the Shadow of Sectarianism*; Robson, *Colonialism and Christianity in Mandate Palestine*.

2. Roberts, *Rethinking the Status Quo*. For instance, in his study of settlement patterns in the Ottoman Empire, Donald Quataert has argued that occupation and wealth were more significant factors than religious affiliation in determining the distribution of urban populations. See Quataert, *The Ottoman Empire*, 177–78.

3. In the late Ottoman period, *millet* was a legal category applied to many non-Muslim communities; they typically maintained a large degree of internal autonomy and often administered their own social services. Robson, *Colonialism and Christianity in Mandate Palestine*.

4. Roberts, *Rethinking the Status Quo*, 60.

5. Evelyn Baring, the First Earl of Cromer who served as consul general in Egypt from 1882 to 1907, frequently references the Christian core of European civilization in his *Modern Egypt* and goes as far as to doubt that any colonial subject could truly adopt the fruits of this civilization without also accepting Christianity. Cromer, *Modern Egypt*, 2:538.

6. For the full text of the Mandate for Palestine, see "The Palestine Mandate," Avalon Project, Yale Law School, 2008, http://avalon.law.yale.edu/20th_century/palmanda.asp.

7. Government of Palestine, "Religious Communities Organization Ordinance."

8. The legislation, which created the administrative mechanism for recognizing the Va'ad Leumi as Palestinian Jewry's official representative body, had as one of its main objectives "to provide the means by which the Jewish community could impose levies on its members for such purposes as education." See "Memorandum: Jewish Education in Palestine. Government Assistance," July 1, 1933, TNA, CO 733/234/11.

9. "Palestine Government Promulgates Religious Communities Ordinance," and "Palestine Communities Ordinance: Text," *Jewish Telegraphic Agency Mail Service*, Jerusalem, February 18 and March 12, 1926, respectively.

10. For a more detailed discussion of this shift and the factors that propelled it, see "The Jewish Political Center," in Horowitz and Lissak, *Origins of the Israeli Polity*, chap. 3.

11. Agudat Israel combined forces with the chief rabbi of the Ashkenazic Old Yishuv, Rabbi Sonnenfeld, and other members of the Va'ad ha-Ir (City Council of the Old Yishuv) to oppose the Religious Communities Organization Act and the corresponding recognition of the Zionist faction as the official Jewish community. See Vaad Ha'ir of the Ashkenazic Jewish Community to Secretary of State for the Colonies, April 24, 1925, TNA, FO 371/10839. See also the protests of Agudat Yisrael and the Va'ad Ha-Ir Ashkenazi of Jerusalem to the PMC in Permanent Mandates Commission, *Minutes of the Eleventh Session*, 213, and *Minutes of the Thirteenth Session*, 54.

12. Draft Agreement by the Vaad Leumi, Enclosure III, TNA, FO 371/18959.

13. Draft Agreement by the Agudath Israel, Enclosure IV, TNA, FO 371/18959.

14. Harry Charles Luke, chief secretary for Palestine, 1927. Quoted and discussed at length in Robson, *Colonialism and Christianity in Mandate Palestine*, 44–74.

15. Government of Palestine, Department of Education, *Annual Report 1934*.

16. A. G. Wauchope to Colonial Office, July 12, 1935, TNA, FO 371/18959.

17. Rabbi Hershel Schachter recorded the following anecdote regarding the Brisker

Rav, who famously avoided involvement in political disputes: "I heard that [R. Joseph Solovetichik] mentioned at that point how his uncle (R. Yitzchak Zev Solovetichik) did not usually participate in controversy and demonstrations, such as when there was an attempt to open mixed [gender] swimming pools in Jerusalem, or matters that include violations of Shabbos, because those are [just] specific sins. Only when they wanted to erect a Sanhedrin in the Heikhal Shlomo building—on this he loudly protested in order to end the matter, because he saw in it a much greater matter, namely, *ziyuf ha-Torah* [misrepresentation of Torah]." Schachter, *Be-ikvei ha-tzon*, 23.

18. The Sanhedrin was the assembly of judges in ancient Israel that ruled on *halachic* matters. Each city was entitled to a Sanhedrin of twenty-three judges, and a single Great Sanhedrin with seventy-one judges acted as a court of final appeal. The Sanhedrin was dissolved in 358 CE, and various attempts to revive it—most famously by Napoleon but also by segments of the Jewish community—have been met with widespread hostility. The normative Orthodox position is that the Sanhedrin cannot be reconvened until the days of the Messiah.

19. J. G. Ward minute, August 31, 1935, TNA, FO 371/18959.

20. In his critique of the Mandatory government and its education policies, Abdul Latif Tibawi dryly notes that laws regarding antiquities, customs, and cinema censorship were promulgated long before an ordinance relating to education. Tibawi, *Arab Education in Mandatory Palestine*, 134.

21. The Council of the League of Nations, "The Palestine Mandate," Avalon Project, Yale Law School, July 24, 1922, http://avalon.law.yale.edu/20th_century/palmanda.asp.

22. Robson, *Colonialism and Christianity in Mandate Palestine.*

23. Tibawi, *Arab Education in Mandatory Palestine*, 134–35.

24. It is telling that in her extended account of Hebrew education in Ottoman Palestine, Rachel Elboim-Dror has little to say about the Ottoman government. The chapter on the crucial years 1912–13, when the Ottoman Education Act was promulgated, is wholly devoted to the conflicts *within* the Jewish community. Elboim-Dror, *ha-Ḥinuch ha-Ivri be-Eretz-Yisrael.*

25. Louis Barlassina to Colonial Office, August 16, 1928, TNA, CO 733/146/8.

26. Tibawi, *Arab Education in Mandatory Palestine*, 30.

27. Norman Bentwich, "Explanatory Note on the Education Ordinance," May 17, 1927, TNA, CO 733/141/17.

28. Until the late nineteenth century, most schools in England were maintained by the Anglican Church. Certain exceptions included the "public schools," which were public in the sense that they were open to anyone who passed the entrance examination and could afford their steep fees. LEAs were first founded in England as a result of the 1902 (coincidentally named) Balfour Education Act. The law established LEAs to replace local school boards, which had proved popular among liberals, nonconformists, and radicals because they allowed for the creation of nonsectarian schools for areas and populations not served by Anglican or public schools. Local education taxes funded the new school boards, and Anglican schools were ineligible for any portion of these rates. In 1902 the Conservative government abolished school boards and transferred respon-

sibility to open and maintain schools, pay teacher salaries, and provide textbooks and equipment to LEAs. Digby and Searby, *Children, School, and Society*, 18–20.

29. Government of Palestine, "An Ordinance Relating to Education," *Palestine Gazette*, October 16, 1927.

30. Humphrey Bowman, diary entry, November 13, 1927, MEC, Humphrey Bowman Collection, Box 3B.

31. T. I. K. Lloyd, "Draft Education Ordinance, Etc.," November 28, 1928, TNA, CO 733/146/8.

32. Ibid.

33. Digby and Searby, *Children, School, and Society*.

34. T. I. K. Lloyd minute, July 30, 1928, TNA, CO 733/146/7.

35. Quoted in Sengupta, *Pedagogy for Religion*, 15.

36. Government of Palestine, Department of Education, *Annual Report 1945–46*.

37. Lord Plumer to Sec. of State Amery, January 12, 1928, TNA, CO 733/146/7.

38. Louis Barlassina to Colonial Office, August 16, 1928, TNA, CO 733/146/8.

39. Ibid.

40. Ibid.

41. T. I. K. Lloyd, "Draft Education Ordinance, Etc."

42. Ibid. (emphasis in original).

43. S. Wilson minute, December 24, 1928, TNA, CO 733/146/8.

44. T. I. K. Lloyd to Foreign Office, March 1, 1929, TNA, CO 733/165/5.

45. Roberts, *Rethinking the Status Quo*, 216.

46. Jerome Farrell, "J. Farrell's Comments [on the Draft Education Ordinance]," TNA, CO 733/191/2. The document is undated, though this passage is quoted almost verbatim in a letter to the Foreign Office dated September 19, 1930 (letter number 77198/30 in the same folder), which would probably place Farrell's comments in the summer of 1930.

47. W. W. Hunter's *The Indian Musalmans* was written in the aftermath of Barelvi's rebellion. For a more detailed account of his movment and its legacy, see Roy, *Islam and Resistance in Afghanistan*. On the Mahdist revolt in the Sudan, see Holt, *The Mahdist State in the Sudan*.

48. Roberts, *Rethinking the Status Quo*, 83.

49. Cromer, *Modern Egypt*, 2:63–64. As we have seen in more recent days, the practice of discrediting political acts by claiming that they stem from religious fanaticism has outlived Britain's empire. For a recent example, see Bret Stephens, "Palestine: The Psychotic Stage," *Wall Street Journal*, October 12, 2015.

50. Cromer, *Modern Egypt*, 2:133–34.

51. Roberts, *Rethinking the Status Quo*, 216.

52. Zionist Organization, "Palestine Education Ordinance," December 14, 1928, TNA, CO 733/146/8.

53. Government of Palestine, "Education Ordinance, 1933." The second clause of the ordinance states, "In his discharge of his functions in regard to any group of public schools established or maintained in part by a Local Authority or an association, the Director shall consult with such authority or association." Officials inserted this clause in

a compromise with the Zionist Organization, which demanded that in his dealings with the Hebrew Public System, the director of education consult with the Jewish Agency's Education Department. See Zionist Organization memorandum, "Palestine Education Ordinance 1928," December 14, 1928, TNA, CO 733/146/8.

54. Colonial Office, "Palestine Education Ordinance and Regulations," draft memo for the Advisory Committee on Education in the Colonies, January 1929, TNA, CO 733/146/8.

55. Council of Ashkenazic Jewish Community to Officer Administering the Government, August 13, 1928, TNA, CO/146/8.

56. Zionist Organization Memorandum, September 14, 1928, TNA, CO 733/146/8.

57. E. Mills to Zionist Executive, letter no. 16122/28, October 6, 1928, TNA, CO 733/146/8.

58. Sir Luke minute, October 22, 1941, TNA, CO 733/442/17.

59. Jerome Farrell, "The Distribution of Educational Benefits in Palestine," December 17, 1945, MEC, Jerome Farrell Collection.

60. Zionist Organization Memorandum, "Palestine Education Ordinance," December 14, 1928.

61. Ibid.

62. Sir John Shuckburg minute, November 11, 1930, TNA, CO 733/191/2.

63. Government of Palestine, "Education Ordinance 1933," pt. 1, clause 2.

64. Dror and Reshef, *ha-Ḥinukh ha-Ivri bi-yamei ha-bayit ha-leumi*, 160.

65. Haj Muhammad Amin al-Husseini to Chief Secretary, August 19, 1928, TNA, CO/733/146/8.

66. Ibid.

67. Ibid.

68. Ibid.

69. Jerusalem Municipal Council memorandum, August 16, 1928, TNA, CO 733/146/8.

70. Ibid.

71. Hanna, *British Policy in Palestine*, 89.

72. Khalidi, *The Iron Cage*, 55.

73. Robson, *Colonialism and Christianity in Mandate Palestine*. 65.

74. For a detailed discussion of the girls' schools maintained by the SMC, see Greenberg, *Preparing the Mothers of Tomorrow*.

75. In 1945, the schools maintained by the SMC educated 2,023 pupils, and the Arab Public System, 81,042. Note that 1936–37 is the last school year for which statistics for the Arab Public System are divided according to religion of the pupils. See Government of Palestine, Department of Education, *Annual Report 1945–46*, 2, 12. The Ottoman public schools were officially open to all, but in actuality they served the Muslim community almost exclusively. Tibawi, *Arab Education in Mandatory Palestine*, 19.

76. Ibid., 78.

CHAPTER 4

1. For a review of literary and autobiographical depictions of the *ḥeder*, see Holtzman, "Ben hoka'ah le-hitrafkut."

2. Quoted in ibid., 78–79.

3. Gottlober, *Zichronot mi yamei ne'uri*. Originally published as a serial in the Hebrew Journal *Boker Ore* between 1879 and 1886.

4. Levine, "Zichron ba-sefer—rishumim mi-toldodtai ve-korotai"; Holtzman, "Ben hoka'ah le-hitrafkut," 81–82.

5. Zerubavel, *Recovered Roots*. The notion that Jewish history in the diaspora was not "real" history because it was characterized by passivity rather than sovereignty also found expression in the Hebrew literature, most famously in Haim Hazaz's short story "The Sermon." The story centers around Yudka, a Russian immigrant and reticent man who makes an unexpected announcement before a Haganah committee that he "objects to Jewish history." As he explains, "You see, we never made our own history, the Gentiles always made it for us. Just as they turned out the lights for us and lit the stove for us and milked the cow for us on the Sabbath, so they made history for us the way they wanted and we took it whether we liked it or not. But it wasn't ours, it wasn't ours at all!" Hazaz, "The Sermon," 236.

6. In our contemporary context, the impulse to return to the core or fundamental principles of Islam is most likely to be associated with conservative *Salafi* movements, yet during the period of *nahḍa* the same conceptual move helped propel liberal strains of Islamic thought. The relationship between these two very different kinds of fundamentalists has yet to be explored in detail. For a detailed examination of Islamic modernism's development and influence in Greater Syria, see Commins, *Islamic Reform*.

7. Tibawi, *Islamic Education*, 36.

8. Musawi, *Islam on the Street*.

9. Hussein, *The Days*, 38. Originally published in Arabic in 1929.

10. Darwaza, *Durūs al-tārikh al-'arabi min aqdam al-azmina ila al-ān*, 292.

11. The classical account of this fraught relationship appears in Raphael Mahler's *Hasidism and the Jewish Enlightenment*, which, despite its plainly ideological bent, reviews many important sources related to the conflict between *maskilim* and Hasidism. For a more detailed account of these battles, many of which appeared at the communal level, see Wodziński, *Haskalah and Hasidism in the Kingdom of Poland*.

12. Pelli, *The Age of Haskalah*, 133n5. As Yaakob Dweck has shown, the embrace of Maimonides as a bulwark against mysticism was already apparent in seventeenth-century Venice. See Dweck, *The Scandal of Kabbalah*.

13. Holtzman, "Ben hoka'ah le-hitrafkut," 79.

14. Hussein, *The Days*, 57.

15. Mantena, *Alibis of Empire*, 6.

16. Ibid., 151.

17. Bowman, "Rural Education in the Near and Middle East."

18. Scholars of Palestine have sometimes failed to apprehend the ways in which the Mandatory government's educational policies diverged from those developed in India by Lord Macaulay. Thus, in her otherwise excellent book on the Palestinian women's movement, Ellen Fleischmann conflates the two approaches and argues that British officials strove to create a class of upper-class civil servants to serve as "interpreters"

between the government and the masses. Such interpreters were in fact wholly out of place in a colony under direct rule and within which administrators devoted almost all of their meager resources toward maximizing access to primary education. For more on Fleischmann's argument, see *The Nation and Its "New" Women*, 36–40.

19. Maine, *Ancient Law.*

20. Lugard, *The Dual Mandate in British Tropical Africa.*

21. Ibid., 425–26.

22. Bowman, "Rural Education in the Near and Middle East," 402–3.

23. Ibid.

24. For example, for the 1929–30 school year, there were 353 pupils enrolled in government secondary schools. However, at a time when Jews represented less than 20 percent of the population, the Hebrew Public System included 1,465 pupils in secondary and approximately 1,200 more in training or commercial schools. The Department of Education was highly critical of the Jewish system of secondary schools, which it viewed as both too restrictive (accessible chiefly to fee-paying students) and too extensive in size. Government of Palestine, Department of Education, *Annual Report 1929–30*, 26, 34.

25. There were eighty pupils enrolled in the Government Arab College in 1925–26 and eighty-eight in 1945–46. Government of Palestine, Department of Education, *Annual Report 1925–26* and *Annual Report 1945–46.*

26. Bowman, "Rural Education in the Near and Middle East," 407.

27. For an extended discussion of the duties of educators beyond the classroom and the social status that they enjoyed as a result of the scarcity of teachers, see Kalisman, "Schooling the State."

28. This characterization of *katātīb* remained consistent in the Department of Education's annual reports throughout the Mandate period. Compare, for instance, Government of Palestine, Department of Education. *Annual Report, 1929–30*, 14; *1940–41*, 6; and *1945–46*, 11

29. Bowman, "Rural Education in the Near and Middle East," 407.

30. Nadan, *Palestinian Peasant Economy under the Mandate.* For an alternative viewpoint arguing that Palestinian agriculture improved during the Mandate period, see Metzer, *The Divided Economy of Mandate Palestine.*

31. On the mixed record of the Department of Education in implementing agricultural training in schools, see Miller, *Government and Society in Rural Palestine*, 108–12; and Tibawi, *Arab Education in Mandatory Palestine*, 235–38.

32. For example, the Government of Palestine agreed to extend preferential breaks on customs duties for raw materials needed for Jewish industry, even those produced locally. An extended discussion appears in B. Smith, *The Roots of Separatism in Palestine.*

33. Government of Palestine, Department of Education, *Syllabus for State Elementary Schools for Boys*, 6 (emphasis in original).

34. In rural schools, "Religion and Reading of Koran" was allotted six hours in the first year, seven in the second, and nine in the third (out of thirty-four, thirty-nine, and thirty-nine total hours, respectively). Arabic was taught twelve hours in the first and second classes and eleven hours in the third. See Totah, "Education in Palestine," 157.

35. Town schools allocated three hours to "Religion" in the second year and only one hour (of twenty-nine to thirty-three total hours) for the third through sixth classes. Ibid., 158.

36. Tibawi, *Arab Education in Mandatory Palestine*, 27.

37. Government of Palestine, Department of Education, *Annual Report, 1940–41* and *1945–46*.

38. Suleiman Beidas, "al-Ta'lim fi al-qurah," *Filisṭīn*, July 16, 1911. The figure of Hubnaqa is allegedly based on the example of Yazid ben Thurwan and has for centuries served as a model for foolishness and stupidity. The medieval writer Ibn al-Jawzi immortalized the figure of Hubnaqa and his follies by featuring him in his *Akhbar al-hamqa wa al-mughallafin* (Annals of fools and the uncivilized [literally, uncircumcised]).

39. Government of Palestine, Department of Education, *Elementary School Syllabus*, 10.

40. Totah, "Education in Palestine," 165. Totah was himself a Christian, but his comment is indicative of the extent to which educators of his generation viewed the modernizing of schooling, even in communal settings, as a grave *national* concern.

41. Government of Palestine, Department of Education, *Syllabus for State Elementary Schools for Boys*, 6.

42. Ela Greenberg's excellent study of the girls' schools maintained by the SMC notes a similar proclivity by the SMC to gear female education around motherhood and "domestic science." Greenberg, *Preparing the Mothers of Tomorrow*. In a similar vein, Ellen Fleischmann points out that it was "rather odd" to teach subjects like gardening and poultry keeping in the Rural Teachers College given that "most village women learned such skills from their mothers or mothers-in-law without the need for special schooling." Fleischmann, *The Nation and Its "New" Women*, 40.

43. Bowman, "Rural Education in the Near and Middle East," 403.

44. See Hassan al-Siba'i Application for Employment, October 24, 1922, CZA, J177295, No. 96/2.

45. Inspection report for Sh. Hassan Siba'i, January 1, 1926, CZA, J177295, No. 16.

46. Inspection report for Hassan Siba'i, February 2, 1928, CZA, J177295.

47. Inspection report for Hassan Saba'i, July 15, 1930, CZA, J177295, No. 45.

48. Inspection reports for Hassan Saba'i, CZA, J177295, Nos. 54, 67. The documents are undated, but judging from dates on the other papers in the series, they are most likely for the 1931–32 school year.

49. See, for example, "Confidential Report on Teachers" (in Arabic), May 29, 1944; May 29, 1945; and June 19, 1949, CZA, J177295.

50. Education Inspector to Headmaster of the Ja'uneh school, Sefad: "Subject: The Teaching Situation in Your School" (in Arabic), October 30, 1943, CZA, J177295, No. 192.

51. Director of Education to Chief Secretary, "Appointments—Hasan Eff. Siba'i," March 25, 1947, CZA, J177295, No. 228.

52. In her study of government schoolteachers in the British Mandate territories of Palestine, Iraq, and Transjordan, Hilary Falb Kalisman has uncovered a similar pattern wherein the scarcity of teachers resulted in retaining those who were otherwise deemed

to be unfit for service, often by requesting their transfer to another school. Yet the lack of teachers meant that even that was not always possible. See Kalisman, "Schooling the State," 75–77.

53. See "Confidential Report on Teachers," January 1, 1926; July 15, 1930; and September 4, 1944, CZA, J177295.

54. Joseph Bentwich, "Summary of Activities for Jerusalem Orthodox Schools Committee, 1942–1947," October 27, 1947, ISA, 1057/24-mem.

55. For the 1941–42 school year, LP 4,200 was distributed, which included an LP 1,200 grant to schools maintained by Alliance Israélite Universelle. In 1945–46, the last year for which a complete report exists, this aid reached LP 10,800. Government of Palestine, Department of Education, *Annual Report 1941–42* and *Annual Report 1945–46*.

56. Bowman, *Middle-East Window*, 255. Bowman's comment most likely applied only to the inspectors who overlapped with his own tenure as education director, as Goitein was born in Germany but did not begin his work as an inspector until 1938.

57. Jerome Farrell, "Notes on Jewish Education and the McNair Report," November 30, 1946, TNA, CO/733/476/2, sec. 36.

58. Roth and Jaffe, "Bentwich Family."

59. In this respect, Bentwich's later activities may shed some light on his views of Judaism and religion more broadly. In the late 1950s, Bentwich founded the Amanah Group "to study and promote new interpretations of Judaism." Amanah rejected the narrow equation of religion (*dat*) with ritual observance and insisted on an ethical understanding of Judaism's core. "You want to know if someone is 'religious' or not. You look if he wears a kippah on his head, restrains from traveling on Shabbat, eats kosher foods [*shomer kashrut*]. It is not important if he is honest in his speech and his exchanges, if he is loyal to others or only worries for himself. . . . If he performs the 'positive commandments' that are in the Shulḥan Aruch, he is a religious Jew." In contrast, Bentwich encouraged the association of religiosity with ethical conduct, cooperation with one's neighbor, and interreligious tolerance. See, for example, Bentwich's introductory remarks given at the group's annual meeting in *Dinim ve-ḥeshbonot al kinuse ḥug Amanah ba-shanim 5722–5724*," 4, 78–83.

60. A partial biography of Goitein, particularly attentive to his involvement with the Cairo Geniza, is available in Hoffman, *Sacred Trash*, chap. 10.

61. For more on Goitein's encouragement of Arabic study, see Halperin, "Orienting Language." Within Goitein's own body of scholarship, a number of publications address the historic and linguistic connections that linked Jewish and Arab peoples (and the study of them). See "ha-Yachas el ha-shilton ba-islam u va-yahadut."

62. For instance, Goitein claimed that Yemenite Jews "remain very much the same as they had been at the end of the Talmudic period" and thus offered a window into the original form of Jewish education. "Jewish Education in Yemen."

63. Goitein, *Hora'at ha-tanakh ba-vait ha-sefer ha-'amami ve-ha-tichoni*; Goitein, "Limud tefilah bi-kitah dalet ha-'amamit: tefilah ha-chag."

64. Interview with Elon Goitein, January 25, 2012, Herzaliya Petuach, Israel.

65. Interview with Ayala (Goitein) Gordon, January 24, 2012, Jerusalem.

66. Eric Ormsby, "The 'Born Schulmeister,'" *New Criterion*, September 2003.

67. High Commissioner MacMichael to Secretary of State for the Colonies, August 14, 1942, TNA, CO 733/435/18.

68. Ibid.

69. Oranborne to Colonial Office, "Summary of Meeting with Deputation from Agudat Israel," October 23, 1942, TNA, CO 733/435/18.

70. Ibid.

71. Oranborne to High Commissioner MacMichael, October 23, 1942, TNA, CO 733/435/18.

72. Jerome Farrell to the Chairman and Executive Education Committee of the Va'ad Leumi, June 13, 1939. Reprinted in *Palestine Review* 4, no. 35 (1940).

73. "Notes and Comments," *Palestine Review* 4, no. 35 (1940).

74. Rabbi M. Blau to W. J. Farrell, September 18, 1942, ISA RG 8, 1057/23-mem.

75. S. D. Goitein, "New Schools to Be Admitted to the Aguda System," August 16, 1942, ISA, RG 8, 1057/23-mem (emphasis in original).

76. Untitled inspection report, November 23, 1946, ISA, RG 8, 1053/8-mem.

77. hanhelet ha-va'ad ha-leumi to District Commissioner, Jerusalem, April 8, 1935, ISA, RG 8, 1016/1-mem (in Hebrew).

78. "Batei sefer ha-'amamiyim be-Yerushaliyim le-or ha-tzrachim," *Ha-aretz*, August 30, 1938.

79. For more on Sarah Schenirer and the history of Bais Ya'akov, see Benisch, *Carry Me in Your Heart*; and Weissman, "Bais Ya'akov."

80. Avinoam Yellin, "Report: Bait Hinnukh Yeladim," November 4, 1926, ISA, RG 8, 1034-mem.

81. "T. T. Histadrut Haredeim, Tel Aviv," February 10, 1941, ISA, RG 8, 1060/39-mem.

82. Ibid.

83. "Alon shel histadrut he-ḥaredim be-tel aviv," June 9, 1933, ISA, RG 8, 1060/39-mem.

84. Berkson, *The Zionist School System*.

85. Elboim-Dror, *ha-Ḥinuch ha-Ivri be-Eretz-Yisrael*, 2:228–41. The term *edah* usually denoted a Jewish community from a specific region, such as the Iranian *edah* and appears to have undergone its own transformation during the Mandate period as the Zionist Organization promoted the notion of a unified Jewish nation. By the late 1930s, the term *ha-edah ha-yehudit* (the Jewish *edah*) entered circulation, suggesting an attempt to overturn the particularistic undertones usually associated with the term. See, for example, hanhelet ha-va'ad ha-leumi to Chief Secretary of the Government, August 10, 1939, ISA, RG 8, 1016/1-mem.

86. Brill, *The School Attendance of Jewish Children in Jerusalem*.

87. Goitein, "Jewish Education in Yemen," 109–10.

88. Eliezer Cohen to M. Lifshitz, "Sekira al avodat beit ha-sefer," 1924, CZA, J179702.

89. See, for example, "Appeal for Support for Education of Yemenite Children," April 30, 1919, CZA, S23981 (in Hebrew).

90. Avinoam Yellin minute, November 8, 1926, ISA, RG 8, 1034/9-mem.

91. See, for instance, Letter no. 2575, Director of Education to Secretary of Central

Agudat Israel, November 26, 1926, ISA, RG 8, 1034/9-mem. After several notices, Agudat Israel claimed to have transferred control to the Yemenite community, which registered the school as an independent entity. See, in the same folder, "Form of Application for Permission to Open a School," December 5, 1926.

92. Director of Education to Deputy District Commissioner, Jerusalem, December 23, 1926, in ibid.

93. Director of Education to Deputy District Commissioner, Jerusalem, March 4, 1927, in ibid.

94. Note from Sgd. J. L. B, September 10, 1928, ISA, RG 8, 1034/9-mem-48.

95. Memorandum from Senior Medical Officer, February 22, 1929, ISA, RG 8, 1034/9-mem.

96. Petition to Director of Education of the Government of Palestine from Yemenite Community, Jerusalem, August 16, 1927, in ibid. (in Hebrew).

97. "Inspection Note on Talmud-Tora 'Tora Or' for Yemenites," December 14, 1937, in ibid.

98. Ibid.

99. Both quotes are taken from discussions regarding Talmud Torah Urphalim, which served the Jewish community from Eastern Anatolia. See S. D. Goitein, "Final Allocation of Grants to Jerusalem Orthodox Schools for the School Year 1945–46," November 30, 1945; and S. D. Goitein, *Talmud torah shel ha-Urphalim, Yerushaliyim,* April 1, 1946, both in ISA, RG 8, 1057/24-mem.

100. S. D. Goitein, "Final Allocation of Grants to Jerusalem Orthodox Schools for the School Year 1945–46," November 30, 1945, in ibid.

101. Joseph Goldschmidt, *Talmud torah ashurim shechonat Zichron Ya'akov*, October 29, 1946, in ibid.

102. S. D. Goitein, *Pegisha im va'adat ha-rabanim shel talmud torah torat aharon*, October 14, 1947, in ibid.

103. Elboim-Dror, *ha-Ḥinuch ha-Ivri be-Eretz-Yisrael*, 2:243.

104. For an extended discussion of the relationship between schools serving children from *edot ha-mizraḥ* and the Mizraḥi educational system, see Katz, "Dat, edah, ve-ḥinuch be-yamei ha-yishuv."

105. Minute from J. L. Bloom to Director of Education, August 17, 1942, ISA, RG 8, 1057/23/mem.

106. Ibid.

107. Ibid.

108. High Commissioner MacMichael to Secretary of State for the Colonies, August 14, 1942, TNA, CO 733/435/18.

109. Moshe Aharon Bejel, untitled, undated memorandum (most likely 1940–41), CZA, J174996 (in Hebrew).

110. Dror and Reshef, *ha-Ḥinuch ha-Ivri bi-yamei ha-bayit ha-leumi*, 63.

111. Riger, *ha-Ḥinuch ha-Ivri be-Eretz Yisrael*, 46.

112. The inspection reports for *talmudei-torah* and *ḥederim* offer numerous examples in this regard; see, for instance, ISA RG 8, 1057/24-mem, which includes Avinoam

Yellin, "Report: Bait Hinnukh Yeladim," November 4, 1926; S. D. Goitein, "Talmud torah shel ha-urphalim, Yerushaliyim, bikur b'yom 1 b'April 1946," April 1, 1946. See also S. D. Goitein to Talmud-Torah Megen David, September 27, 1945, ISA, RG 8, 1034/14-mem (in Hebrew).

113. Maḥleket ha-ḥinuch shel ha-hanhala ha-tzioni be-Eretz Yisrael, 20.

CHAPTER 5

1. Starrett, *Putting Islam to Work*; Asad, *Formations of the Secular*.

2. Berkey, "Madrasas Medieval and Modern," 46 (emphasis in original).

3. Asad, *Genealogies of Religion*, 28–29.

4. On the related emergence of "politics" and "economy" as sites of state management and social action, see Mitchell, *Rule of Experts*; Mitchell, "Rethinking Economy." On the concept of modern state space, see Lefebvre, *The Production of Space*. Manu Goswami is one author who has productively applied Lefebvre's theory to explain the ways in which "colonial state space" was produced. Gaswami, *Producing India*.

5. Government of Palestine, Department of Education, *Annual Report 1924*, 5.

6. "The teacher of Quran and Moslem Religious Instruction should read carefully pages 15 and 17 of the *'Irshadatu al 'Amalieh* [*sic*] on the teaching of Quran and Moslem Religion." Government of Palestine, Department of Education, *Elementary School Syllabus*, 71. *Irshādāt al-'amaliya* was a handbook originally published in 1920 by the Royal Printing Press in Cairo.

7. Bowman, *Middle-East Window*, 50.

8. Brownson, "Colonialism, Nationalism."

9. See, for example, the directives in the manual distributed to Palestinian teachers: Government of Egypt, Ministry of Public Education, *Irshādāt al-'amaliya*. The acquisition of permanent literacy was a primary goal of the Department of Education throughout the period. Palestine Royal Commission, "Testimony of Mr. H. E. Bowman."

10. Government of Palestine, Department of Education, *Elementary School Syllabus*, 8–9.

11. Government of Palestine, Department of Education, *Syllabus for State Elementary Schools for Boys*, 32.

12. In a similar vein, advocates of Islamic revival argued that the return of the caliphate to Arab hands was crucial to restoring Islam's former grandeur. See, for example, Blunt, *The Future of Islam*.

13. For example, after the publication of *Zaynab* in 1913, widely considered the first modern Arabic novel, Taha Hussein lamented its use of colloquial Arabic for dialogue, noting that the colloquial was not "a suitable instrument for mutual understanding and a method for realizing the various goals of our intellectual life." Quoted in Allen, *The Arabic Novel*, 35.

14. Government of Palestine, Department of Education, *Elementary School Syllabus*, 72.

15. Asad, *Formations of the Secular*, 201.

16. The most extensive, and recent, of these is the study of Palestinian and Zionist historiographical production during the Mandate years. See Furas, "In Need of a New Story."

17. According to Tibawi's account, Arab nationalists never ceased to argue that the history syllabus "insisted in its content and tone on the international rather than the national character of Palestine." Tibawi, *Arab Education in Mandatory Palestine*, 88. More recently, Rashid Khalidi has implicated this fact (and the educational structure as a whole) in accounting for the failure of Palestinian state formation during the Mandate period. Khalidi, *The Iron Cage*. For a useful overview of and supplement to Tibawi's argument, see Brownson, "Colonialism, Nationalism."

18. Government of Palestine, Department of Education, *Elementary School Syllabus*, 37.

19. Ibid., 30–37. As this list suggests, the syllabus was entirely devoid of great women, though this was interestingly not the case in curricular materials prepared by ʿIzzat Darwaza. His Arab history textbook included a discussion of Khula bint al-Azwar, who led a group of women in the Battle of Yarmouk, and invited students to compare her heroic deeds with the lowly condition of Muslim women in their day. Darwaza, *Durūs al-tārikh al-ʿArabi min aqdam al-azmina ila al-ān*, 95.

20. Government of Palestine, Department of Education, *Elementary School Syllabus*, 40–41.

21. Ibid., 40.

22. Government of Palestine, Department of Education, *Syllabus for State Elementary Schools*, 16.

23. In the first two grades, students spent five hours a week on religious instruction, five hours on arithmetic, and a whopping fourteen hours on Arabic, out of a total thirty hours in school each week. In grades three and four, religious instruction commanded four hours, which was further reduced to three hours in the final two years. Ibid., 6.

24. Tibawi, *Arab Education in Mandatory Palestine*, 149.

25. See "Hassam al-Din Jarallah," in Hamada, *Aʿlām Filasṭīn* , 133–34. On the elections to chose the grand mufti, see Al-Hout, *al-Qiyādāt wa al-muʾassassāt al-siyāsiya fi Filasṭīn 1917–1948*, 203–5.

26. *Government of Palestine Civil Service List 1939*.

27. Ellen Fleischmann interviewed Saʿida Jarallah in 1994 while researching the Palestinian women's movement. The complete transcript is available at https://www.scribd.com/document/12534656/Interview-with-Sa-ida-Jarallah.

28. Ibid.

29. Government of Palestine, Department of Education, *Syllabus for State Elementary Schools for Boys*, 32.

30. Government of Egypt, Ministry of Public Education, *Irshādāt al-ʿamaliya*,15.

31. Ibid., 17.

32. Sheehan, *The Enlightenment Bible*, chap. 9.

33. Hefner, "Introduction," 12.

34. ʿAbduh, "Lāʾiḥa iṣlāḥ al-taʿlīm al-ʿOthmānī."

35. Government of Palestine, Department of Education, *Syllabus for State Elementary Schools for Boys*, 34–35.

36. Furas, "In Need of a New Story," chap. 3.

37. Tibawi, *Arab Education in Mandatory Palestine*, 184.

38. The attempt to avoid fueling sectarian conflicts is also evident in the treatment of Christian religious instruction, in which teachers are expressly forbidden to use any text other than the Bible "unless the children are all of the same community." Government of Palestine, Department of Education, *Syllabus for State Elementary Schools for Boys*, 36.

39. "al-Madāris fi Filisṭīn," *Filisṭīn*, July 5, 1911.

40. 'Abduh, "Lā'iḥa iṣlāḥ al-ta'līm al-'Othmānī," 3:71–85. The original letter dates from 1887.

41. Ibid., 75.

42. Ibid., 72.

43. Sengupta, *Pedagogy for Religion*, 124–25.

44. 'Abduh, "Lā'iḥa iṣlāḥ al-ta'līm al-'Othmānī," 78.

45. Gesink, "Islamic Reformation." For an extended treatment of al-Azhar's central place within modern reform efforts, see Gesink, *Islamic Reform and Conservativism*.

46. 'Abduh, "Lā'iḥa iṣlāḥ al-ta'līm al-'Othmānī," 78.

47. Fortna, *Imperial Classroom*.

48. From "The Diary of Ihsan Turjman," in Tamari, *The Year of the Locust*, 110.

49. The term is borrowed from Albert Hourani's *Arabic Thought in the Liberal Age*.

50. *Barnamaj al-Najāḥ al-wataniya Nablusi*, 2. For a general history of the school, including information about its enrollment numbers, funding sources, and relationship to other Palestinian bodies, see Abdoh, "Educational Conditions in Nablus during the British Mandate" (in Arabic).

51. Matthews, *Confronting an Empire, Constructing a Nation*, 51.

52. *Barnamaj al-Najāḥ al-wataniya Nablusi*, 5.

53. According to one report, approximately 10 percent of students at al-Najāḥ were Christian during the 1926–27 school year. See Abdoh, "Educational Conditions in Nablus during the British Mandate," 129.

54. Darwaza chronicled his involvement with the school in his memoir: Darwaza, *Muthakkirāt Muhammad 'Izzat Darwaza*, 1:317–18, 520–47.

55. Darwaza's memoir includes a review of his publications and claims not only that his history texts were used widely in private schools in Palestine but also that government history teachers depended on them in preparing their lessons. According to his memoir, Darwaza's textbooks were also used in public schools in Jordan and Iraq. Ibid., 19.

56. Darwaza, *Durūs al-tārīkh al-'Arabi min aqdam al-azmina ila al-ān*; Darwaza, *Durūs al-tārīkh al-qadīm*; Darwaza, *Durūs al-tārīkh al-mutawassaṭ wa al-hadīth*.

57. Darwaza, *Durūs al-tārīkh al-mutawaṣsat wa al-hadīth*, 268.

58. Ibid., 269.

59. Government of Palestine, Department of Education, *Elementary School Syllabus*, 10.

60. al-Ashqar and 'Inani, *Ṣafwat durūs al-dīn wa al-akhlāq*.

61. *'Ibādāt* and *mu'āmalāt* are legal categories within sharia: *'ibādāt* are ritual actions relating to the relationship between humans and God, whereas *mu'āmalāt* consist of laws governing relations between individuals, often of a commercial or contractual nature.

62. Starrett, *Putting Islam to Work*, 38.

63. H. Boyle, "Memorization and Learning in Islamic Schools," 185.

64. Government of Egypt, Ministry of Public Education, *Irshādāt al-'amaliya*.

65. 'Auda et al., *Mabāda fi al-dīn al-Islamī*, 18.

66. Ibid., 21.

67. Ibid., 29–30.

68. For instance, the eleventh-century scholar Muhammad Bakar Majlisi includes this justification in section 96 of his *Biḥār al-Anwār*. The same sentiment was also attributed to the eighth Shia imam, 'Ali ibn Musa al-Rida, in the compendium *Wasa'il al-Shī'a*, which is dated to the late sixteenth or early seventeenth century. I express my gratitude to Hossein Kamaly of Barnard College for bringing these sources to my attention.

69. 'Auda et al., *Mabāda fi al-dīn al-Islāmī*, 33.

70. This should not, however, be taken to mean that either party is actually able to monopolize the religious discourse. As Gregory Starrett has shown in his study of Egypt, the process of habituating students to adopt correct Muslim behavior is complicated by the functionalist terms "that actively encourage students to draw connections between the world of this life and the world of texts," adding that "once the possibility of this sort of interpretation is opened, the construction of additional, or alternate, readings of Muslim practice is inevitable." Starrett, *Putting Islam to Work*, 129. For an analysis of the contemporary Saudi case, including its missionary attempts to spread Wahhabi Islam, see Commins, *The Wahhabi Mission and Saudi Arabia*.

71. Matthews, *Confronting an Empire*, 116.

72. Darwaza, *Muthakkirāt Muhammad 'Izzat Darwaza*, 1, 9, 520.

73. Darwaza, *Durūs al-tārīkh al-'Arabi min aqdam al-azmina ila al-ān*, 63.

74. Ibid., 71.

75. Ibid., 66, 85, 111.

76. *Barnamaj al-Najāḥ al-wataniya Nablusi*, 4–5.

77. Khayr al-Din, 'Inani, and Mansur, *Kitāb al-dīn al-Islāmī*.

78. *Barnamaj al-Najāḥ al-wataniya Nablusi*, 18–19.

79. Khayr al-Din, 'Inani, and Mansur, *Kitāb al-dīn al-Islāmī*, 135.

80. Ibid., 139. Considered among the founding generation of Muslim modernists, Jamal al-Din al-Afghani famously accepted Spencer's condemnation of Christianity as irrational but argued that religion per se was not. On the contrary, he argued, the principles of Islam were fully harmonious with—and even only appreciated through—the use of human reason. For an extended discussion, see Hourani, *Arabic Thought in the Liberal Age*, chap. 5.

81. Ibid., 137–38.

82. Qur'an, Sura al-A'ref, 31–32. Adapted from the translation by 'Ali, *The Meaning of the Holy Qur'an*.

83. Khayr al-Din, 'Inani, and Mansur, *Kitāb al-dīn al-Islāmī*, 221.
84. Ibid., 97.
85. Ibid., 100.
86. Sheehan, *The Enlightenment Bible*, xi.

CHAPTER 6

1. The *mitzvot ma'asiot* encompass a broad variety commandments that are materially enacted, such as ritual hand washing or cooking food in a kosher manner, rather than metaphysical ones, such as recognizing the singularity of God or remembering the Exodus from Egypt.

2. Meeting minutes of the Board to Clarify the Questions of Religious Education, May 29, 1928, CZA, J16110 (in Hebrew).

3. It still remains commonplace to recount that "the modern Zionism that emerged in the late nineteenth century was clearly a secular nationalist movement," with very little engagement regarding what bundle of behaviors and assumptions the term "secular" is meant to convey. See Novak, *Zionism and Judaism*, 48. For scholars of education in the *yishuv*, this framing also remains dominant. For instance, "From 1920 until 1953 (when the "State Education Law" was passed), organized Zionist education was divided into three main ideological subdivisions. Two of them were secular and one was religious: the 'General [Zionist] Trend,' the central-liberal one; the 'Workers' Trend,' Zionist-socialist, run by the 'Histadrut' (Workers' Union); and the 'Mizrahi Trend,' Zionist-religious." Dror, "From 'Negation of the Diaspora' to 'Jewish Consciousness,'" 58.

4. Shimoni, *The Zionist Ideology*, 295.

5. Scholars conducting research on India have been at the forefront of trying to articulate, both for the sake of historical nuance and contemporary political life, what alternative forms secularism might assume in non-European contexts. Chief questions addressed by this group of scholars are also central to this inquiry, such as, "How far can a distinction between religion and cultural practice be drawn in societies dominated by religions that emphasize practice rather than belief? Where religious and cultural practice is more or less indistinguishable, does the politics of multiculturalism assume the form of the politics of secularism? . . . More generally, is there a difference between Western and Eastern secularism? Is the Indian version a mere specification of an idea with Western origin and imprint?" and so on. See Bhargava, "Introduction," in *Secularism and Its Critics*, 6.

6. Ibid., sec. 36 (emphasis in original).

7. "On the Question of Strengthening the Spirit of Religion and Torah in Schools: A Presentation of Rabbi Shlomo Ha-Cohen Aronsohn during the Board of Education Meeting from March 19, 1928," CZA, J16110, 2 (in Hebrew).

8. Zionist Organization Central Office to Henrietta Szold, June 17, 1929, CZA, S4824.

9. Dr. I. B. Berkson to Henrietta Szold, July 5, 1929, CZA, S4824.

10. "On the Question of Strengthening the Spirit of Religion and Torah in Schools: A Presentation of Rabbi Shlomo Ha-Cohen Aronsohn during the Board of Education Meeting from March 19, 1928," CZA, J16110, 2 (in Hebrew).

11. Ibid.

12. Meeting minutes, Committee to Clarify the Question of Religious Education, May 29, 1928, CZA, J16110 (in Hebrew).

13. Ibid.

14. In 1929–30, there were 1,506 pupils in Labor schools; 6,392 in Mizraḥi schools; and 13,133 in General schools. See Government of Palestine, Department of Education, *Annual Report 1929–1930*, 30.

15. Quoted in Dror and Reshef, *ha-Ḥinukh ha-Ivri bi-yamei ha-bayit ha-leumi*, 61–62.

16. Shimoni, *The Zionist Ideology*, 295.

17. Meeting minutes, Committee to Clarify the Question of Religious Education, May 29, 1928, CZA, J16110 (in Hebrew).

18. Meeting minutes, Committee to Clarify the Issue of Religion Education, May 3, 1928, CZA, J16110 (in Hebrew).

19. "On the Question of Strengthening the Spirit of Religion and Torah in Schools" (in Hebrew).

20. Meeting minutes, Committee to Clarify the Question of Religious Education, May 29, 1928, CZA, J16110 (in Hebrew).

21. *Tashlich*, meaning "to cast off," is a custom typically performed on Rosh Hashanah wherein Jews symbolically cast off their sins by throwing small pieces of bread into a body of water.

22. Meeting minutes, Committee to Clarify the Question of Religious Education, May 29, 1928, CZA, J16110, 6 (in Hebrew). The image of Satan as a court prosecutor appears prominently in the liturgy for Yom Kippur. I have chosen a more idiomatic translation, but the original terminology is noteworthy given the context.

23. Meeting minutes, Committee to Clarify the Question of Religion Education, May 3, 1928, CZA, J16110, 1 (in Hebrew).

24. Meeting minutes, Committee to Clarify the Question of Religious Education, May 29, 1928, CZA, J16110 (in Hebrew).

25. Ibid.

26. As Yael Zerubavel's work shows, the creation of a specific genre of "constructive" children's literature was also a favorite practice of the Zionist left, particularly among schoolteachers. Zerubavel, *Recovered Roots*, 82.

27. As later articulated in Segal's *Biblical Values—Human Values* (1959). Quoted in Dror, "Teaching the Bible in the Schools of the Labor and Kibbutz Movements," 188. Segal was a leading figure in Labor education circles and the "founding father" of education within kibbutz Meuhad. For an extended discussion of kibbutz education, see Dror, *History of Kibbutz Education*.

28. The term "religious subjects" is admittedly unsatisfactory. In this discussion, its use is meant as shorthand for the Hebrew Bible, Mishna, Talmud, and associated works of commentary. It also includes instruction in elements of ritual practice, usually indicated in syllabi as *tefilah* (prayer), *dinim*, or *halacha* (law).

29. The Waad Leumi [*sic*] of Keneset Yisrael, *The Jewish Public School System of Palestine*, 12.

30. Maḥleket ha-ḥinuch, "Sekirah al ha-ḥinuch be-Eretz Yisrael ba-shnot 1920–1923," CZA, J178536.

31. Amit, "The Study of the Hebrew Bible in Israel," 200.

32. Shapira, *The Bible and Israeli Identity*, 1.

33. For instance, "Hebrew culture from the pre-state period suggests that this shift from the religious to the national was pervasive. This was clearly manifested in the transformation of biblical or traditional allusions to God into a reference to the people of Israel." Zerubavel, *Recovered Roots*, 24.

34. Shimoni, *The Zionist Ideology*, 311. Other examples of work on Zionism that employ the concept of civil religion include Don-Yehiya and Liebman, *Civil Religion in Israel*; Almog, *The Sabra*; Saposnik, *Becoming Hebrew*.

35. Yosef Azaryahu, "Our Goal in Teaching the Bible," cited in Amit, "Study of the Hebrew Bible in Israel," 203.

36. Dror, "Teaching the Bible in the Schools of the Labor and Kibbutz Movements," 188.

37. Bentwich, *Education in Israel*, 24. For an extended analysis of the place of biblical criticism early in the Zionist movement, see Arkush, "Biblical Criticism and Cultural Zionism."

38. Shimony, "Teaching the Bible as Common Culture," 163.

39. Maḥleket ha-ḥinuch shel ha-hanhala ha-tzionit be-Eretz Yisrael, *Tokhnit batei ha-sefer ha-amamiyim ha-ironiyim*, 28.

40. The concept of *moledet* could include everything from the animal life and historic sites of Palestine to nature study more generally and ethnographic accounts of one's surroundings. Within the Mizraḥi system, *moledet* assumed an overtly theological character, for instance, in the directive that students should discuss "subjects mentioned in the Book of Genesis: land, heavens, moon, stars, seas, rivers, day and night, trees, vineyard, garden, shepherd and his flock, etc." See Maḥleket ha-ḥinuch shel ha-sokhnut ha-Yehudit le-Eretz Yisrael, *Tokhnit ha-limudim ha-nehugah be-vatei ha-sefer ha-amamiyim shel ha-mizrachi*, 18.

41. For an extended discussion, see Shimony, "Teaching the Bible as Common Culture," 163.

42. Schoneveld, *The Bible in Israeli Education*. More recently, Yuval Dror has revisited Schoneveld's categorization of Labor schools and offered his own. See Dror, "Teaching the Bible in the Schools of the Labor and Kibbutz Movements."

43. Ibid., 195.

44. Ravnitski, Bialik, and Ben-Zion, *Sipurei ha-Mikra* (1919).

45. Ravnitski, Bialik, and Ben-Zion, *Sipurei ha-Mikra* (1928), 3, 40. This particular edition includes a Hebrew-English glossary, attesting to the international exchange of Jewish textbooks that already existed by the 1920s.

46. Ravnitski, Bialik, and Ben-Zion, *Sipurei ha-Mikra* (1919), 176. Translation adapted from Jewish Publication Society, *Hebrew-English Tanakh*.

47. This trend was not unique to Labor schools. For instance, General Zionist schools began the formal study of Tanakh in the fourth class. Thus, students in General

schools did not begin their formal study of the Torah until their sixth year of schooling, though the formal curriculum for Hebrew Bible commenced in year four. The curriculum includes the Books of Joshua, Judges, Ruth, Samuel I and II, and Esther. Maḥleket ha-ḥinuch shel ha-hanhala ha-tzionit be-Eretz Yisrael, *Tokhnit batei ha-sefer ha-amamiyim ha-ironiyim*, 20.

48. ha-Histadrut ha-klalit shel ha-ovdim ha-Ivrim be-Eretz Yisrael, mirkaz ha-ḥinuch, *Kavim alef*, 11.

49. Feiner, *Haskalah and History*.

50. Maḥleket ha-ḥinuch, "Sekirah al ha-ḥinuch be-Eretz Yisrael ba-shnot 1920–1923," CZA, J178536. This document appears to have been submitted to the Department of Education of the Government of Palestine (stamped July 17, 1923).

51. For an alternative interpretation of the history curriculum, see Porat, "Between Nation and Land." Porat argues that the syllabus adopted Dubnov's idea of "shifting autonomous centers," leading to subject headings like "the Jews in Spain," and "the Jews in Babylon" rather than an overwhelming focus on the Land of Israel itself.

52. Maḥleket ha-ḥinuch shel ha-hanhala ha-tzionit be-Eretz Yisrael, *Tokhnit batei ha-sefer ha-amamiyim ha-ironiyim*, 29–30.

53. Maḥleket ha-ḥinuch shel ha-sokhnut ha-yehudit le-Eretz Yisrael, *Tokhnit ha-limudim ha-nehugah be vatei ha-sefer ha-amamiyim shel ha-Mizraḥi*, 19–20.

54. Ibid., 18–19.

55. That secular history often bears traces of a theological, specifically Christian, teleology is clear enough from Lowith's work. See Lowith, *Meaning in History*. For a more detailed account of the historiographical practices that emerged among European *maskilim*, see Feiner, *Haskalah and History*.

56. Volcani articulated his critique of "national theology" in an article published by the journal *ha-Poel ha-tza'ir*, which was directed against the "circle of cultural Zionist thinkers who were perennially locked in debate about the purpose of Jewish national life." See Shimoni, *The Zionist Ideology*, 295–96.

57. Maḥleket ha-ḥinuch shel ha-hanhala ha-tzionit be-Eretz Yisrael, *Tokhnit batei-ha-sefer ha-amamiyim ha-ironiyim*, 41.

58. Maḥleket ha-ḥinuch shel ha-sokhnut ha-Yehudit le-Eretz Yisrael, *Tokhnit ha-limudim ha-nehugah be-vatei ha-sefer ha-amamiyim shel ha-Mizraḥi*, 20.

59. ha-Histadrut ha-klalit shel ha-ovdim ha-Ivrim be-Eretz Yisrael, mirkaz ha-ḥinuch, *Kavim alef*, 21.

60. For example, Zionist immigrants in late Ottoman Palestine instituted outdoor Passover celebrations that included music and sporting competitions. These celebrations "consciously stressed the (fearless) rediscovery of the out-of-doors and nature by the new Hebrew and the reassertion of a culture of the body that was ostensibly so foreign to the Jew of the Diaspora, for whom the centerpiece of the festival was (and is) the study of text around the Seder table." Saposnik, *Becoming Hebrew*, 109.

61. Shimoni, *The Zionist Ideology*, 209, 307.

62. Here I must disagree with Porat's argument that General and Mizraḥi schools did not emphasize the Land of Israel in an ideological fashion and did not aim to indoc-

trinate students in any particular political program. The absence of socialist ideas within the curricula did not render General or Mizraḥi Zionist schools apolitical; Zionism itself already involved a very precise form of politics that found expression in almost every element of the curricula (e.g., which Mishnayot were taught). See Porat, "Between Nation and Land," 258–61.

63. For an excellent analysis of the reciprocal relationship between the "redemption" of the land and the revival of the Jewish spirit, see Zakim, *To Build and Be Built*.

64. Avraham Shlonsky, "Metropolis," part of the poem cycle "Masa," in *Avnei bohu*. The latter quotation is taken from *birkat ha-mazon*, the traditional blessing recited after meals.

65. Maḥleket ha-ḥinuch shel ha-hanhala ha-tzionit be-Eretz Yisrael, *Tokhnit batei ha-sefer ha-amamiyim ha-ironiyim*, 47.

66. Ibid., 2.

67. Bentwich, *Education in Israel*, 24.

68. This is not to say that Mizraḥi schools did not emphasize the importance of *Eretz Yisrael*, and no contemporary observer of religious Zionism in Israel would be surprised to find that the corpus of Jewish texts offered no shortage of material that served this purpose. In the words of Rabbi Yakov Berman, who served as an inspector for Mizraḥi schools from 1924 to 1944, "The Hebrew Bible is the center of our study, and if it does not unfold in relation to Eretz Yisrael, we are not properly transmitting its content." Berman wrote these words in response to critics who worried that Zionism was not being sufficiently emphasized in Mizraḥi schools and therefore called for the introduction of a new prayer to fill the alleged void. Berman's response was telling: "Our prayers are full of love of the land and there is no need to add a new, distinct prayer." *Hartza'at ha-Rav Y. Berman*, 1926, CZA, J17931.

69. For a scholarly account that embraces this interpretation, see Elboim-Dror, "British Educational Policies in Palestine."

70. Moshe Aharon Bejel, untitled, undated memorandum (most likely 1940–41), CZA, J174996 (in Hebrew).

71. This characterization appears consistently in evaluations of the Zionist school system; see, for example, Jerome Farrell, "Relations between the Government of Palestine and the Jewish School System 1918–1941," November 26, 1943, TNA, CO 733/453/4, sec. 21.

72. Though government administrators were highly critical of the Zionist school system, threats to withhold the block grant if certain reforms were not executed proved to be empty. For instance, writing five years after the grant was initiated, the high commissioner noted, "Though the [Jewish] Agency has expressed its general agreement with the [reform] principles laid down, it has found itself unable to make any substantial progress toward giving effect to them." High Commissioner Wauchope to Sir Philip Cunliffe-Lister, Secretary of State for the Colonies, April 9, 1932, TNA, CO 733/224/11. However, the grant was never suspended, and the government soon agreed to act as a guarantor for the Va'ad Leumi when the latter applied for a loan of LP 100,000 for new school construction. See High Commissioner Wauchope to Sir Philip Cunliffe-Lister, Secretary of State for the Colonies, April 19, 1935, TNA, CO 733/274/4.

73. High Commissioner Wauchope to Secretary of State for the Colonies, September 29, 1941, TNA, CO 733/442/17.

74. Joseph Ahronovitz, "Le-sheilah kiyum batei sefer be-Eretz Yisrael," *ha-Poel ha-tza'ir* 12 (1920), in Elboim-Dror, *ha-Ḥinuch ha-Ivri be-Eretz-Yisrael*, 2:4.

75. See, for example, Farrell's memorandum of November 26, 1943, "Relations between the Government of Palestine and the Jewish School System, 1918–1941," TNA, CO 733/453/4. Farrell earlier expressed his views directly to the Va'ad Leumi and urged the body to undertake numerous pedagogic and administrative reforms. See Farrell, "Jewish Education Administrative Reform," June 13, 1939, TNA, CO 733/435/18.

76. Confidential letter from Arnold D. McNair to Secretary of State for the Colonies, March 26, 1946, TNA, CO 733/453/8.

77. Palestine Royal Commission, *The System of Education of the Jewish Community in Palestine*, 7.

78. Ibid., 76.

79. Ibid., 5.

80. Anglo-American Committee of Inquiry, *Report to the United States Government and His Majesty's Government*, sec. 9.

81. Jerome Farrell, "Notes on Jewish Education and the McNair Report," November 30, 1946, TNA, CO/733/476/2, sec. 8.

82. Ibid.

83. Jerome Farrell to District Commissioner of Haifa, August 25, 1943, ISA, RG 8 1056/35-mem.

84. Jerome Farrell, "Notes on Jewish Education and the McNair Report," November 30, 1946, TNA, CO/733/476/2, sec. 5.

85. Ibid., sec. 16.

86. Ibid., sec. 61.

87. Humphrey Bowman, diary entry, August 28, 1929, MEC, Humphrey Bowman Collection, Box 4A.

88. Jerome Farrell, "Notes on Jewish Education and the McNair Report," November 30, 1946, TNA, CO/733/476/2, sec. 6.

89. See undated memorandum regarding the report in the same folder, TNA, CO 733/476/2.

90. "Memorandum of the Department of Education of the Jewish Agency on the Proposals of the Director of Education regarding Reform of the Jewish Schools System," received December 12, 1932, TNA, CO 733/224/11.

91. H. S. Scott memorandum, March 11, 1944, TNA, CO 733/453/4.

92. Department of Education, "Report to the General Council and to the Administrative Committee of the Jewish Agency for Palestine," 1930, CZA, J13735; Executive Committee of the Va'ad Leumi, "Hebrew Education in *Eretz Israel*" (in Hebrew), October 22, 1945, CZA, J178374.

93. Sir John Shuckburgh minute, November 28, 1941, TNA, CO 733/442/17.

94. Jerome Farrell, "Relations between the Government of Palestine and the Jewish School System, 1918–1941," November 26, 1943, TNA, CO 733/453/4.

95. In one of his many critiques directed to the Va'ad Leumi, Farrell stated, "The goal of this department is to support the study of religion as an integral [*bilti nifrad*] part of the basic curriculum, that all students must participate in, with the exception of those whose parents have expressed in writing their desire to exempt their children." He further implored the Va'ad Leumi to inform him "what steps you recommend to implement in order to advance the study of religion in General and Labor schools." Jerome Farrell to the Chairman of the Executive Committee of the Va'ad ha-Leumi (in Hebrew), July 4, 1940, CZA, J174996.

96. Anita Shapira, for instance, has argued that with the emergence of a new generation of Israelis not connected to their socialist roots, "Jewish identity in Israel lost its link with a universalistic worldview," leading to a more chauvinistic form of Zionism. See Shapira, *Land and Power*, 367. It is perhaps no coincidence that Shapira's latest project is a biography of David Ben-Gurion. More recently, Michael Walzer has also embraced the notion of a golden age of Zionist secularity in contrast to the growing dominance of Orthodox Judaism evident today. Walzer, *The Paradox of Liberation*.

97. In her ethnography of the Gaza settlements, Joyce Dalsheim has reached a similar conclusion by demonstrating that, rather than represent an aberration of liberal Zionism, the contemporary settlement movement shares many fundamental assumptions with its leftist critics. Dalsheim, *Unsettling Gaza*.

98. From a letter to Franz Rosenzweig, quoted in Ohana, *Modernism and Zionism*.

99. Gorenberg, *The Unmaking of Israel*.

CONCLUSION

1. Ben-Gurion, "Status-Quo Agreement." At the time that the nascent state of Israel exempted *yeshiva* students from military service, there were approximately 400 of them. It is unlikely that state leaders could have envisioned our present reality, in which (during the 2013–14 school year) there were approximately 125,000 men in *yeshivot* and *kollels*. "Yeshiva Students, by Type of Institution and Citizenship," Central Bureau of Statistics, State of Israel, September 10, 2015, http://www.cbs.gov.il/reader/shnaton/templ_shnaton.html?num_tab=st08_40&CYear=2015.

2. J. S. Bennet minute, March 4, 1938, TNA, CO 733/362/2.

3. *Palestine Royal Commission Report*, 342.

4. H. S. Scott, "On Memorandum by Jerome Farrell," November 3, 1944, TNA, CO 733/453/4.

5. Somel, *The Modernization of Public Education*.

6. Miller, *Government and Society in Rural Palestine*.

7. *Palestine Royal Commission Report*, 341–42.

8. J. S. Bennet minute, March 4, 1938, TNA, CO 733/362/2.

BIBLIOGRAPHY

ARCHIVES

The British National Archives (TNA)
CO 733: Colonial Office, Palestine Original Correspondence
CO 742: Colonial Office, Palestine Government Gazettes
CO 765: Colonial Office, Palestine Acts
CO 814: Palestine Sessional Papers
FO 371: Foreign Office, Political Departments: General Correspondence
Central Zionist Archives (CZA)
J1: General Counsel (Va'ad Leumi) of the Jews of Palestine
J17: Education Department of the Va'ad Leumi
S2: Education Department of the Palestine Office, Zionist Commission and Jewish Agency
S48: Office of Henrietta Szold
Haifa Municipal Archives (HMA)
7: Jewish Education Committee
The Institute for Palestine Studies, Beirut
Institute for the Revival of Islamic Research and Heritage, Abu Dis
Israel State Archive (ISA)
RG 8: Department of Education of the Government of Palestine
Jewish National and University Library, Jerusalem
The Middle East Centre at St. Antony's College, Oxford (MEC)
Humphrey Bowman Collection
Jerome Farrell Collection
Abdul Latif Tibawi Collection
The Aviezer Yellin Archives of Jewish Education in Israel and the Diaspora, Tel Aviv University

NEWSPAPERS

Filiṣṭīn (Jaffa)
Ha-aretz (Tel Aviv)
Mirat al-Sharq (Jerusalem)
Official Palestine Gazette (Jerusalem)
The Times (London)

PUBLISHED PRIMARY SOURCES

'Abduh, Muhammad. "Lā'iḥa iṣlāḥ al-ta'līm al-'Othmānī. In *al-A'māl al-kāmila lil-imām al-sheikh Muhammad 'Abduh*, edited by Muhammad 'Imarah. Beirut: Dar al-Shuruq, 1993.

Anglo-American Committee of Inquiry. *Report to the United States Government and His Majesty's Government in the United Kingdom*. Washington, DC: United States Government Printing Office, 1946.

Annual Report for Palestine and Transjordan for the Year 1928. London: His Majesty's Stationery Office, 1929.

al-Ashqar, 'Atiyah, and Mustafa 'Inani. *Ṣafwat durūs al-dīn wa al-akhlāq*. Cairo: al-Maṭba'a al-Raḥmāniya, 1932.

'Auda, 'Ali Hasn, Ahmed al-Khalifa, 'Abd al-Hamid al-Sā'iḥ, and Ibrahim Sanwir. *Mabāda fi al-dīn al-Islāmī*. Jaffa: Maktaba al-Tāhir Ikhwān, 1947.

Barnamaj al-Najāḥ al-wataniya Nablusi. Jerusalem: Dar al-Aytām al-Islāmiya, 1939.

Ben-Gurion, David. " 'Status-Quo Agreement' (June 19, 1947)." In *Israel in the Middle East*, edited by Itamar Rabinovich and Jehuda Reinharz, 58–59. Waltham, MA: Brandeis University Press, 2007.

Bentwich, Joseph, ed. *Dinim ve-ḥeshbonot al kinuse ḥug 'Amanah' ba-shanim 5722–5724*. Jerusalem: R. Mas, 1965.

Berkson, Isaac Baer *The Zionist School System*. Jerusalem: Department of Education of the Jewish Agency for Palestine, 1930.

Bialik, Hayyim Nahman. "Aftergrowth." In *Aftergrowth and Other Stories*. Philadelphia Jewish Publication Society of America, 1939.

Blunt, Wilfred Scawen. *The Future of Islam*. London: Paul, 1882.

Bowman, Humphrey Ernest. *Middle-East Window*. London: Longmans, 1942.

———. "Rural Education in the Near and Middle East." *Journal of the Royal Central Asian Society* 26 (1939): 402–14.

Brill, M. *The School Attendance of Jewish Children in Jerusalem*. Jerusalem: Hebrew University Press Association, 1941.

Cromer, Evelyn Baring. *Modern Egypt*. Vol. 2. London: Macmillan, 1908.

Darwaza, Muhammad 'Izzat. *Durūs al-tārīkh al-'Arabi min aqdam al-azmina ila al-ān*. Cairo: al-Maṭba'a al-Salafiya, 1929.

———. *Durūs al-tārīkh al-qadīm*. al-Quds: Maṭb'a dār al-Aytām al-Islāmiya al-Ṣanā'iya, 1936.

———. *Durūs al-tārīkh al-mutawassaṭ wa al-hadīth*. Cairo: al-Maṭba'a al-Salafiya, 1930.

———. *Muthakkirāt Muhammad 'Izzat Darwaza*. Vol. 1. Beirut: Dār al-gharb al-Islāmī, 1993.

Goitein, Shlomo Dov. ha-Yachas el ha-shilton ba-Islam u-va-Yahadut." *Tarbiz* 19, no. 3–4 (1948): 153–59.

———. *Hora'at ha-tanakh ba-vait ha-sefer ha-'amami ve-ha-tichoni: maṭarot, shita, tochnit*. Jerusalem: Hebrew University, 1942.

———. "Jewish Education in Yemen as an Archetype of Traditional Jewish Education." In *Between Past and Future, Essays and Studies on Aspects on Immigrant Absroption in Israel*, edited by C. Frankestein. Jerusalem: Henrietta Szold Foundation for Child and Youth Welfare,1953.

———. "Limud tefilah be-kitah dalet ha-'amamit: tefilah ha-chag." *hed ha-ḥinuch* 18, no. 5 (1944): 18–22.

Gottlober, Avraham Bar. *Zichronot mi yemei ne'urai*. Edited by Ruven Goldberg. Jerusalem: Mosad Bialik, 1976.

Government of Egypt, Ministry of Public Education. *Irshādāt al-'amaliya*. Cairo: Royal Printing Press, 1920.

Government of Palestine. "Education Ordinance, 1933." Jerusalem: Greek Conv. Press, 1933.

———. "Religious Communities Organization Ordinance of February 15, 1926." *Official Gazette of the Government of Palestine*, no. 157. Jerusalem, 1926.

Government of Palestine, Department of Education. *Annual Report*. Jerusalem, 1923–24–1945–46.

———. *Elementary School Syllabus*. Rev. ed. Jerusalem, 1925.

———. "Note on Education in Palestine 1920–1929." Jerusalem, 1929.

———. "Syllabus for State Elementary Schools for Boys in Towns and Villages." Jerusalem, 1921.

Government of Palestine Civil Service List 1939. Rev. to January 1, 1939. Alexandria: Whitehead Morris Limited, 1939.

Hanna, Paul. *British Policy in Palestine*. Washington, DC: American Council on Public Affairs, 1942.

Hazaz, Haim. "The Sermon." Translated by Hillel Halkin. In *The Sermon and Other Stories*, edited by Dan Miron. New Milford, CT: Toby Press, 2005.

ha-Histadrut ha-klalit shel ha-ovdim ha-Ivrim be'Eretz Yisrael, mirkaz ha-ḥinuch. *Kavim Alef*. Tel Aviv: ha-Histadrut ha-klalit shel ha-ovdim ha-Ivrim be'Eretz Yisrael, 1937.

Hebrew Education in Erez Israel. Jerusalem: Keren ha-Yesod, 1930.

Hussein, Taha. *The Days*. Cairo: American University in Cairo Press, 1997.

Jewish Publication Society. *Hebrew-English Tanakh*. Philadelphia: Jewish Publication Society, 2003.

Khayr al-Din, 'Abd al-Wahab, Mustafa 'Inani, and Hasn Mansur. *Kitāb al-dīn al-Islāmī*. Cairo: Dār al-Kuttub, 1930.

Levine, Yehuda Lieb. "Zichron ba-sefer—rishumim mi-toldotai ve-korotai (1910)." In *Zichronot ve-higayonot*, edited by Yehuda Slotzky. Jerusalem: Mosad Bialik, 1968.

Lugard, Frederick John Dealtry Baron. *The Dual Mandate in British Tropical Africa*. 5th ed. London: F. Cass, 1965.

Macaulay, Thomas Babington. "Minute on Education, 1835." In *Selections from Educational Records, Part I (1781–1839)*, edited by H. Sharp. Delhi: National Archives of India, 1965.

Maḥleket ha-ḥinuch shel ha-hanhala ha-tzionit be-Eretz Yisrael. *Tokhnit batei ha-sefer ha-amamiyim ha-ironiyim*. Jerusalem: Maḥleket ha-ḥinuch shel ha-hanhala ha-tzionit be-Eretz Yisrael, 1923.

———. *Tokhnit ha-limudim ha-nehugah be-vatei ha-sefer ha-amamiyim shel ha-Mizraḥi.* Jerusalem: Maḥleket ha-ḥinuch shel ha-hanhala ha-tzionit be-Eretz Yisrael, 1933.

Maine, Henry Sumner. *Ancient Law: Its Connection with the Early History of Society and Its Relation to Modern Ideas.* London: J. Murray, 1887.

Nardi, Noah. *Education in Palestine, 1920–1945.* Washington, DC: Zionist Organization of America, 1945.

Nathan, David ben. "A Sermon contra Wessely." In *The Jew in the Modern World,* edited by Paul R. Mendes-Flohr and Jehuda Reinharz. Oxford: Oxford University Press, 1980.

Palestine Royal Commission. *Summary of Report.* London: His Majesty's Stationery Office, 1937.

———. *The System of Education of the Jewish Community in Palestine: Report of the Commission of Enquiry Appointed by the Secretary of State for the Colonies in 1945.* London: His Majesty's Stationery Office, 1946.

———. "Testimony of Mr. H. E. Bowman, C.M.G., C.B.E., Director of Education. November 27, 1936." In *Palestine Royal Commission Minutes of Evidence Heard at Public Sessions.* London: His Majesty's Stationery Office, 1937.

Palestine Royal Commission Report: Presented by the Secretary of State for the Colonies to Parliament by Command of His Majesty July 1937. London: His Majesty's Stationery Office, 1937.

Permanent Mandates Commission. *Minutes of the Eleventh Session.* Geneva: League of Nations, 1927.

———. *Minutes of the Thirteenth Session.* Geneva: League of Nations, 1928.

Riger, Eliezer. *ha-Ḥinuch ha-Ivri be-Eretz Yisrael.* Tel Aviv: Dvir, 1940.

Segal, Mordecai. *Oraḥot ḥinuch.*Tel Aviv: Kibbutz Meuḥad, 1992.

Shlonsky, Avraham. "Masa." In *Avnei bohu.* Tel Aviv: Yahdav, 1934.

Talmud Bavli (The Babalonian Talmud). *Tractates* Shabbat, Bava Batra, Gittin.

Totah, Khalil. "Education in Palestine." In "Palestine: A Decade of Development," special issue, *Annals of the American Academy of Political and Social Science* 164 (November 1932): 156–66.

The Waad Leumi [*sic*] of Keneset Yisrael. *The Jewish Public School System of Palestine.* Jerusalem: R. H. Cohen's Pres, 1932.

SECONDARY SOURCES

Abdoh, Majd Abed-al-Fatah. "*al-Ouḍā' al-ta'līmiya fi Nablus ibān al-intidāb al-Briṭāni.*" Master's thesis, Al-Najah National University, 1998.

Abu-Lughod, Ibrahim. *Arab Rediscovery of Europe: A Study in Cultural Encounters.* Princeton, NJ: Princeton University Press, 1963.

Aksakal, Mustafa. *The Ottoman Road to War in 1914.* Cambridge: Cambridge University Press, 2010.

'Ali, 'Abdullah Yusuf. *The Meaning of the Holy Qur'an.* Beltsville, MD: Amana, 1999.

Allen, Roger. *The Arabic Novel: An Historical and Critical Introduction.* Manchester, UK: University of Manchester, 1982.

Almog, Oz. *The Sabra: The Creation of the New Jew*. The S. Mark Taper Foundation Imprint in Jewish Studies. Berkeley: University of California Press, 2000.

Amit, Yairah. "The Study of the Hebrew Bible in Israel—between Love and Knowledge." *Jewish History* 21, no. 2 (2007): 199–208.

Anidjar, Gil. "Secularism." *Critical Inquiry* 33, no. 1 (2006): 52–77.

Antonius, George. *The Arab Awakening: The Story of the Arab National Movement*. Philadelphia: J. B. Lippincott, 1939.

Arkush, Allan. "Biblical Criticism and Cultural Zionism prior to the First World War." *Jewish History* 21, no. 2 (2007): 121–58.

Asad, Talal. *Formations of the Secular: Christianity, Islam, Modernity*. Stanford, CA: Stanford University Press, 2003.

———. *Genealogies of Religion: Discipline and Reasons of Power in Christianity and Islam*. Baltimore: Johns Hopkins University Press, 1993.

Assaf, Immanuel, and David Etkes, eds. *ha-Ḥeder: meḥkarim, te'udot, pirkei sifrut ve-zichronot*. Tel Aviv: Institute for Polish Jewry, Tel Aviv University, 2010.

Ayalon, Ami. *Reading Palestine: Printing and Literacy, 1900–1948*. Austin: University of Texas Press, 2004.

Bar-Lev, Mordechai. *ha-Ḥinuch ha-dati ba-ḥevra ha-Yisraelit*. Jeruslaem: Center for Study and Documentation of Israeli Society, Hebrew University, 1986.

Bashkin, Orit. "'When Mu'awiya Entered the Curriculum'—Some Comments on the Iraqi Education System in the Interwar Period." In *Islam and Education: Myths and Truths*, edited by Wadad Kadi and Victor Billeh. Chicago: University of Chicago Press, 2007.

Batnitzky, Leora. *How Judaism Became a Religion*. Princeton, NJ: Princeton University Press, 2011.

Benisch, Pearl. *Carry Me in Your Heart: The Life and Legacy of Sarah Schenirer*. Jerusalem: Feldheim Publishers, 2003.

Bentham, Jeremy. *A Fragment on Government*. 1776. Reprint, New York: Cambridge University Press, 1988.

Bentwich, Joseph S. *Education in Israel*. Philadelphia: Jewish Publication Society of America, 1965.

Ben-Yosef, Yaakov. *Milḥemet ha-safot: (ha-ma'avak le-'Ivrit, 1914)*. Tel Aviv: Otzar ha-moreh, hotza'at ha-sefarim shel histadrut ha-morim be-Yisrael, 1984.

Berkey, Jonathan P. "Madrasas Medieval and Modern: Politics, Education, and the Problem of Muslim Identity." In *Schooling Islam: The Culture and Politics of Modern Muslim Education*, edited by Robert W. Hefner and Muhammad Qasim Zaman. Princeton, NJ: Princeton University Press, 2007.

Bhargava, Rajeev, ed. *Secularism and Its Critics*. Oxford: Oxford University Press, 1998.

Biale, David, and Michael Galchinsky, and Susannah Heschel. *Insider/Outsider: American Jews and Multiculturalism*. Berkeley: University of California Press, 1998.

Billeh, Victor, and Wadad Kadi, eds. *Islam and Education: Myths and Truths*. Chicago: University of Chicago Press, 2007.

Boucher, David, and Andrew Vincent. *British Idealism and Political Theory*. Edinburgh: Edinburgh University Press, 2000.

Boyarin, Daniel. "Was There Judaism in Pre-modernity? The Terms of the Debate." Paper presented at the Bampton Lectures in America, Columbia University, March 23, 2015.

Boyle, Helen N. "Memorization and Learning in Islamic Schools." In *Islam and Education Myths and Truths*, edited by Wadad Kadi and Victor Billeh, 172–89. Chicago: University of Chicago Press, 2007.

Boyle, Susan Silsby. *Betrayal of Palestine: The Story of George Antonius*. Boulder, CO: Westview Press, 2001.

Brownson, Elizabeth. "Colonialism, Nationalism, and the Politics of Teaching History in Mandate Palestine." *Journal of Palestine Studies* 43, no. 3 (2014): 9–25.

Burke, Edmund. *Reflections on the Revolution in France*. Oxford: Oxford University Press, 2009.

Calhoun, Craig, Mark Juergensmeyer, and Jonathan VanAntwerpen, eds. *Rethinking Secularism*. Oxford: Oxford University Press, 2011.

Calhoun, Craig, Eduardo Mendieta, and Jonathan VanAntwerpen, eds. *Habermas and Religion*. Cambridge: Polity Press, 2013.

Campos, Michelle. *Ottoman Brothers: Muslims, Christians, and Jews in Early Twentieth-Century Palestine*. Stanford, CA: Stanford University Press, 2011.

Casanova, José. *Public Religions in the Modern World*. Chicago: University of Chicago Press, 1994.

Chidester, David. *Savage Systems: Colonialism and Comparative Religion in Southern Africa*. Charlottesville: University of Virginia Press, 1996.

Commins, David. *Islamic Reform: Politics and Social Change in Late Ottoman Syria*. New York: Oxford University Press, 1990.

———. *The Wahhabi Mission and Saudi Arabia*. New York: I. B. Tauris, 2006.

Dalsheim, Joyce. *Unsettling Gaza*. Oxford: Oxford University Press, 2011.

Davis, Rochelle. "Commemorating Education: Recollections of the Arab College in Jerusalem, 1918–1948." *Comparative Studies of South Asia, Africa and the Middle East* 23, no. 1–2 (2003): 190–204.

Digby, Anne, and Peter Searby. *Children, School, and Society in Nineteenth-Century England*. New York: Macmillan, 1981.

Dirks, Nicholas B. *Castes of Mind: Colonialism and the Making of Modern India*. Princeton, NJ: Princeton University Press, 2001.

Dogan, Mehmet Ali, and Heather Sharkey, eds. *American Missionaries and the Middle East: Foundational Encounters*. Salt Lake City: University of Utah Press, 2011.

Don-Yehiya, Eliezer, and Charles Liebman. *Civil Religion in Israel: Traditional Judaism and Political Culture in the Jewish State*. Berkeley: University of California Press, 1983.

Doumani, Beshara. *Rediscovering Palestine*. Berkeley: University of California Press, 1995.

Dror, Yuval. "From 'Negation of the Diaspora' to 'Jewish Consciousness': The Israeli Educational System, 1920–2000." *Israel Studies Forum* 18, no. 2 (2003): 58–82.

———. *The History of Kibbutz Education: Practice into Theory*. Bern, Switzerland: Peter Lang, 2001.

———. "Teaching the Bible in the Schools of the Labor and Kibbutz Movements, 1921–1953." *Jewish History* 21, no. 2 (2007): 179–97.

Dror, Yuval, and Zehavit Gross, eds. *Dor le dor: kovtzim le-ḥeker ve-leti'ud toldot ha-ḥinuch ha-Yahudi be-Yisrael u-ve-tfutzot*, no. 44. Tel Aviv: Tel Aviv University, 2013.

Dror, Yuval, and Shimon Reshef. *ha-Ḥinuch ha-Ivri be-yamei ha-bayit ha-leumi, 1919–1948*. Jerusalem: Mosad Byalik, 1999.

Dueck, Jennifer. *The Claims of Culture at Empire's End*. Oxford: Oxford University Press, 2010.

Duncan, James. *In the Shadows of the Tropics: Climate, Race and Biopower in Nineteenth Century Ceylon*. Aldershot, UK: Ashgate, 2007.

Dweck, Yaakob. *The Scandal of Kabbalah: Leon Modena, Jewish Mysticism, Early Modern Venice*. Princeton, NJ: Princeton University Press, 2011.

Elboim-Dror, Rachel. "British Educational Policies in Palestine." *Middle Eastern Studies* 36, no. 2 (2000): 28–47.

———. *ha-Ḥinuch ha-Ivri be-Eretz-Yisrael*. Sifriyah le-Toldot ha-Yishuv ha-Yehudi be-Eretz-Yisrael. Jerusalem: Yad Yitshak Ben-Tsevi, 1986.

———. "Maslulei modernizatsia be-ḥinuch: mi ha-ḥeder le-vait ha-sefer." In *ha-Ḥeder: meḥkarim, te'udot, pirkei sifrut ve-zichronot*, edited by David Assaf and Immanuel Etkes. Tel Aviv: Institute for the History of Polish Jewry, Tel Aviv University, 2010.

Feiner, Shmuel. *"Haskalah" and History: The Emergence of a Modern Jewish Historical Consciousness*. Oxford: Oxford University Press, 2002.

———. "Programot ḥinuchiot ve-idialim ḥevratiyim: beit ha-sefer 'Ḥinuch Ne'arim' be-Berlin 1778–1825." *Zion* 60, no. 4 (1995): 393–424.

Feiner, Shmuel, and David Sorkin, eds. *New Perspectives on the "Haskalah."* London: Littman Library of Jewish Civilization, 2001.

Figueira, Dorothy. *Aryans, Jews, Brahmins: Theorizing Authority through Myths of Identity*. Albany: SUNY Press, 2002.

Fitzgerald, Timothy. *The Ideology of Religious Studies*. Oxford: Oxford University Press, 2000.

———. *Religion and Politics in International Relations: The Modern Myth*. London: Continuum 2011.

———, ed. *Religion and the Secular: Historical and Colonial Formations*. London: Equinox, 2007.

Fleischmann, Ellen. *The Nation and Its "New" Women: The Palestinian Women's Movement, 1920–1948*. Berkeley: University of California Press, 2003.

Fortna, Benjamin C. *Imperial Classroom: Islam, the State, and Education in the Late Ottoman Empire*. Oxford: Oxford University Press, 2002.

Foucault, Michel. "Governmentality." In *Power*, edited by James D. Faubion. New York: New Press, 2000.

Friedman, Menachem. *Ḥevra ve-dat: ha-orthodoxia ha-lo tzionit be-Eretz Yisrael 1918–1936*. Jerusalem: Yad Ben-Zvi, 1978.

Fromkin, David. *A Peace to End All Peace*. New York: Owl Books, 2001.

Furas, Yoni. "In Need of a New Story: Writing, Teaching and Learning History in Mandatory Palestine." PhD diss., University of Oxford, 2015.

Gaswami, Manu. *Producing India*. Chicago: University of Chicago Press, 2004.

Gellner, Ernest. *Nations and Nationalism*. Ithaca, NY: Cornell University Press, 1983.

Gelvin, James. "The 'Politics of Notables' Forty Years After." *Middle Eastern Studies Association Bulletin* 40, no. 1 (2006): 19–29.

Gesink, Indira Falk. *Islamic Reform and Conservativism: Al-Azhar and the Evolution of Modern Sunni Islam*. London: I. B. Tauris, 2014.

———. "Islamic Reformation: A History of Madrasa Reform and Legal Change in Egypt." In *Islam and Education: Myths and Truths*, edited by Wadad Kadi and Victor Billeh. Chicago: University of Chicago Press, 2007.

Gordon, Peter, and John White. *Philosophers as Educational Reformers: The Influence of Idealism on British Educational Thought and Practice*. New York: Routledge, 1979.

Gorenberg, Gershom. *The Unmaking of Israel*. New York: HarperCollins, 2011.

Greenberg, Ela. *Preparing the Mothers of Tomorrow: Education and Islam in Mandate Palestine*. Austin: University of Texas Press, 2010

Gribetz, Jonathan. *Defining Neighbors: Religion, Race, and the Early Zionist-Arab Encounter*. Princeton, NJ: Princeton University Press, 2014.

Habermas, Jürgen. *An Awareness of What Is Missing: Faith and Reason in a Post-secular Age*. Cambridge: Polity Press, 2010.

———. "Notes on Post-secular Society." *New Perspectives Quarterly* 25, no. 4 (2008): 17–29.

Halperin, Liora. *Babel in Zion: Hebrew and the Politics of Language in Palestine*. New Haven, CT: Yale University Press, 2014.

———. "The Battle over Jewish Students in the Christian Missionary Schools of Mandate Palestine." *Middle Eastern Studies* 50, no. 5 (2014): 737–54.

———. "Orienting Language: Reflections on the Study of Arabic in the Yishuv." *Jewish Quarterly Review* 96, no. 4 (2006): 481–89.

Hamada, Muhammad 'Amr. *A'lām Filasṭīn min al-qurn al-awal hata al-khāmis 'ashar*. Damascus: Dar Qutaybah, 1985.

Hanna, Paul. *British Policy in Palestine*. Washington, DC: American Council on Public Affairs, 1942.

Hefner, Robert W. "Introduction: The Culture, Politics, and Future of Muslim Education." In *Schooling Islam: The Culture and Politics of Modern Education*, edited by Robert W. Hefner and Huhammad Qasim Zaman. Princeton, NJ: Princeton University Press, 2007.

Hefner, Robert W., and Muhammad Qasim Zaman, eds. *Schooling Islam: The Culture and Politics of Modern Education*. Princeton, NJ: Princeton University Press, 2007.

Hertzberg, Arthur. *The French Enlightenment and the Jews*. New York: Columbia University Press, 1968.

Hess, Jonathan. *Germans, Jews and the Claims of Modernity*. New Haven, CT: Yale University Press, 2002.

Hoffman, Adina. *Sacred Trash: The Lost and Found World of the Cairo Geniza*. Edited by Peter Cole and S. Schechter. New York: Nextbook, 2011.

Holt, Peter. *The Mahdist State in the Sudan, 1881–1898: A Study of Its Origins, Development, and Overthrow*. Oxford: Oxford University Press, 1970.

Holtzman, Avner. "Ben hoka'ah le-hitrafkut: ha-ḥeder be-sifrut ha-zichronot u-ve-sifrut ha-Ivrit." In *ha-Ḥeder: meḥkarim, te'udot, pirkei sifrut ve-zichronot*, edited by David Assaf and Immanuel Etkes. Tel Aviv: Institute for the History of Polish Jewry, Tel Aviv University, 2010.

Horowitz, Dan, and Moshe Lissak. *Origins of the Israeli Polity: Palestine under the Mandate*. Chicago: University of Chicago Press, 1978.

Hourani, Albert. *Arabic Thought in the Liberal Age, 1798–1939*. Cambridge: Cambridge University Press, 1983.

———. "Ottoman Reform and the Politics of Notables." In *Beginnings of Modernization in the Middle East: The Nineteenth Century*, edited by William R. Polk and Richard L. Chambers. Chicago: University of Chicago Press, 1968.

al-Hout, Bayan Nuwayhed. *al-Qiyādāt wa al-mu'assassāt al-siyāsiya fi Filasṭīn 1917–1948*. 3rd ed. Beirut: Institute for Palestine Studies, 1986.

Hunter, W. W. *The Indian Musalmans (1871)*. Delhi: Indological Book House, 1969.

Jacobson, Abigail. *From Empire to Empire: Jerusalem between Ottoman and British Rule*. Syracuse, NY: Syracuse University Press, 2011.

Kalisman, Hilary Falb. "Schooling the State: Educators in Iraq, Transjordan and Palestine: c. 1980–c. 1960." PhD diss., University of California, Berkeley, 2015.

Katz, Malka. "Dat, edah, ve-ḥinuch be-yamei ha-yishuv: sephardim, bnei edot ha-mizraḥ ve-temanim be-zerem ha-ḥinuch shel 'mizraḥi' be-yamei ha-bayit ha-leumi, 1918–1948." In *Dor le dor: kovtzim le-ḥeker ve-leti'ud toldot ha-ḥinuch ha-Yahudi be-Yisrael u-ve-tfutzot*, vol. 44, edited by Yuval Deror and Zehavit Gross. Tel Aviv: Tel Aviv University, 2013.

Khalaf, Samir. *Protestant Missionaries in the Levant: Ungodly Puritans, 1820–1860*. Routledge Studies in Middle Eastern History. Oxford: Routledge, 2012.

Khalidi, Rashid. *The Iron Cage: The Story of the Palestinian Struggle for Statehood*. Boston: Beacon Press, 2006.

———. *Palestinian Identity: The Construction of Modern National Consciousness*. New York: Columbia University Press, 1997.

Khalidi, Rashid, Lisa Anderson, Muhammad Muslih, and Reeva Simon, eds. *The Origins of Arab Nationalism*. New York: Columbia University Press, 1993.

Khan, Sayyid Ahmad. "Sir Sayyid Ahmad Khan on Islam and Science." In *Textual Sources for the Study of Islam*, edited by Andrew Ruppin and Jan Knappert. Chicago: University of Chicago Press, 1990.

Khoury, Philip S. *Syria and the French Mandate: The Politics of Arab Nationalism, 1920–1945*. Princeton, NJ: Princeton University Press, 1987.

King, Richard. *Orientalism and Religion: Postcolonial Theory, India and "the Mystic East."* London: Routledge, 1999.

Kupferschmidt, Uri M. *The Supreme Muslim Council: Islam under the British Mandate for Palestine.* Leiden, Netherlands: New York, 1987.

Latour, Bruno. *Science in Action: How to Follow Scientists and Engineers through Society.* Cambridge, MA: Harvard University Press, 1988.

———. *We Have Never Been Modern.* Cambridge, MA: Harvard University Press, 1993.

Lee, Daniel. *Pétain's Jewish Children.* Oxford: Oxford University Press, 2014.

Lefebvre, Henri. *The Production of Space.* Translated by Donald Nicholson-Smith. Malden, MA: Blackwell, 1991.

Levy, Lital. "The Nahḍa and the Haskala: A Comparative Reading of 'Revival' and 'Reform.'" *Middle Eastern Literatures* 16, no. 3 (2013): 300–316.

Li, Tania Murray. *The Will to Improve: Governmentality, Development, and the Practice of Politics.* Durham, NC: Duke University Press, 2007.

Locke, John. "An Essay concerning Toleration (1667)." In *Political Writings*, edited by David Wootton. Indianapolis: Hackett Publishing, 2003.

Lockman, Zachary. *Comrades and Enemies: Arab and Jewish Workers in Palestine, 1906–1948.* Berkeley: University of California Press, 1996.

Lopez, Donald S., Jr., ed. *Curators of the Buddha: The Study of Buddhism under Colonialism.* Chicago: University of Chicago Press, 1995.

Lowith, Karl. *Meaning in History.* Chicago: University of Chicago Press, 1949.

Mahler, Raphael. *Hasidism and the Jewish Enlightenment: Their Confrontation in Galicia and Poland in the First Half of the Nineteenth Century.* Philadelphia: Jewish Publication Society of America, 1984.

Mahmood, Saba. *Politics of Piety: The Islamic Revival and the Feminist Subject.* Princeton, NJ: Princeton University Press, 2011.

———. *Religious Difference in a Secular Age: A Minority Report.* Princeton, NJ: Princeton University Press, 2016.

Makdisi, Ussama Samir. *The Culture of Sectarianism: Community, History, and Violence in Nineteenth-Century Ottoman Lebanon.* Berkeley: University of California Press, 2000.

Mantena, Karuna. *Alibis of Empire: Henry Maine and the Ends of Liberal Imperialism.* Princeton, NJ: Princeton University Press, 2010.

Masuzawa, Tomoko. *The Invention of World Religions; or, How European Universalism Was Preserved in the Language of Pluralism.* Chicago: University of Chicago Press, 2005.

Matthews, Weldon C. *Confronting an Empire, Constructing a Nation: Arab Nationalists and Popular Politics in Mandate Palestine.* London: I. B. Tauris, 2006.

McLaughlin, T. H. *Liberalism, Education and Schooling.* Exeter, UK: Imprint Academic, 2008.

Mendes-Flohr, Paul, and Jehuda Reinharz, eds. *The Jew in the Modern World: A Documentary History.* 2nd ed. Oxford: Oxford University Press, 1995.

Messick, Brinkley. *Calligraphic State.* Berkeley: University of California Press, 1996.

Metzer, Jacob. *The Divided Economy of Mandate Palestine.* Cambridge: Cambridge University Press, 1998.

Mill, John Stuart. "On Liberty." In *On Liberty and Other Essays*, edited by John Gray. Oxford: Oxford University Press, 1991.
Miller, Ylana N. *Government and Society in Rural Palestine 1920–1948*. Modern Middle East Series. Austin: University of Texas Press, 1985.
Mitchell, Timothy. *Colonizing Egypt*. Berkeley: University of California Press, 1991.
———. "Rethinking Economy." *Geoforum* 39, no. 3 (2008): 1116–21.
———. *Rule of Experts: Egypt, Techno-politics, Modernity*. Berkeley: University of California Press, 2002.
Mufti, Aamir. *Enlightenment in the Colony*. Princeton, NJ: Princeton University Press, 2007.
Musawi, Muhsin Jasim. *Islam on the Street: Religion in Modern Arabic Literature*. Lanham, MD: Rowman & Littlefield, 2009.
Nadan, Amos. *The Palestinian Peasant Economy under the Mandate: A Story of Colonial Bungling*. Harvard Middle East Monograph Series. Cambridge, MA: Harvard University Press, 2006.
Nongbri, Brent. *Before Religion*. New Haven, CT: Yale University Press, 2013.
Novak, David. *Zionism and Judaism: A New Theory*. Cambridge: Cambridge University Press, 2015.
Ohana, David. *Modernism and Zionism*. Hampshire, UK: Palgrave Macmillan, 2012.
Ormsby, Eric. "The 'Born Schulmeister.'" *New Criterion*, September 2003. https://www.newcriterion.com/issues/2003/9/the-ldquoborn-schulmeisterrdquo.
Pederson, Susan. *The Guardians: The League of Nations and the Crisis of Empire*. Oxford: Oxford University Press, 2015.
Pelli, Moshe. *The Age of "Haskalah."* Leiden, Netherlands: Brill, 1979.
Porat, Dan. "Between Nation and Land in Zionist Teaching of Jewish History, 1920–1954." *Journal of Israeli History* 27, no. 2 (2008): 253–68.
Porat, Reuven. *The History of the Kibbutz: Communal Education, 1904–1929*. Kibbutz Studies Book Series. Ramat Efal, Israel: Yad Tabenkin, 1985.
Pursley, Sara. *Familiar Futures: Time, Selfhood, and Sovereignty in Iraq, 1920–63*. Stanford, CA: Stanford University Press, forthcoming.
Quataert, Donald. *The Ottoman Empire, 1700–1922*. Cambridge: Cambridge University Press, 2000.
Ramirez, Francisco O., and John Boli. "The Political Construction of Mass Schooling: European Origins and Worldwide Institutionalization." *Sociology of Education* 60 (1987): 2–17.
Ravnitski, Yehoshua, Chaim Nahman Bialik, and S. Ben-Zion. *Sipurei ha-Mikra*. Odessa, Ukraine: Moriah, 1919.
———. *Sipurei ha-Mikra*. New York: Hebrew Publishing, 1928.
Rawls, John. *Political Liberalism*. New York: Columbia University Press, 1993.
Ridder-Symoens, Hilde de, ed. *A History of the University in Europe*. Vol. 1, *Universities in the Middle Ages*. Cambridge: Cambridge University Press, 1992.
Roberts, Nicholas. *Rethinking the Status Quo: The British and Islam in Palestine, 1917–1929*. New York: New York University Press, 2010.

Robson, Laura. *Colonialism and Christianity in Mandate Palestine*. Jamal and Rania Daniel Series in Contemporary History, Politics, Culture, and Religion of the Levant. Austin: University of Texas Press, 2011.

Roth, Cecil, and Benjamin Jaffe. "Bentwich Family." In *Encyclopedia Judaica*, edited by Michael Berenbaum and Fred Skolnik. Detroit, MI: Macmillan Reference USA, 2007.

Roy, Olivier. *Islam and Resistance in Afghanistan*. Cambridge: Cambridge University Press, 1990.

Saposnik, Arieh Bruce. *Becoming Hebrew: The Creation of a Jewish National Culture in Ottoman Palestine*. New York: Oxford University Press, 2008.

Schachter, R. Hershel. *Be-ikvei ha-tzon*. Jerusalem: Beit ha-Midrash de-Flatbush, 1997.

Schilcher, Linda S. "The Famine of 1915–1918 in Greater Syria." In *Problems of the Modern Middle East in Historical Perspective*, edited by P. Spagnolo. Oxford: Oxford University Press, 1992.

Schneider, Suzanne. "Monolingualism and Education in Mandate Palestine." *Jerusalem Quarterly* 52 (2013): 68–74.

Schoneveld, Jacobus. *The Bible in Isreali Education*. Amsterdam: Assen, 1976.

Schor, Laura. *The Best School in Jerusalem: Annie Landau's School for Girls, 1900–1960*. Waltham, MA: Brandeis University Press, 2013.

Scott, David. "Colonial Governmentality." *Social Text* 43 (1995): 191–220.

Sedra, Paul. *From Mission to Modernity: Evangelicals, Reformers and Education in Nineteenth Century Egypt*. London: I. B. Tauris, 2011.

Segev, Tom. *One Palestine, Complete: Jews and Arabs under the Mandate*. New York: Metropolitan Books, 2000.

Sengupta, Parna. *Pedagogy for Religion: Missionary Education and the Fashioning of Hindus and Muslims in Bengal*. Berkeley: University of California Press, 2011.

Shafir, Gershon. *Land, Labor, and the Origins of the Israeli-Palestinian Conflict, 1882–1914*. Updated ed. Berkeley: University of California Press, 1996.

Shapira, Anita. *The Bible and Israeli Identity*. Jerusalem: Magnes Press, 2006.

———. *Land and Power*. Stanford, CA: Stanford University Press, 1992.

Sheehan, Jonathan. *The Enlightenment Bible*. Princeton, NJ: Princeton University Press, 2005.

Shemesh, David. *Beit ha-midrash le-morim "Mizraḥi": masad la-ḥinuch ha-dati ha-leumi*. Jerusalem: ha-Mikhlalah ha-datit le-morim `a.sh. R.A.M. Lifshits, 1991.

Shimoni, Gideon. *The Zionist Ideology*. Hanover, NH: Brandeis University Press, 1995.

Shimony, Tali Tadmor. "Teaching the Bible as Common Culture." *Jewish History* 21, no. 2 (2007): 159–78.

Sluglett, Peter. *Britain in Iraq, 1914–1932*. London: Ithaca Press, 1976.

Smith, Barbara J. *The Roots of Separatism in Palestine: British Economic Policy, 1920–1929*. Contemporary Issues in the Middle East. Syracuse, NY: Syracuse University Press, 1993.

Smith, Jonathan Z. "Religion, Religions, Religious." In *Relating Religion: Essays in the Study of Religion*, 179–96. Chicago: University of Chicago Press, 2004.

Somel, Selçuk Akşin. *The Modernization of Public Education in the Ottoman Empire, 1839–1908: Islamization, Autocracy, and Discipline.* Leiden, Netherlands: Brill, 2001.
Starrett, Gregory. *Putting Islam to Work.* Berkeley: University of California Press, 1998.
Straumann, Benjamin. "The Peace of Westphalia as a Secular Constitution." *Constellations: An International Journal of Critical & Democratic Theory* 15, no. 2 (2008): 173–88.
Symonds, R. *Oxford and Empire.* Oxford: Oxford University Press, 1986.
Tamari, Salim. *The Year of the Locust.* Berkeley: University of California Press, 2011.
Taylor, Charles. *A Secular Age.* Cambridge, MA: Harvard University Press, 2007.
Thompson, Elizabeth. *Colonial Citizens: Republican Rights, Paternal Privilege, and Gender in French Syria and Lebanon.* New York: Columbia University Press, 2000.
Tibawi, Abdul Latif. *Arab Education in Mandatory Palestine: A Study of Three Decades of British Administration.* London: Luzac, 1956.
———. *Islamic Education: Its Traditions and Modernization into the Arab National Systems.* London: Luzac, 1972.
———. "Religion and Educational Administration in Palestine of the British Mandate." *Die Welt des Islams* 3, no. 1 (1953): 1–14.
Totah, Khalil. "The Contribution of the Arabs to Education." PhD diss., Columbia University, 1926.
Turniansky, Chavah. "Limud ba-ḥeder be-et ha-ḥadasha ha-mukdemet." In *ha-Ḥeder: meḥkarim, te'udot, pirkei sifrut ve-zichronot*, edited by David Assaf and Immaneul Etkes. Tel Aviv: Institute for the History of Polish Jewry, Tel Aviv University, 2010.
van der Leest, Charlotte. "Conversion and Conflict in Palestine: The Missions of the Church Missionary Society and the Protestant Bishop Samuel Gobat." PhD diss., Leiden University, 2008.
Walzer, Michael. *The Paradox of Liberation: Secular Revolutions and Religious Counterrevolutions.* New Haven, CT: Yale University Press, 2015.
Wasserstein, Bernard. *The British in Palestine: The Mandatory Government and the Arab-Jewish Conflict 1917–1929.* Royal Historical Society Studies in History Series. London: Royal Historical Society, 1978.
Weber, Eugen. *Peasants into Frenchmen: The Modernization of Rural France, 1870–1914.* Stanford, CA: Stanford University Press, 1976.
Weiss, Max. *In the Shadow of Sectarianism: Law, Shi'ism, and the Making of Modern Lebanon.* Cambridge, MA: Harvard University Press, 2010.
Weissman, Deborah. "Bais Ya'akov—a Women's Educational Movement in the Polish Jewish Community: A Case Study in Tradition and Modernity." Master's thesis, New York University, 1977.
———. "Ḥinuch banot datiyot be-Yerushalayim be-tekufat ha-shilton ha-Briti: hitmasdutan ve-hitgabshutan shel ḥamesh ideologiyot ḥinuchiyot." PhD diss., Hebrew University, 1993.
Wessely, Naphtali Herz. "Words of Peace and Truth." Translated by S. Weinstein and S. Fischer. In *The Jew in the Modern World*, ed. Paul R. Mendes-Flohr and Jehuda Reinharz, 70–74. Oxford: Oxford University Press, 1995.

Williams, Raymond. *The Sociology of Culture*. New York: Schocken Books, 1981.
Wodziński, Marcin. *"Haskalah" and Hasidism in the Kingdom of Poland: A History of Conflict*. Oxford: Littman Library of Jewish Civilization, 2005.
Zakim, Eric Stephen. *To Build and Be Built: Landscape, Literature, and the Construction of Zionist Identity*. Philadelphia: University of Pennsylvania Press, 2006.
Zerubavel, Yael. *Recovered Roots: Collective Memory and the Making of Israeli National Tradition*. Chicago: University of Chicago Press, 1995.

INDEX

'Abbasid Empire, 157
'Abd al-Qadir al-Jaza'iri, 136
'Abduh, Muhammad, 137, 210n53; on Islamic religious education, 141–45, 150
Abu Bakr, 139
Abu-Lughod, Ibrahim: *Arab Rediscovery of Europe*, 207n2
Adnani, Muhammad, 147
Advisory Committee on Education in the Colonies, 61, 106
al-Afghani, Jamal al-Din, 157, 229n80
Agudat Israel, 76, 117–18, 122, 197, 213n46, 216n11, 225n91; relations with Va'ad Leumi, 74–75, 113, 116
Ahad Ha'am, 46
Ahmad bin 'Abdallah, Muhammad, 85
'Ali, Muhammad, 20, 42–43, 136
Alliance Israélite Universelle, 45, 116, 223n55
Alterman, Natan, 167
Alterman, Yitzhak, 161, 167–69, 171, 172
Altschuler girl's school, 120
Amanah Group, 223n59
Amery, Lord, 57
Amin, Qasim, 144
Amit, Yairah, 175
'Amr ibn Madi Karib, 135
Anatolian Jewish community, 125
Anglo-American Committee of Inquiry, 187, 189
Anglo-Jewish Association, 45
Anidjar, Gil, 3
anti-Semitism, 10–11, 13, 68
Antonius, George: *The Arab Awakening*, 207n2
Arab Executive, 14
Arab history, 130, 134–37, 139, 227n17, 228n55
Arabic language, 48, 98, 115, 137, 149–50, 199, 209n52, 213n51, 226n13; and Arab nationalism, 46, 55–56; role in Arab Public System, 53–56, 67, 109, 133–34, 227n23
Arab *nahḍa* (renaissance), 67, 100, 134, 207n3, 220n6
Arab nationalism, 44, 47, 58–59, 71, 78, 102, 129, 132, 134–35, 187, 202, 215n91, 227n17; and Arabic language, 46, 55–56; of Muhammad 'Izzat Darwaza, 3, 136, 147, 148–49, 154–56, 159; relationship to Islam, 146, 154–57, 158–59. *See also* al-Najāḥ National School
Arab Public System, 65–66, 67, 78, 90–96, 97, 129, 215n91; vs. al-Najāḥ National School, 136, 145–46, 150, 151, 152, 154, 158–59; curricula in, 38, 44, 61–62, 65–66, 67, 109–10, 130, 132–40, 144, 146, 149, 150, 152, 177, 182, 221n34, 222n35, 227nn17,19,23; educational uniformity in, 141–42, 144, 152; enrollment in, 57, 80, 109, 213n59, 219n75, 221n24; female education in, 61–62; vs. Hebrew Public System, 48–49, 53–54, 58–59, 60–61, 68, 72, 80, 88, 92–93, 94, 106, 150, 164,

177, 179, 182, 186, 188, 189; Islam and, 88, 109–11, 130, 140, 150–52; Mandatory government funding for, 53, 57, 63, 67, 109; role of Arabic language in, 53–56, 67, 109, 133–34, 227n23; rural education, 38, 50–51, 59–60, 98, 104–13, 125–26, 128, 132–33, 214n67, 221n34, 222n35; teachers in, 106–7, 108, 110, 111–12, 139, 140, 144, 188, 222n52
Arab Revolt of 1936, 66–67
Aronsohn, Rabbi Shelomo, 161, 164, 166, 167–68, 170–71, 172
Asad, Talal, 3, 130, 131, 134, 210n53
al-Ashqar, 'Aṭiyah, 150–51
Assyrian Jewish community, 125
'Auda, 'Ali Hasn, 151
Ayalon, Ami, 37
Azaryahu, Joseph, 166–67, 171, 176
al-Azhar, 150–51

Bais Ya'akov network of schools, 119
Balfour, Lord: visit of 1925, 65
Balfour Declaration, 10, 11, 13, 15, 48, 141
al-Banna, Hassan, 151
Barchihu, Aharon Michal, 166
Barelvi, Syed Ahmed, 85, 210n65, 218n47
Bar Gottlober, Avraham, 99
Barlassina, Louis (Latin patriarch of Jerusalem), 81–82
Bar-Lev, Motti, 205n7
Batnitzky, Leora, 30
Beijel, Moshe Aharon, 186
Ben-Gurion, David, 88, 197
Bennet, J. S., 201
Bentham, Jeremy, 27; panopticon of, 26
Bentwich, Joseph, 14, 114; and Amanah Group, 223n59; *Education in Israel*, 20
Bentwich, Norman, 114, 207n27
Berkey, Jonathan, 21
Berkson, Isaac, 165
Berman, Rabbi Ya'akov, 172–73, 234n68
Bialik, Hayyim Nahman, 178; "Safiaḥ" (Aftergrowth), 99
Bloom, J. L., 114, 126–27
Blunt, Wilfred Scawen: *The Future of Islam*, 210n8
Boli, John, 26, 208n17

Bowman, Humphrey, 27–28, 37, 83, 104–5, 112, 122–23, 207n28; on Arab primary education, 59, 60; on Arab rural education, 50–51, 106, 107–8, 110–11, 132–33; on Education Ordinance, 79; on Farrell, 13–14; vs. Farrell, 13–14, 55, 67, 186–87, 191; on female education, 61, 62; on Jewish school inspectors, 114, 223n56; on language and education, 55; on Orthodox Jews, 191; on politics and education, 66; on public service, 64
Brisker Rav, 216n17
British Mandatory government in Palestine. *See* Mandatory government
Brit Shalom, 115
Brownson, Elizabeth, 133

Calhoun, Craig, 3
Campos, Michelle, 37, 58
Casanova, José: *Public Religions in the Modern World*, 3
Catholic Church: and education, 25, 76, 79, 80–82, 83–84, 86, 90, 211n14; Locke on, 33
Central Asian Jews, 120–21
Christianity, 35–36, 130, 190, 208n27, 216n5, 229n80; and colonialism, 34, 72; ethical core, 139, 191; missionary schools, 17, 36–37, 45–46, 52, 56, 76, 77–78, 79, 83–84, 205n1, 211nn14,15; Palestinian Christians, 3, 46, 71; Protestantism, 25, 30, 34, 138, 154, 164; and secularism, 4, 5. *See also* Catholic Church
colonialism, 28, 32, 33, 145, 146, 159, 209n52; and Christianity, 34, 72; and education, 27, 29, 34–35, 37–40, 41, 50, 129, 131–32, 134–35, 151, 154, 163, 197, 202; indirect rule in, 12, 103–4, 105; and

modernity, 148; relationship to Zionism, 185–95; role of sectarianism in, 71–72
Colonial Office, 58, 75, 76, 78, 86, 87, 89–90, 114, 116; relations with Mandatory government, 13, 54, 56–57, 79–80, 82–84, 117, 189, 191, 192, 201, 203
Committee to Clarify the Question of Religious Education, 161, 164, 166–74, 176–77
conceptual boundaries, 146, 166; politics-education, 8–9, 64, 67, 116, 129–30, 159, 190, 200; religious-secular, 4, 5, 16, 17, 21, 31–33, 72, 129–31, 133–34, 140–41, 177, 200; transgression of, 9, 17, 27, 67, 116, 129, 163, 190, 200; universal-particular, 3, 29, 32, 134, 200
Cromer, Lord: on Christianity, 216n5; on Islam, 85; on the Mahdi, 85; *Modern Egypt*, 60, 216n5; policies regarding education in Egypt, 133

Dalsheim, Joyce, 236n97
Dar al-'Ulum/Kuliya Dar al-'Ulum, 151
Darwaza, Muhammad 'Ali, 146
Darwaza, Muhammad 'Izzat, 110, 197; at al-Najāḥ National School, 3, 17, 101, 146, 147; Arab nationalism of, 3, 136, 147, 148–49, 154–56, 159; on Islam and Arab nationalism, 3, 155–56, 159; *Lessons in Ancient History*, 148; *Lessons in Arab History from Antiquity to the Present*, 147–48, 155, 227n19; *Lessons in Medieval and Modern History*, 148; on modernity and colonialism, 148; textbooks written by, 101–2, 136, 145, 147–48, 228n55
Darwish, Ishaq, 144
Dawkins, Richard, 203
de Bunsen, Bernard, 14
Dror, Yuval, 178, 206n11, 230n3, 232n42
dual society narrative, 5–6
Dubnov, Semen Markovich, 233n51
Duruy, Jean Victor, 43
Dusturiyya school, 46
Dweck, Yaakob, 220n12

Egypt: Coptic leaders in, 39–40; education in, 19, 22–23, 39–40, 42–43, 105, 106, 107, 109, 132–33, 150, 151, 229n70; Islamic Jihad in, 197; mass politics in, 37–38; vs. Palestine, 2, 37–38, 39–40, 41, 59–60, 66, 103, 106, 107, 109, 130, 132–33, 145, 150, 151; revolution of 1919, 37–38; Sadat assassination, 197; during WWI, 11
Elazari-Volcani, Benjamin, 182, 233n56
Elboim-Dror, Rachel, 125, 206n9, 217n24
Eliahu, Rabbi Ovadya, 118
Epstein, Itzhac, 55
European liberalism, 2, 33, 114, 129–30, 190, 193, 200
European nationalism, 25–26
European public education, 25–28
Evelina de Rothschild School for Girls, 45

Faisal, Emir, 147
Fanus, Akhnukh, 40
al-Farabi, 135
Farrell, Jerome, 114, 159; vs. Bowman, 13–14, 55, 67, 186–87, 191; on Education Ordinance, 84–85; on Jewish education, 88; on language and education, 55, 67; on Nazism, 68, 190; on religious education, 117, 163; on Zionist education, 68–69, 113, 182, 189–91, 192, 193, 194, 235n75, 236n95
Federation of Heredi Jews, 120
Feiner, Shmuel, 181
female education, 61–63, 119–20, 137–38, 214n76, 215n85, 222n42
Filisṭīn, 141
First Arab Congress, 213n51
Fitzgerald, Timothy, 3, 32
Fleischmann, Ellen, 214n81, 220n18, 222n42, 227n27

Fortna, Benjamin, 35; *Imperial Classroom*, 210n4
Foucault, Michel, 145; on governmentality, 25, 26, 208nn14,20; on self-discipline, 171
France: and Catholic schools in Palestine, 79, 81; education in, 28; Islam in, 33; Mandate in Lebanon and Syria, 52; Sykes-Picot Agreement, 11–12
Furas, Yoni, 206n16

Gellner, Ernest, 4, 25, 205n5
General Federation of Jewish Labor (Histadrut), 178
General Zionists, 167, 173; schools of, 47, 126, 161, 165, 169, 175, 177–78, 181, 182–83, 184–85, 186, 187, 188, 194, 230n3, 232n47, 233n62, 236n95
Germany: educational theory in, 19; Nazism in, 68, 190; Orthodox Jews in, 173
al-Ghazali, 20, 24, 135, 139
Goitein, Shlomo Dov, 14, 114, 125, 126, 223nn56,61; on Agudat Israel, 117–18; *Hora'at ha-tanakh*, 115; on Yemenite Jews, 115, 121, 223n62
Gordon, A. D., 183–84
Gordon, Charles George, 85, 135
Goswami, Manu, 226n4
Government Arab College, 59, 107, 125, 221n25
grand mufti of Palestine, 14, 15, 85–86, 93, 137
Great Britain: Anglican schools in, 28, 80, 86–87, 217n28; Balfour Education Act, 217n28; LEAs in, 217n28; vs. Palestine, 80, 81–82, 86–87, 138, 152, 189; public schools in, 217n28; religious education in, 28, 34–35, 138, 152; Sykes-Picot Agreement, 11–12. *See also* Colonial Office; Mandatory government
Greater Syria, 47–48, 141, 147, 156
Green, T. H., 208n27
Gribetz, Jonathan, 215n98; on nationalism, 4
Guttmann, Simhah Alter, 178–79

Ha-aretz, 119
Habermas, Jürgen, 3
Haifa: Jewish vs. Arab school enrollment in, 60; Reali School, 115
Haifa Technion, 47
Halperin, Liora, 55
Hapsburg Empire, 31
Harris, Sam, 203
ha-shomer ha-tza'ir (Young Guard), 128
Hasidism, 102, 220n11
Haskalah (enlightenment), 160, 207n3; Jewish enlighteners (*maskilim*), 19, 20, 30–32, 98–99, 102, 181, 220n11, 233n55
Hazaz, Haim: "The Sermon", 220n5
Hebrew Bible, 231n28; Torah, 1, 21–22, 24, 31, 115, 118–19, 120, 127–28, 165, 173, 179, 180, 182, 195, 233n47; and Zionism, 99–100, 118–19, 127–28, 166, 168–69, 175–82, 183, 232n47, 234n68. *See also* Torah
Hebrew language, 21–22, 124, 199; and Zionism, 45, 46, 47, 53–55, 99, 121, 127, 171, 172, 175, 191, 195, 211n13
Hebrew Public System: vs. Arab Public System, 48–49, 53–54, 58–59, 60–61, 68, 72, 80, 88, 92–93, 94, 106, 150, 163–64, 177, 179, 182, 186, 188, 189; autonomy of, 40, 48, 49, 53, 58, 72, 86–90, 92, 94, 97, 113, 186, 188–89, 191–93, 198; as belonging to a religious community, 77, 86–88, 94, 116; curricula and textbooks, 177–83, 184–85, 232n45, 233nn51,62; enrollment in, 60, 61, 80, 165, 183, 213n59, 221n24; funding from abroad, 170, 177, 212n27; funding from Jewish taxation, 58, 87; funding from Mandatory government, 53–58, 86, 87, 115, 187, 192, 213n46, 234n72; Jewish inspectors for, 114–15, 118, 119, 125, 126–27, 192; legacy of, 194–95; role of Hebrew Bible in, 127–

28, 168–69, 175–82, 183, 232n47, 234n68; secularism in, 117, 161–62, 163, 165, 174, 194; teachers, 47, 187, 188; Zionist nationalism/politicization in, 113, 117, 186–91, 193–94. *See also* Va'ad Leumi (National Council); Zionist Executive
Hebrew University, 115
Hebron, 100
hed ha-ḥinuch, 115
Hefner, Robert, 34
Herzl, Theodor, 46; *Der Judenstaat*, 10
Herzliya Gymnasium, 177
Hess, Jonathan: *Germans, Jews and the Claims of Modernity*, 209n44
Hinduism, 34, 35–36, 38–39
Hitchens, Christopher, 203
Holtzman, Avraham, 99
Horovitz, Joseph, 115
Horowitz, Dan, 5
Hourani, Albert: *Arabic Thought in the Liberal Age*, 207n1, 228n49; on politics of notables, 36, 210n56
Hubnaqa, 110, 222n38
Hunter, W. W.: *The Indian Musalmans*, 38–39, 210n65, 218n47
al-Husayni, Hamdi, 154
Hussaini, Jamal, 191
Hussein, Taha, 146, 197; *al-Ayyam* (The days), 101; on colloquial Arabic, 226n13; on Sufism, 103
Hussein bin Ali, 12
al-Husseini, Haj Amin, 14, 66, 85–86, 137, 144

Ibn al-Jawzi, 222n38
Ibn al-Walid, Khalid , 135
Ibn Ziyad, Tariq, 135
Ibrahim Pasha, 136
imperial ideologies, 103–4, 113
'Inani, Mustafa, 150–51; *Kitāb al-dīn al-Islāmī* (Book of the Islamic Religion), 151, 156–59
India, 11, 19; Bengal, 28–29, 38–39, 143; education in, 28–29, 34, 38–39, 105, 106, 107, 143; Muslims in, 33, 38–39, 85, 143, 210n65; mutiny of 1857, 38, 105; vs. Palestine, 2, 29, 41, 59–60, 80, 103, 105, 106, 107, 143, 220n18; secularism in, 230n5
indirect rule, 12, 103–4, 105
Iraq, 12, 150, 222n52, 228n55; Jewish community in, 125
Islam: idea of fundamental core, 34, 100, 102–3, 139, 191, 220n6; hadith, 22, 137, 140, 152, 155; Hajj, 153; *hirjah* to Medina, 155; jihad, 203; Muhammad, 22, 136, 137–38, 139, 140, 143, 153, 155, 156; permissible (*ḥalāl*) vs. prohibited (*ḥarām*), 143; Ramadan, 153, 229n68; relationship to Arab nationalism, 146, 154–57, 158–59; relationship to science, 157–58; ritualistic elements ('ibadāt), 151, 152–53, 154, 156, 157, 229n61; sharia, 130, 197, 229n61; *shura* (consultation), 158; socioethical elements (*mu'āmalāt*), 151, 152–53, 154, 156, 229n61; Sunna, 138, 142. *See also* Qur'an
Islamic religious education: communal religious schools (*katātīb*), 21, 22–23, 24, 34, 43, 44, 62, 94, 97–98, 100–103, 108, 109–10, 111, 112, 118, 119, 125, 128, 133–34, 137, 139, 140, 150, 152, 198, 205n1, 221n28; vs. education in Christian Europe, 25; vs. Jewish religious education, 2, 3, 6–7, 9, 17, 19–21, 23–24, 40, 98, 100, 118, 119, 125; madrasas, 20, 21, 34, 44, 133, 143–44, 157, 203; memorization in, 34–35, 98, 101, 110, 112, 133–34, 138, 152; reform of, 15–16, 19–20, 24, 34–35, 43–44, 95, 97–98, 100–103, 108, 109–10, 118, 128, 137–40, 144–45, 152, 198–99; relationship to politics, 2, 3, 9, 21, 29, 36, 84–85, 129–32; relationship to social and political stability, 21, 29, 36, 131; role of Qur'an in, 22, 34–35, 44, 84, 101, 109, 132, 133–34, 138, 140, 150; standardized curricula in, 35; texts studied, 21,

23, 34–35, 101, 109, 110; traditional curricula, 19, 24, 137; uniformity in, 141–42, 143; views of ʿAbduh on, 141–45, 150
Israel, State of: education in, 20, 178; Gaza policies, 197; impact of Jewish-Arab relations on, 6; Ministry of Education, 178; religious education in, 205n7; settlement movement, 194, 203, 236n97; ultra-Orthodox communities in, 1, 24–25, 87, 194; *yeshiva* students in, 236n1
Istiqlāl (Independence) Party, 147
Italy, 79

Jacobson, Abigail: *From Empire to Empire*, 206n16
Jaffa Government Boys' School, 49
Jahiliyya period, 135, 142
al-Jāḥiẓ, 100
Jamal Pasha, 47
Jarallah, Saʿida, 137, 227n27
Jarallah, Sheikh Hussam al-Din, 14, 137–38
Jerusalem: Government Arab College, 59, 107, 125, 151, 221n25; Municipal Council, 92, 93; Orthodox Schools Committee, 114; Torat Aharon, 125; Western Wall, 14
Jewish Agency, 14, 15, 59, 73, 86, 126, 165, 192, 212n27, 234n72; Department of Education, 87–88, 90, 91, 94, 121, 219n53
Jewish agricultural economy, 108, 221n32
Jewish-Arab relations, 5–7, 16, 94, 187, 197, 200–203, 206n16, 215n98; Nebi Musa riots (1920), 85; riots of 1929, 14, 65
Jewish enlighteners (*maskilim*), 19, 20, 30–32, 98–99, 102, 181, 220n11, 233n55
Jewish identity, 173, 174, 175, 236n96; and Zionism, 3, 17, 121, 162–63, 166–67, 170, 177, 178, 185, 194, 224n85
Jewish religious education: Committee to Clarify the Question of Religious Education, 161, 164, 166–74, 176–77; communal religious schools (*ḥederim*), 20, 21, 22, 24, 46, 97–99, 113, 117, 118, 119, 128, 162, 171, 198, 205n1; vs. education in Christian Europe, 25; as *ḥinuch*, 21–22; vs. Islamic religious education, 2, 3, 6–7, 9, 17, 19–21, 23–24, 40, 98, 100, 118, 119, 125; memorization in, 98; and mysticism, 102; reform of, 15–16, 19–20, 24, 30–31, 35, 46, 95, 97–100, 103, 113–28, 198–99; role of Torah in, 1, 21–22, 24, 31, 115, 119, 120, 127–28; *talmud torah* schools, 22, 98, 113, 117–18, 119, 120, 122–25, 205n1; texts studied, 20–22, 23, 99, 118–19, 120, 126–27, 168; traditional curricula, 19, 24; *yeshivot*, 22, 113, 126, 170, 203, 236n1
Jewish Telegraph Agency (JTA), 73
Jews from *edot ha-mizraḥ*, 120–25
Jordan, 137, 151
Joseph II's Edict of Toleration, 31
Judaism, 209n44, 223n59; diasporic Judaism, 164–65, 169–70, 178, 185, 190, 220n5, 233n60; ethical core, 139; *halachot*, 22, 75, 119, 125, 165, 166, 173, 185, 217n18; *kashrut*, 24; modern emergence as religion, 30–32, 33–34; Passover, 233n60; practical commandments (*mitzvot maʿasiot*), 161, 169, 170, 171, 172, 173, 230n1; Rosh Hashanah, 185, 231n21; and secularism, 33–34, 169–70; Shabbat, 24, 172, 173, 185; Yom Kippur, 231n22; in Zionism, 68–69. *See also* Hebrew Bible; Mishnah; Talmud; Torah
Juergensmeyer, Mark, 3

Kalisman, Hilary Falb, 222n52
Khalidi, Rashid, 93, 227n17
al-Khalifa, Ahmad, 151
Khan, Sayyid Ahmad, 19
Khayr al-Din, ʿAbd al-Wahab, 151, 156
kibbutz farming, 6, 178, 231n27
Kilani, Kamil: *Qusūs atfāl*, 149–50
Kitāb al-dīn al-Islāmī (Book of the Islamic Religion), 151, 156–59
Knesset Israel, 14, 15, 73, 77, 212n27

Kurdish Jews, 121–22

Labor movement, 115, 169–70, 174, 231n27; schools of, 47, 161, 163, 165, 173, 175, 176, 178–81, 182, 183–84, 186, 187, 188, 194, 230n3, 232n47, 236n95
Landau, Annie, 45
Lane-Poole, Stanley, 85
Latour, Bruno: on God, 8; on Modern Constitution, 7–8, 129; on modernity, 7–8, 9, 72; *We Have Never Been Modern*, 7–8
Lawrence, Susan, 65–66
League of Nations: League Covenant, 12; Mandate system, 12–13, 58–59; Permanent Mandates Commission, 53, 56, 57, 106, 206n25. *See also* Mandate for Palestine
LEAs. *See* local education authorities
Lebanon, 12, 52
Levine, Yehuda Lieb, 99
Levy, Lital, 207n3
Lipshitz, Eliezer Meir, 166
Lissak, Moshe, 5
literary education, 59–60, 62, 105, 106
Lloyd, T. I. K., 56–57, 80, 83, 84
local education authorities (LEAs), 78, 86, 87, 93, 190, 217n28; and Education Ordinance, 51, 89, 91–92, 213n62
Locke, John: on Catholic Church, 33; on religious tolerance, 33
Lockman, Zachary, 6
London Times, 37
Lowith, Karl, 233n55
Lugard, Lord, 105–6
Luke, Sir Harry Charles, 88
Luria, Joseph, 47, 169

Mabāda fi al-dīn al-Islāmī (Principles of the Islamic Religion), 147, 151
Macaulay, Lord, 220n18; *Minute on Indian Education*, 105
MacMichael, Sir Harold, 116–17
Magnes, Judah, 115
Mahdi, 85
Mahler, Raphael: *Hasidism and the Jewish Enlightenment*, 220n11
Mahmood, Saba, 3
Maimon, Shelomo, 98–99
Maimonides, Moses, 102, 125, 220n12
Maine, Henry, 105
Majlisi, Muhammad Bakar, 229n68
Mandate for Palestine, 50, 80, 82–83, 203; Article 4, 14; Article 15, 77, 78, 79; Article 16, 79, 83; and Balfour Declaration, 13, 15; communities in, 77, 78; recognition of national rights for Jews vs. Arabs in, 13, 15, 58, 72, 201–2. *See also* League of Nations
Mandatory government, 6, 12, 212n25; Department of Education, 13–14, 16, 20, 48, 50–52, 53–54, 58, 61, 62, 63, 66, 68, 78, 79, 81, 82, 83, 86, 87, 89, 91, 92, 93, 94, 98, 104–5, 106, 107–8, 111, 112, 113–14, 115–16, 118–19, 120, 122–27, 128, 132–33, 134, 140, 151, 163, 185–95, 218n53, 221n24; financial resources for education, 50–58, 63, 67, 80, 86, 87, 109, 114, 115–18, 120, 127, 187, 192, 212n32, 213n46, 223n55, 234n72; High Commissioner, 53, 54, 65, 66, 73, 75, 79, 81, 88, 91, 116–17, 234n72; Jewish national home as project of, 10, 13, 14, 59, 78, 104, 188–89, 192, 193; Jewish vs. Arab attitudes regarding, 90, 92; vs. Ottoman Empire, 41–42, 44, 48, 52, 59, 77–78, 81, 82, 94, 202, 203; policies regarding Arab primary education, 49–51, 59–60, 61, 64, 106–7, 221n18; policies regarding Arab rural education, 38, 50–51, 59–60, 98, 104–13, 125–26, 128, 132–33, 214n67, 221n34, 222n35; policies regarding Arab secondary education, 106–7; policies regarding Christian schools, 9, 17, 200–201, 202; policies regarding educational monolingualism, 54–56,

65, 67; policies regarding educational reform, 103–28; policies regarding female education, 61–63; policies regarding Orthodox Jewish education, 113–28, 187, 193, 213n46, 223n55; policies regarding preservation of tradition, 2, 62, 67, 71–72, 98, 103, 106, 108, 111, 112–13, 126, 130, 159, 194, 198, 202, 214n81; policies regarding religious education, 2–3, 5, 7, 9, 15, 16–17, 28, 29, 33, 34–35, 36, 40, 76–95, 97–98, 103–9, 110, 113–28, 129–30, 132, 137, 138–41, 144–45, 146, 159, 163–64, 174–75, 177, 187, 193–94, 197–98, 221n34, 222n35, 236n95; policies regarding school sanitation, 83–84, 118, 122–24; policy of decentralization of education, 50–51; policy of equalization regarding Jews and Arabs, 49; and politics of denial, 9, 16, 17, 42, 64–68, 85–86, 116, 129–30, 185–95, 200; recognition of Zionist schools as public entities, 52, 54; relations with Colonial Office, 13, 54, 56–57, 79–80, 82–84, 117, 189, 191, 192, 201, 203; role of sectarianism in, 71–72, 76–86, 94, 116, 140, 141, 164, 191–92, 197, 198, 228n38; school inspectors, 14, 114–15, 118, 119, 122, 123–24, 125, 126–27, 192, 223n56. *See also* Bowman, Humphrey; Farrell, Jerome; Palestine Education Ordinance of 1933; Religious Communities Organization Ordinance
Mansur, Hassan, 151, 156
Mantena, Karuna, 103–4
mass politics, 15, 16, 20, 64–70; relationship to religious education, 2–3, 4–5, 9, 36, 39–40, 67–68, 84–86, 128, 129–32, 140–41, 144–45, 146, 153–57, 158–59, 163, 177, 187, 193–94, 197–98, 199–200, 203, 204; rise of, 21, 36–40
Masuzawa, Tomoko, 3
Matthews, Weldon, 37
McMahon, Sir Henry, 12
McNair Commission, 187–89
Mendelssohn, Moses: *Jerusalem*, 30
Messick, Brinkley, 35
Middle Eastern Jews, 113, 120–21
Mill, John Stuart, 33
Miller, Ylana, 65
Mishnah, 22, 167, 168, 184–85, 231n28
Mitchell, Timothy, 22–23
Mizraḥi (Religious Zionists) Party, 163, 165, 169; Mizraḥi schools, 116, 117, 124–25, 126–27, 163, 172, 173, 174, 175, 181, 182–83, 184, 185, 186, 187, 188, 194, 230n3, 232n40, 233n62, 234n68
modernity: biblical criticism in, 164, 173, 177; and colonialism, 148; concept of religion in, 29–34, 35; education in, 8–9, 16, 19, 21, 22–23, 25–27, 77, 98, 101–3, 104, 106, 108, 112–13, 120, 126, 129, 134, 135, 137–38, 144–45, 150, 151–52, 153–54, 159, 171, 199, 222n40; and history, 135; secularization in, 3–4, 16, 17, 21, 31–34, 72, 129–31, 133–34, 140–41, 158, 177, 197; and tradition, 1–2, 19–20, 34
Mohliver, Yosef, 166, 171
moledet, 178, 232n40
Mufti, Aamir, 33
Muslim Brotherhood, 197
al-Mutanabbi, 135

Nablus, 14, 17; Arab Club, 146. *See also* al-Najāḥ National School
Nadan, Amos, 108
al-Najā National School, 130–31, 145–52, 191; vs. Arab Public System, 136, 145–46, 150, 151, 152, 154, 158–59; curriculum and textbooks, 146–47, 149–56; Darwaza at, 3, 17, 101, 146, 147; moral fashioning at, 145–46
al-Namari, 24
Nashashibi, Is'af, 144
Nebi Musa riots (1920), 85
New Atheists, 203
newspapers and periodicals, 37

New Yishuv, 205n1
Nigeria, 41, 78, 105
Nizam al-Mulk, 157
Nongbri, Brent, 3, 209n52
Nordau, Max, 10
North African Jews, 120–21

Old Yishuv, 5, 46, 48–49, 87, 98, 114, 116, 121, 205n1, 216n11. *See also* Agudat Israel
Organization of Talmudic Education, 126–27
Ormsby, Eric, 115
Ottoman Empire, 11–12, 215n98, 216n2; Arab nationalists in, 44, 46; vs. British Mandate in Palestine, 41–42, 44, 48, 52, 59, 77–78, 81, 82, 94, 202, 203; Constitutional era (Second), 58, 141, 213n51; Decentralization Party, 213n51; Education Act of 1913, 77; education in, 7, 35, 41–48, 52, 56, 59, 77, 81, 90, 101–2, 141–44, 202, 203, 205n1, 208n11, 210n4, 211n11, 217n24, 219n75; *millet* system, 71, 77, 216n3; policies regarding Armenians, 47; political life in Arab provinces, 36–37, 210n56, 213n51; Regulation of Public Education, 43; sheikh al-Islam, 142, 144, 150; Sublime Porte, 77, 78, 81, 141; Turkish language in, 44, 56; during WWI, 47–48

Palestine Education Ordinance of 1933, 58, 76–95, 192, 218n53; autonomy of religious schools in, 16, 83–84, 130; categories of private religious schools in, 83–84; and LEAs, 51, 89, 91–92, 213n62
Palestine Liberation Organization, 197
Palestine Royal Commission (PRC) 51, 55, 59, 61in, 83, 200–201, 202, 215n91
Parsitz, Shoshana, 166
Passerfield White Paper of 1930, 89
Pederson, Susan, 206n25
Peel Commission, 50, 187
Plato: on education, 27–28; *Laws*, 27–28
Plumer, Lord, 53–55, 56, 57, 79, 82
politics of denial: definition, 9, 72, 116, 203–4; and Mandatory government, 9, 16, 17, 42, 64–68, 85–86, 116, 129–30, 185–95, 200. *See also* mass politics
Porat, Dan, 233nn51,62
postcolonial studies, 26
practical education, 107–8, 133; vs. religious education, 24–25, 67, 97, 103, 110, 118, 119, 128, 157–58, 175, 199, 208n11
Protestantism, 25, 30, 34, 138, 154, 164

Quataert, Donald, 216n2
Qur'an, 24, 142, 149, 199, 221n34; memorization of, 34–35, 101, 133–34, 150, 152; role in Islamic religious education, 22, 34–35, 44, 84, 101, 109, 132, 133–34, 138, 140, 150; Sura al-A'rāf, 157; Sura al-Baqara, 157
Qutb, Sayyid, 151

Ramah, 23
Ramirez, Francisco, 26, 208n17
Rashi, 127–28
Ravnitski, Yehoshua, 178–79
Rawls, John, 26
Religious Communities Organization Ordinance, 14, 73–76, 77, 86–87, 116, 191–92, 193, 216nn8,11
religious education: definition, 5; Mandatory government policies regarding, 2–3, 5, 7, 9, 15, 16–17, 28, 29, 33, 34–35, 36, 40, 76–95, 97–98, 103–9, 110, 113–28, 129–30, 132, 137, 138–41, 144–45, 146, 159, 163–64, 174–75, 177, 187, 193–94, 197–98, 221n34, 222n35, 236n95; as moral fashioning, 21, 24, 34–35, 39–40, 64, 67–69, 84–85, 97, 130–31, 136, 138, 139, 145–46, 153, 154, 159, 198; vs. practical education, 24–25, 67, 97, 103, 110, 118, 119, 128, 157–58, 175, 199, 208n11; relationship

to mass politics, 2–3, 4–5, 9, 36, 39–40, 67–68, 84–86, 128, 129–32, 140–41, 144–45, 146, 153–57, 158–59, 163, 177, 187, 193–94, 197–98, 199–200, 203, 204; relationship to nationalism, 2, 16, 170–71, 173, 198; relationship to political radicalism, 17, 203–4. *See also* Islamic religious education; Jewish religious education
religious tolerance, 33–34
Reshaf, Shimon, 206n11
Riger, Eliezer, 127–28
rightly guided caliphs, 135
riots of 1929, 14, 65
Roberts, Nicholas, 71, 72, 84, 85
Robson, Laura, 71, 77, 93–94
Rosenberg, Alfred, 68
Rosenzweig, Franz, 195
Rothschild, Baron de, 185
Royal Central Asian Society, 104–5, 106, 108

Sadat, Anwar, 197
Ṣafwat durūs al-dīn wa al-akhlāq (Primary lessons in religion and morals), 151, 152–53
al-Sa'ih, 'Abd al-Hamid, 147, 151
al-Sakakini, Khalil, 46, 144; *al-Jahīd fi qirā'a al-'Arabiya*, 149
Salafi movements, 220n6
Salah al-Din, 135
Samuel, Herbert, 206n27
Sanhedrin, 75, 217n18
Sanwir, Ibrahim Mahmud, 151
Saposnik, Arieh, 47
Saudi Arabia, 154, 229n70
Schachter, Rabbi Hershel, 216n17
Schenirer, Sarah, 119
Scholem, Gershom, 115, 195
Schoneveld, Jacobus, 178, 232n42
Scott, H. S., 192, 201
Second Aliyah, 11, 46–47, 162, 164, 169–70, 182
secularism, 4–5, 8, 200; and Edict of Toleration, 31; in Hebrew School System, 117, 161–62, 163, 165, 174; and Judaism, 33–34; and politics, 32, 33; and reason, 3, 31–32, 146; relationship to Zionism, 32, 47, 161–63, 164–65, 175–76, 178, 185, 194, 230n3; secularization in modernity, 3–4, 17, 31–34, 158, 197; vs. utilitarian use of secular education, 119; of Va'ad Leumi, 15
Sedra, Paul, 39–40, 142
Segal, Mordechai, 174, 176, 231n27
Segev, Tom, 10, 206n22
Sengupta, Parna, 28–29, 34, 35–36, 143
Sephardic Jews, 113, 120–21
al-Shafi'i, 135, 136
Shafir, Gershon, 6
Shapira, Anita, 175, 236n96
Sheehan, Jonathan, 138, 158
Shimoni, Gideon, 162, 169–70
Shlonsky, Avraham: "Amal" (Toil), 184; "Metropolis", 184
Shuckburg, Sir John, 89–90
al-Siba'i, Hassan, 111–12
Sipurei ha-Mikrah (Bible stories), 178–80, 183
al-Siqilli, Jawhar, 135
SMC. *See* Supreme Muslim Council
Smith, Jonathan Z., 29
Sonnenfeld, Rabbi Yosef Chaim, 216n11
Spencer, Herbert, 157, 229n80
Starrett, Gregory, 34, 35, 130, 152, 229n70
Sudan, 11, 13, 85, 135
Suez Canal, 11
Sufism, 102–3
Supreme Muslim Council (SMC), 15, 71, 85, 90–92, 93–94, 104, 151; Education Committee, 90–91; schools run by, 5, 219n75, 222n42; vs. Va'ad Leumi, 59
Sykes-Picot Agreement, 11–12
Syria, 12, 52
Szold, Henrietta, 166, 170, 173

al-Ta'ī, Hatim, 135
Talmud, 22, 24, 100, 120, 126–27, 168, 169, 172, 231n28
Tamari, Salim, 211n22
tashlich, 172, 231n21
Taylor, Charles, 3
Thompson, Elizabeth, 52
Tibawi, Abdul Latif, 14, 20, 48, 77, 138, 140; *Arab Education in Mandatory Palestine*, 205nn1,6, 217n20, 227n17
Torah, 118–19, 165, 173, 179, 180, 182, 195, 233n47; role in religious education, 1, 21–22, 24, 31, 115, 119, 120, 127–28. *See also* Hebrew Bible; Talmud
Totah, Khalil, 59, 110, 222n40
transgression of boundaries, 9, 17, 27, 67, 116, 129, 163, 190, 200
Transjordan, 12, 145, 150, 222n52, 228n55
Tuqan, Qudri, 147
Turjman, Ihsan, 144

Ussishkin, Menahem, 55

Va'ad Leumi, and Knesset Israel, 14, 15, 77
Va'ad Leumi (National Council), 16, 58, 73, 87, 88, 89, 90, 114, 119, 124, 216n8; Department of Education, 117, 121, 125, 165, 212n38; and Knesset Israel, 14–15, 77; relations with Agudat Israel, 74–75, 113, 116; relations with Mandatory government, 115–16, 117, 175, 187, 190, 192, 193, 234n72, 235n75, 236n95; vs. SMC, 59. *See also* Hebrew Public System
VanAntwerpen, Jonathan, 3
volunteerism in education, 40, 41, 60, 80

Wasserstein, Bernard, 52
Wauchope, Arthur, 65, 66
Weber, Eugen, 25
Weizmann, Chaim, 206n22
Wessely, Naphtali Herz: "Divrei shalom ve-emet" (Words of peace and truth), 31–32; on Torah of God vs. Torah of man, 31–32
Williams, Raymond, 199
Women's Teacher College (WTC), 63
World War I, 2, 47–48, 205n1, 211n22

Yazid ben Thurwin, 222n38
Yemen, 35
Yemenite Jews, 115, 121, 122–24, 223n62, 225n91
Yiddish, 1, 98, 100
Yitzhaki, Rabbi Shelomo, 127–28
Young Men's Christian Association (YMCA), 65

Zaghlul, Said, 37
al-Zarnuji, 24
Zerubavel, Yael, 231n26, 232n33
Zionism, 5, 64, 116, 129, 231n26; and anti-Semitism, 10–11, 13, 68; and Arab economy, 6; and Balfour Declaration, 10, 11, 12; vs. diasporic Judaism, 164–65, 169–70, 178, 190, 220n5, 233n60; and Hebrew Bible, 99–100, 118–19, 127–28, 166, 168–69, 175–82, 183, 232n47, 234n68; and Hebrew language, 45, 46, 47, 53–55, 99, 121, 127, 171, 172, 175, 191, 195, 211n13; and Jewish identity, 3, 17, 121, 162–63, 166–67, 170, 177, 178, 185, 194, 224n85; and Jews from *edot ha-mizraḥ*, 120–25; labor in, 183–84; Land of Israel in, 10, 11, 47, 100, 162, 170, 175, 176, 180, 181–83, 195, 233nn51,62, 234n68; vs. Nazism, 68, 190; relationship to British colonialism, 185–95; relationship to secularism, 32, 47, 161–63, 164–65, 175–76, 178, 185, 194, 230n3; role of education in, 46–47, 99–100; role of religion in, 46–47; the sabra in, 46. *See also* General Zionists; Hebrew Public System; Labor movement; Mizraḥi (Religious Zionists) Party
Zionist Executive: Board of Education, 164, 166, 170–71, 173; Department of

Education, 47, 53, 61, 90, 91, 121, 169, 175, 181, 212n38; and Mandate for Palestine, 14. *See also* Hebrew Public System
Zionist historiography, 161–62; and British colonialism, 185; self-sufficiency in, 6
Zionist Organization, 14, 15, 52, 73, 125, 175, 181, 212n27, 224n85; relations with Agudat Israel, 75–76; relations with Mandatory government, 16, 48, 53–54, 57–58, 77, 78, 86–90, 92, 94, 187, 189–90, 219n53. *See also* Zionist Executive
Zionist Teachers Association, 47, 187
Zu'aytir, Akram, 146, 147
Zurayq, Jalal, 146

The authorized representative in the EU for product safety and compliance is:
Mare Nostrum Group
B.V Doelen 72
4831 GR Breda
The Netherlands

www.ingramcontent.com/pod-product-compliance
Lightning Source LLC
Chambersburg PA
CBHW031803220426
43662CB00007B/508
* 9 7 8 1 5 0 3 6 0 4 1 5 5 *